Praise for *A BREAK IN THE CHAIN*

'This is a warm, lively, empathetic novel full of fascinating social history'
Sydney Morning Herald

'At the core of the book is Judaism and what it means when affection strays beyond religious barriers. Tansley records the lives of her ancestors, not in dry prose but in an imaginative, fictive construct.'
The Sunday Age

'An engaging story that will resonate with anyone who has ever witnessed the deep, astonishing antagonism to an interfaith relationship, and the permanent damage to family ties that such antagonism can cause.'
Bracha Rafael, *Galus Australis*

'A bold and imaginative history, told with the dedication of the historian and the imaginative flair of the novelist...A well-written and gripping book and far more than the story of a migrant family...'
Novelist, columnist and literary critic Alan Gold

'A beautifully written imagining of three generations of her family.'
Herald Sun

'Richly researched, splendidly illuminating. A Break in the Chain *offers insider history, the private story beyond the public history, an emotionally dense and intriguing Australian story of high achievement, and of cultures and traditions in rich conflict.'*
Writer and academic Michael Meehan

A QUESTION OF BELONGING

By turns heartbreaking and joyful, A Question of Belonging *is a deceptively intimate novel in which tumultuous outward events imbue the fraught intertwined lives of just a handful of characters with a rich universality.'*
William Yeoman, *The West Australian*.

'*Tangea Tansley's deeply engaging narrative will have you reflecting on your own sense of belonging.*'
Writing WA

'*At the deepest level Ronnie is interrogating her identity in relation to place, history, family and responsibility... where does she belong? This is a novel of few major characters but those few are beautifully drawn to reveal their own difficulties around where, and how, they belong — not just physically but emotionally.*'
Carmel Bendon, *Verity La*

'*An engrossing story of a strong woman and her attachment to place. The characters come to life as does the country she inhabits. Thoroughly enjoyable!*'
Di Rowling

PERSPECTIVES: STORY & MEMOIR

'*With vivid imagination and sharp intelligence, Tangea Tansley's stories probe the struggle of being "human in a not-always-humane" world... Tansley's writing is writing of great maturity, tensions held in balance, drama often matched with humour, and not a word wasted.*'
Emeritus Professor Dennis Haskell, AM

'...a substantial compilation, impressive in its range of different narrative methods.'
Writer and critic Ian Reid

FOR WOMEN WHO GRIEVE

'Our culture, by and large, is not comfortable with this kind of reality. We prefer not to think about death, loss or loneliness, but keep ourselves busy and working hard at being happy. That is why this book is important, and for all of us, not just those who have recently lost a partner.'
From foreword by noted writer and academic: the late
The late Sister Veronica Brady

'Tansley's warm personal disclosures will undoubtedly assist women who mourn; those who feel lost and dejected will find joy and hope in place of despair, and a sense of purpose for the future'
Canberra Times

'...the clear message from one grieving woman to others is that "you are not alone" and that "your experience is valued and normal"...'
Australian Health Review

'...an essential and valuable addition to any collection of books on the painful and sensitive subject of death, dying, and the process of grieving.'
Midwest Book Review

'...this is a sensible, sensitive approach to the grieving process that would be as helpful to a man as to a woman whose spouse has died...'
Fifty-Plus

Tangea Tansley was born in Zimbabwe and lived and worked around the world before settling in Perth, Western Australia over thirty years ago. She holds a PhD in cross-cultural literature from Murdoch University and is the author of three novels, a hybrid collection of short stories/memoir and three works of non-fiction. Her first novel, *A Break in the Chain,* was longlisted for One Country Reading and the second, *Out of Place,* shortlisted in the Penguin-Varuna unpublished manuscript competition. Her stories and essays have been published in journals, newspapers and gazettes both in Australia and overseas, and have won awards in a number of national competitions.

A Break in the Chain

The Early Kozminskys

Tangea Tansley

Text and copyright © Tangea Tansley
All rights reserved. No part of this publication may be reproduced without prior permission.

First published by Affirm Press in 2011
1 Jacksons Road, Mulgrave VIC 3170
www.affirmpress.com.au

Second printing 2022

National Library of Australia Cataloguing-in-Publication entry:
Tansley, Tangea
A Break in the Chain: The Early Kozminskys / Tangea Tansley
978-0-9941625-9-5 (pbk.)
978-0-9941625-8-8 (e-book)
Historical Fiction A823.4

Cover image courtesy of the National Gallery of Victoria:
Frederick McCubbin
Australia 1855–1917
Study in blue and gold 1907
Oil on canvas on plywood
114.2 x 86.0 cm
National Gallery of Victoria, Melbourne
Gift of Mr Hugh McCubbin, 1960

This book is for my father

Kenneth William Coton
1908–2008

And for Tammy and Viv

A Break in the Chain

The Early Kozminskys

Tangea Tansley

Contents

Part One: Simon 13

Part Two: Simon and Emma 87

Part Three: Israel 113

Part Four: Isidore 219

Part Five: Francis 311

Postscript 321

Acknowledgements 335

Chronology 339

Part One

Simon

1856

1

Trouble was the last thing on my great-grandfather's mind, as he sat watching his father's cattle on the side of a smooth green hill in Prussia. For one thing, Simon Kosmanske was not much given to negative introspection. He figured that if he kept holy the Sabbath, honoured his father and his father's spouse, and kept his eyes off his neighbours' chattels, goods and wives, then he'd pretty much cover all bases here on earth and the Almighty would look after the rest. But it was impossible to live in the Prussia that had been Poland – fought over, swapped, slashed, divided and conquered – without realising that trouble came calling whether you looked for it or not.

But it was not for dwelling on. Besides, never far from his mind these days were thoughts of the girls in the village. A woman of his own, a wife? No, not yet. Women were for *zadza*, for lusting after. He was not yet ready for the type of tongue-lashing his father Moses received, most times with surprising meekness, from his first wife and then, after her death, from his new wife Sarah. There was plenty of time ahead for worries of that nature, but meanwhile this was playtime and the girls in the village liked Simon's games. And he liked theirs. They particularly liked his beard, his music. He smiled. Even if he travelled the wide world over, like his brother Marks, he doubted he would find their match. Roksanna was good. She knew how to make a man forget his surroundings. But Tola. A-ha! There was a woman! She was well-named: Tola, the priceless one. What skin, what hands. It might almost be possible to change his *zadza-*only rule with such a woman. Almost.

Simon's hands lay softly on the warm wood of his violin. When the cattle were back in the barn for milking he was free to pick up his fiddle and play for anyone who would listen. At gatherings or special nights at the local tavern they paid him in golden *zloty* for his talent and the coins, piled in neat towers, were gradually filling the small chest at the end of his bed. What to do with such a modest but growing fortune was Simon's only other concern, and that was worth some thought. He could use it to buy a cow or two from his father's herd to start one of his own. Or build a house for his one-day wife-to-be.

Sometimes, on days like this when the sun shone and there was no risk of rain, Simon liked to take his fiddle into the pasture, sit against a tree and play to the cattle. He swore it increased the milk, made it creamier, too. Other times, he just sat and dreamed while his hands caressed the rich golden brown of the spruce wood. One day he would buy himself a fiddle like Roman's, the leader of the troupe at the *tawerna*. Perhaps that was how he could spend his *zloty*. The thought that the money earned from his music would be returned to his music pleased him. But would the tunes be any richer, the melody sweeter? He knew enough to know there would be a difference.

From a clump of grass, Simon pulled a shoot and nibbled at it gently. He closed his eyes. Around the hill cattle grazed, the rhythm of their jaws vibrating just as his music did. The stream gushed and tumbled at the base of the valley.

He was about to put aside the fiddle that lay suddenly heavy across his lap when a hand struck his shoulder with the speed and sound of a thunderclap.

'Simon!'

The fiddle tumbled down the hill. Fantasy interrupted, he shot to his feet, his senses so rattled that he thought for an instant it was his brother Marks returned from America, his fortune already made. But one look at old Moses's eyes, dark with disgust, cleared his brain quite magically. There was no mistaking that it was his father standing before him, fists clenched and ready, it would seem, for battle. Simon spat out the blade of grass, tugged at his clothes.

'So this is how my eldest son chooses to spend his days, chewing the cud like the animal he is.' Beneath his beard, the old man's chin trembled. 'Never mind that his father is tilling the fields. Never mind that his new mother is at this moment working her very hands to the bone preparing his evening meal – with everything else she has to do with Abraham only so high and the new babe on the way. This is how the eldest grandson of that great man who fought at the side of Tadeusz Kosciuszko himself at Racławice chooses to spend the day when the weather is set fair for honest work. Phhf, I say to you, Simon, phhf. What do you have to say for yourself? Eh?'

Simon opened his mouth to answer. His father took a sudden step towards him and he closed it again. Moses was not tall, but right now it was clear that he possessed the strength of two good men.

'I'll tell you what you have to say for yourself,' Moses spat. 'Nothing. Isn't that so? Because there is nothing that someone who sits under a tree all day can say. Do you know what happens when a horse can work no longer, Simon? What do I do with that horse? No, don't answer. I will tell you what I do. Quite simply, I shoot him. And what happens when one of my cows no longer calves? Yes, I shoot her, too. So I ask you, what happens when I have begotten a son who does no work? And no...' He raised his hand to stop his son's protest. 'This is not work. It is idle, Simon. Idle. And what is it that the devil finds for idle hands?'

Simon shifted his feet. At least the argument had moved away from shooting and killing. But the day had lost a little of its shine, and he was anxious to see if there was any damage to his fiddle. He sighed.

'You sigh?' Moses cried. 'That is all you can do?'

For a moment he thought Moses was going to strike him, but the old man restrained himself, and sunk instead to one knee. So long did he stay in that position that Simon wondered whether he was ill or praying. He went to him and placed his fingertips on his father's shoulder.

'Father?'

Moses looked up at him and then down again. 'The time has come, my son, for you to leave. No, don't look at me like that. My mind has been made up. You waste your days in idle thought. A person's days add up very soon to a life, and a wasted life is a sin against God.' He pressed his hands together and took a deep breath. When next he spoke, his voice was steadier. 'There is no future in any case in Prussia. This land has been cut up into slices and fought over for so long it is in danger of losing its very soul. Men love war, Simon, but that love contains a sac of poison that can destroy them and all they hold dear.' Moses was silent for a minute and when he spoke again, his voice was softer still. 'I grew up the son of an army surgeon – I grew up on stories of bloodied battlefields the like of which I pray you will never see in your lifetime. I sense that it will not be very long before there is another uprising that will make the revolution look like a tea party.'

Leave Prussia? Leave the farm? His home?

'But I love Prussia,' Simon whispered.

This was enough to bring the old man to his feet, his rough voice dangerously low.

'You love, Simon. Yes, I know you love. You love too much. It's all over Raoskow. You are young, I know, but you are not discreet. This village is too small for you – or rather, Raoskow is too small to contain us both. I like walking tall along the street, and when I am questioned as to the health of my family, my sons, I say something like: "Ah yes, my son Marks is doing very well for himself, very well indeed, with this new thing called a camera in America. He went there for the gold but he is earning his living in a very clever way." I can say that with real pride. But when they ask me about you – what can I say?'

The hills were unusually quiet. Even the cattle were motionless. There seemed, thought Simon, nothing else to be said, and after a moment his father set off down the hill. But about halfway down he stopped and turned. His voice rose up on the breeze.

'A father is the sum of his children, Simon. And don't you ever forget that. They are saying in the tavern that

Australia, too, has its reefs of gold. Go to Australia and make an old man proud.'

Simon watched his father until his cap had disappeared over the rise. His own hands were clenched. It may have been better, he thought, if he had fought a little, stood up for himself instead of playing the submissive son. He was angry, but the anger was directed at himself and as much as it hurt to admit it, he couldn't help feeling he could have prevented this – that he could have worked harder. He knew, too, that once Moses's mind was made up, there was no going back.

'Spilt milk,' he muttered, walking slowly to his favourite cow. 'There's nothing to be done.' The cow dropped her head for him to scratch the poll between her ears, and snuffled green muck through her nostrils. He had always thought of his father's herd as his own. Had never thought further than spending his whole life dairying as his father had before him.

But what had Marks said at the outset of his trip? The train was already whistling, the steam rising as his brother gripped him tight across the shoulders. 'Grow up well, brother. Don't let the old fellow work too hard.'

He bit his lip. Sometimes it seemed to him that Marks was the elder. It was not so much that he was wise in any degree; surely he had not years enough for that. But there was a love of humanity in Marks that invariably provoked a reciprocal feeling in those who knew him.

Now Simon was to leave Raoskow. And this meant, he suddenly realised, leaving Tola, too. It was unthinkable. He would marry her. But maybe his father was right. What, after all, did he have to offer any woman when he could not yet care for himself? He kicked out at a tuft of grass.

Wondering why the petting had stopped, the cow opened her eyes and Simon stared, as he had done since he was a child, at his reflection in the large pupil. Outwardly he may look different now with his beard and his fair hair tied back, but inside he felt just as bewildered as he had then.

Life, in all its important forms, had always arrived at his feet before he was quite ready to meet it. There had been his mother's death, his father's remarriage, the new baby and Marks's departure.

He laid his head against the slope of the cow's withers. If he prayed at all, it was that he would never forget the silkiness of this coat, this particular blend of satin and, up by the mane, the finest corduroy velvet over which he was compelled to run his hands. It never failed to remind him of a fragment of cloth carefully pasted into the family album, a small square that had intrigued them so much as children that it had long since grown frayed and grubby. But the softness was still there, along with the description – *my most important day* – written in his mother's awkward hand. Important day. Neither he nor Marks had thought to ask their mother about her most important day. He swallowed. This might turn out to be *his* most important day, too. Though not quite in the way he would have wished.

The sun's heat had gone and the cattle were turned in his direction, ears pricked, their incessant grinding almost at a halt. Blowing his breath out in short bursts, Simon collected himself. His fiddle, at least, was unharmed. He wiped it gently, picked up the bow. Unless he hurried, he would bring in the cows late for milking.

Playing a tune before leading the cattle home had become a ritual, and he sometimes wondered whether the cows would move without it. It was this music before milking, he was convinced, that produced the sweetest milk in all Prussia. Well, the old man would just have to find that out for himself. Simon raised the fiddle to his shoulder and drew the bow across the strings.

The moment the first note reached her, the lead cow flicked her ears and swung away, heading off towards the barn. One by one the others followed. Hemmed in by the hills, the music echoed back to him, note upon note, the chords lifting, spiralling over one another. But tonight the sound was heavier, strangely fitting for the slow-moving line of black cattle.

In the days that followed, Simon spoke very little to Moses as preparations for the voyage took place. He was to take the train up to Gdansk, and then a ship from there to Liverpool. From Liverpool, he was to take a clipper to Australia. How easy it looked on the map.

'Heh man,' they called out to him in the village. 'I hear about you travelling to the other side of the world. Australia. Ooh yeh! You quite ready for it, Simon, eh? You want to watch out for the convicts and kangaroos in those parts. Watch out, too, for the laughing jackass. And do you know the natives have spears? But there's nothing else there, you know. No women! So why would you go? Oh, the poor Tola. Who will take care of the lovely Tola while you are gone? Who will warm her bed on winter nights? Ooh la la, Simon. Not much to be had on the other side at all.'

A BREAK IN THE CHAIN

He had grown up in this village. It was as much part of him as an arm or a leg. As his music. Everything he ever knew or wanted was here. When he had said he loved Prussia, his father had taken it as a further sign of weakness and Simon had wished the words unsaid. But if this ache he felt for his homeland was not love, what was it?

The night before he left, while he lay tossing in his narrow bed wondering whether Tola would answer a pebble thrown at her window in the hours before dawn, his door creaked open.

'Are you awake?'

Simon lay still, deepened his breathing, and allowed a small snore.

'Ah good. Here, I have something to give you.' Moses sat heavily on the edge of the bed. 'Do you have room in your bag for these?'

Simon raised himself on his elbow, moved to make room. The old man's fingers shook as he placed his candle on the small bedside table and handed across the album with the shabby leather covers that had been mended more than once, but were again unravelling. Across the front, written boldly in his father's hand, was *Zbierajmy Przeszłosci Rozsiane Ciało* – a collection of the cut-up body of the past. Inside these pages were the accounts of Simon's grandfather's exploits. The right-hand pages were blank until about a third of the way through, when his grandfather gave way to his father, who wrote his life in terse lists mainly about his herd: those he had bought, the calving, the illnesses, the sales and those he shot. A few pages later, his mother took her place.

Simon knew each verse, each poem, each story; he knew, too, that as a whole this book was greater than these separate parts, more than a simple record of the lives of his family. As a collection, such an album imagined the life of the Polish nation as it had been and as it would be again. It had sat for as long as he could remember on a tall wooden pedestal in the hallway of the farmhouse, and it was a book to be savoured on Moses's knee.

He couldn't look at his father; took the book, nodding. But there was something else, something bright that caught at the candlelight. Moses smiled at the sudden grin on Simon's face. The surgeon Kosmanske's small brass bleeding cups, long lusted after as proof of blood spilled in battle. If it had been possible, Simon knew the cups would have taken their place in the album along with the drop of blood he knew to be his grandfather's.

Another image floated before him. The day he and Marks had set out to dig through the earth to Australia. They knew it was there, yet it would take time and persistence to dig that deep. They got a long way down, so the ground was just at the level of Marks's chin, when a thought came to them both at the same time.

'If we go down much further, how are we going to get out?' Marks' lips trembled.

Simon looked at his brother. Marks was still a real baby sometimes. He yawned to cover his own concern.

'Oh, I'll stand on your back to jump out first and then pull you out. We might need a pulley system. And buckets.' The look on Marks's face made him suddenly doubtful. 'But maybe this is deep enough for now. We definitely need to put some more thought into it.'

A BREAK IN THE CHAIN

The tunnel to Australia was abandoned and quite forgotten until Moses discovered it by accident. From the tone of his roar, the boys knew that retribution would be swift and stinging. They made good time that day, down the track and out to the forest beyond the cow fields...

Simon's face was hot and prickly with remembering, but his father was now saying something else. He bent his head to listen.

'Attend synagogue,' old Moses muttered. 'Go to *shul*. Say your prayers. And whatever else you do, please don't forget...' His voice trailed off. As Simon put his hand in the hot grip of his father's, he wondered why it had to be this way. How was it that losing something was so often the only way of finding it?

2

Simon trekked between his bunk and the water closet for the fourth time that day. Where Raoskow had been a slice of heaven, this voyage was surely a sample of hell.

What they called a bunk was no more than one of a dozen slings set three to a row down a wood-partitioned section of the ship. The clerk in Gdansk who had taken his money had been insistent that he pay both portions of the voyage at the outset – from Gdansk to Liverpool and onwards to Port Phillip Bay – saying that ticket-holders would be given priority over the thousands queuing for a passage to the goldfields.

'For a little extra, you will get a cabin, a worthwhile investment on such a long voyage. I would strongly advise you to pay this.' The clerk rubbed at his chin.

His hand shaking, Simon slowly counted out extra of the precious *zloty*, the money band around his waist already pitifully light.

When he had complained to Moses that he was voyaging to the other side of the world with so little money, his father had shrugged.

'So? You have your music. And your wits.'

As it turned out, he remembered nothing of the voyage to Liverpool and nothing of the city either, knowing only, after a brief venture along its narrow noisy streets, that he would board the first packet to accept his ticket.

A niggling worry that he might have been overcharged at Gdansk was fast building into tension as he waited in the short queue under a sign 'Black Swan 896 tons'. Eventually it was his turn and a man, all starched whites and glinting brass, took his ticket. He was grand enough, Simon thought, to be the captain.

'Not British?' he snapped.

Simon shook his head.

'Pity. You could have travelled free. Government sponsored. You'll have to go steerage.'

'A cabin?' Simon leaned over the desk and pointed at the ticket. 'It says there, cabin.'

'Not for this sum, I'm afraid. Steerage is steerage. Cheap. Low fare. No cabin.' He slowed his speech. 'Understand? No cabin for this fare. We're not a charity, we're a business. Though you do get access to a water closet. This vessel's a shade better than most in that department. You can cook up on the deck – but you'll need your own pots for that.' He eyed Simon's one bag. 'And more clothes. At least six shirts. It's a long trip. There's a full list over there of what you'll need.' He pointed with a curving fingernail to a sheet pinned to a board under the ship's name. 'If you don't get the full list, you won't be allowed on board. Understand-y? For a cabin I'll need an extra six pounds. Yes or no?'

How quickly he had been fleeced! Simon forced himself to shrug.

'I understand. No cabin.'

'All right. Occupation?'

Simon nudged the fiddle lying on top of his bag. 'Music, you know. Musician.'

The officer lifted an eyebrow. He would have been handsome had his face not been so evenly pockmarked.

'I suggest you purchase some sort of a case for that. It's a little vulnerable.'

'Vulnerable?'

The officer raised his eyes to somewhere over Simon's head. 'Mother of God, preserve me,' he muttered. 'It doesn't matter. Year of birth?'

'I beg pardon?'

'Your age. How old? Boy? Man?'

Simon stood taller. He didn't rightly know. 'Twenty-one,' he guessed.

'Which makes your date of birth around 1835. That right?' He glanced at Simon's long fingers. 'No rings. Single male?'

Simon nodded and the official signed his name at the end of the line and tossed the ticket into a box at his feet. 'Next.'

Three days later he was aboard the *Black Swan*. But his relief was brief. Nothing he had experienced on the voyage from Gdansk to Liverpool had prepared him for what lay ahead. For the first week, as the ship churned through the seas off the west coast, and then down to Land's End and out into the Atlantic, he was dizzy and sick. While lying on his back in the canvas sling was all he had energy for, time lost all meaning. The day curled back on itself as wave after wave of nausea sent him staggering from hammock to latrine and back. No morning-after had prepared him for this. He was helpless, wrapped in the sour smell of excrement and vomit, the stench of fouled bedding.

So it was some time before he realised he had paid a premium for a space that was only just above the waterline. And although the line of portholes down one side relieved the dimness slightly, the one positioned alongside his own bunk only added to his queasiness as the ship rolled and the sea sloshed in front of his eyes. He spent most of his time lying on his side facing into the room with its swaying slings instead. The ceiling was so low that even a person of average height could not fully extend an arm upwards. When food arrived, it unleashed in him a sense of loathing, and he ached for a sip of strong black tea. He wondered how long it took for a man to go mad.

Even worse was the stench of the latrine, a foul fug that formed a blanket of poison that the men breathed back into their lungs and out again through the pores of their skin. In the short breaks when the ship stopped rolling, the portholes were opened and great smacks of cold air blasted through the cabin. But most of the time he breathed shallowly and reluctantly.

Moses had been partly right. It was certainly true that Simon had his fiddle, which he had wedged carefully against the wall behind his bag, but Moses had been wrong in saying he had his music. Music came from the hillside and from the tavern.

And how time stretched on! Simon tried to pray – but God, like his father, appeared to have given up on him. Light and dark threaded into each other arriving and departing without announcement. He knew it was night only because of the release of the coughing and snoring and farting. There was a blessedness in the darkness: he dared to lie facing the porthole because each roll offered only another version of black instead of the swinging horizon. But as the ship progressed further south, presenting its canvas to the north-easterly trades of the Atlantic, the swell was such that he could only hold his breath and count his heartbeats, the water inches from his face. It seemed that it was only by the grace of Almighty God that the ship hauled herself up, staying upright for a count of two before gathering herself to keel over the other way.

There was a group of three or four men who seemed almost cheerful and spent most of their time on deck. Below, no one spoke unless they had to. In between their visits to relieve themselves, or on their rare trips up the narrow treads of the companionway, the other passengers lay much as he did, with an arm twisted behind a head or with hands shielding their eyes as if they played the game from childhood. Maybe they didn't want to be going where they were headed any more than he did? Perhaps this fake bubble of Babel abolished the need on the part of all to communicate?

Finally impelled on deck, Simon took in gulps of air that were fresh and cold and clean. But he was soon dizzy, aware that there was only the railing between him and the swelling, heaving black, the swishing of the ship cutting through the water with the maddening sound of a faucet turned on full and forgotten.

How had he allowed himself to be thrust aside so easily? Without a fight even. What sort of a man was he for not standing up for himself? Why had he not stayed where he was happy? There were places in Raoskow where he could have sought work. Or he could have gone further afield, but still within Prussia. What possibly could be gained by an adventure like this? His father was mad. Or so absorbed by his wife and his new family that he had no time for the old. Or maybe, Simon thought woozily, I am the mad one.

Back in his bunk, his hand touched something hard under his head and he fingered it for a moment before he remembered that it was the album wrapped in his shirt, used as a pillow to keep it safe from the rats prowling the decks at night. There was nothing it contained that he didn't already know, no verse he couldn't recite from memory. No reason, really, for Moses to part with it at all. Just an aberration of an old man's mind.

Simon jerked the book from under his head, freed it from the cloth and held it for a long moment. The cut-up body of the past. He shook his head and clenched his jaw. Ah yes, the past which to his father was so much more important than the present. Flashes of lightning, redder than the blood his surgeon grandfather had ever let, danced before his eyes and for an instant even the creaking of the ship was silenced. Simon's fingers turned white. Had he been lying in a real bunk instead of a sling which tended to dissuade such spontaneity, he would have sat bolt upright and flung the book across the room. The cut-up body of the past. Or his cut-up mind of the present?

He must have fallen asleep and woken in response to the altered motion of the ship. The album had fallen across his chest, open at the page where his mother had pasted the small piece of her wedding gown. Ignoring his father's entry on the left, he concentrated on the piece of cloth. It was, he thought now, a somewhat fragile signpost for the enormity of the journey she was about to undertake, fitting, all the same, for a person who had spent her life worrying about others.

On the next page she had drawn a picture of herself as a smiling young woman, her hair drawn back and piled up high. Underneath she had written Hendel Kosmanske *Matka Polka* – the Polish mother. He wondered if the baby in her arms was him or Marks.

He remembered, one day when he was a boy, coming home hungry for milk and biscuits and she wasn't there. Instead of his mother moving around the kitchen cooking and baking and making a warm and merry clatter, Moses sat on a chair with the baby Marks on his knee, his hand over his eyes. And that was that – she was just gone. Except that Simon missed her a great deal and could not accept that she was no longer there. He had wished he was young enough to suck his thumb like his brother. Instead he had started biting his fingernails. He'd never really wondered whether his father missed her; Moses was always too busy being both mother and father, too busy even to look for his new wife Sarah until a few years ago.

The ship's movement was becoming more violent as Simon turned the page, eager now for distraction from the weaving water at his side. His mother had now restricted her entries to love verse mainly by the poet Adam Mickiewicz, interspersed here and there with Ursyn's poetry. And then, with the book not much more than half-filled, there was suddenly nothing, a sign in itself she had left her life incomplete. He sighed, turning back to the beginning and Moses's wandering rambles of the exploits of 'the incomparable' Kosciuszko as witnessed by his surgeon grandfather.

A BREAK IN THE CHAIN

Apart from the opening line of the national anthem *Jeszcze Polska nie zgineła kiedy my zyjem* – Poland has not yet died as long as we are alive – the sole piece of poetry copied into his father's section of the book was an excerpt from *Pan Tadeusz*, Mickiewicz's epic about Napoleon's invasion of Russia. It was a poem created for the voice and the heart in tandem, to be acted out in grand style in the tavern, on national days or family gatherings. It was, of course, his father's favourite. Here were only a few pages and he had no idea how many verses Moses had committed to memory, only that he would recite for hours, his low, toneless voice strangely infused by the movements of his shoulders and his hands, and the sparks lighting his eyes. Where other families had bedtime stories, the Kosmanskes had their Bible and *Pan Tadeusz*. Now, holding the album towards the glass to catch what little light there was, it became clear that the copy hand was his mother's.

Simon ran his fingers softly over the feathered page. His head was clearer than it had been since he boarded. Maybe not everything in his life would be uncovered too late. But there was another change in the movement of the ship now, which had taken to running forward and stopping before plunging; the weather was changing, too, and it might pay another visit to the latrine before the storm really took hold. With the thought that he might one day put *Pan Tadeusz* to music, Simon left the book open and swung his feet to the ground just as the ship lurched and stopped short, as if it had hit something solid.

A bell and a shout rang out through the sudden quiet.

'Bad weather coming in! Secure all portholes.' And almost immediately a collective flicking and clicking of latches. 'All hands on deck! On deck all. Everyone. On deck! Now!'

A moment, then, of suspension. The sound of glass breaking somewhere. After that, it was just events. The rows of hammocks that had moved back and upwards with the rush of the ship stood at the top of their trajectory. A dozen hands grasped at the foul air when they would have done better to have hung onto the sides of the slings. Some men fell; others were loosed, like stones from a slingshot, against the far wall. Simon slid across the deck just as the porthole above his bunk gave way. A torrent of water poured in, arching gracefully and hanging, just hanging, in the air above his bed.

Over it all, the scream: 'Batten the hatches.'

Amid the grunts and screams and the rush for the stairs before the hatch was dropped and bolted, Simon grabbed at the album to find the copy already dissolving into purple smudges. He took it anyway. His fiddle and bag were among the jumble piling against the far partition and there was no time now to search. He joined the tail of the rush up the treads.

Later, on deck, he wondered at the power of a God who could spin an ocean into such chaos one minute, such calm the next. If it weren't for the confusion around him, it would be easy to believe that he had imagined the fury. Wondering how he'd kept it through the turmoil, he held the spoiled album in his hands. A word here and there was legible, sometimes even a couple of lines intact, but the sodden pages were too fragile to turn and he knew that when it dried, the book would seal itself shut. Maybe it was right that the past remained the past, that it kept its small secrets sealed off from the present. There was, he felt, little point keeping it. He tried to throw it into the water, but it proved not so easy. One part of him stopped the other, and then he started as someone tapped him on the shoulder.

'Yes?'

'Here, mate. Not quite as good as new, but we done our best. It took a fair hammering.' The man's eyes shone out of a leathery skin tanned by a sun harsher than anything they knew in Europe. He had something in his hands and he held it out towards Simon. 'You see, we could all do with a bit of music. Downstairs the men are working on the bow.' When Simon made no move, he offered it to him again.

He nodded, encouragingly. 'Here,' he repeated. 'It's yours.'

For another moment, Simon looked at him. Slowly he placed the wet book on the deck between his feet and took the fiddle in both hands. He had thought it a bird with a broken wing, beyond help.

'You...fix?'

'Yes. Well, sort of. It's still got the dent there, see. And that string's from a gent's guitar. Don't know whether it'll work. None of us knows whether it'll play right.' He put his hand to his forehead to drop down the brim of a hat that wasn't there, shuffled his feet instead. Simon said nothing. Just held the instrument and stared at it. 'Anyway...' The man nodded again, moved off towards the stairs. At the top he turned and called back. 'Bit of a ways to go still. But, as I said, we could all do with some music in the evenings. Liven things up a little – if you know what I mean?'

A BREAK IN THE CHAIN

Simon stayed as he was, staring down at the instrument, until the man disappeared. His eyes were becoming hot and his face wet with something more than sea spray. The violin was still too damp to play, and he doubted whether he'd get a proper tune out of it ever again. But as he leaned there, his back against the railing, he ran his hands over the wood and there was a vibration in the air remarkably akin to the evening song, and he imagined himself away from all this, back in Raoskow on the side of the hill with the fiddle in his lap, and one cow here, another there. Bending to pick up the album and clutching hard at his versions of the cut-up body of the past, he turned back towards the sea.

There was an uneasy attempt at quiet interrupted by scraping chairs and clearing throats that first night Simon played. Initially, he was tentative, drawing the bow across the strings with hesitation, as though it were an old friend to whom he might owe an apology. But then the music claimed him. He cupped his chin to the cool curve of the wood, and very soon the word did the rounds of the ship until it seemed suddenly right to play on deck under the huge cupola of darkness broken only by the flicker of the stars above and the glow of the pipes before him.

His violin would never be the same but then, he figured, neither would he, so one way or another they complemented each other well enough. Sometimes he sang or, on occasions, recited his favourite verses of *Pan Tadeusz*. Even though few understood the words, the story lived in the gleam of his eyes, the lift of his chin, the set of his shoulders. Other times he was joined in song by a young woman with a voice so sweet that if she hadn't had a large, rather hairy husband, Simon would have been tempted to see what other tunes she might be persuaded to sing... Or so he told himself. More real was the unpleasant fact that living in this gap between one life and the unknown, a kind of vacuum filled with its filthy smells and the endless rotation of salt beef with salt pork, was sufficient to kill all thoughts of sex.

But not only the physical was quiescent. Slowly, too, his emotions subsided. The tangle of confusion was replaced by a type of mesmerism that fixed his gaze to the thin line between sea and sky, or drew his eyes down to the foamy trail the clipper left in its wake. He became used to the rock and roll of the vessel, and pitched his stride accordingly. His English improved, too. A little.

Finally, there were signs that the land on the other side of the world really did exist and that this long journey was not just some unpleasant joke of the Almighty. Nothing was said aloud – it was more that there was a calm about the men, not the bruised, closeted silence of before, but one of imagining a future close at hand. They fidgeted less and sometimes sat with their heads at a slight angle, a frown on their faces, listening, animals testing the wind.

There was a change, too, in the bird life. They had not seen an albatross for many days. Instead there were gulls now, and doves perched in the rigging. Fish eagles hovered, always too high, he thought, before proving him wrong and plummeting into the ocean to rise almost instantly stiff-legged with a bright silver fish whipping and glinting in their claws.

One morning the man who had returned his fiddle joined him on deck. 'The name's Jack, by the way.' He put out his hand. 'Going home. Whaling's me occupation down Albany way. Water's teaming with whales 'long the southern tip there. And ships. More than two hundred of 'em.' Once he started talking, Jack stopped only to tamp down his pipe. 'Come from all over, whalers. Mainly Yanks, some Brits and European types, but not your sort. French, Norwegian mostly.' He jabbed the head of his pipe at two dolphins swimming alongside the clipper. 'And if you think they're big, you should see a whale. Weigh up to forty ton apiece. These are small fry in comparison.' He looked Simon over, grinned. 'Healthy chap like you. Why the heck don't you come down? About three hundred mile south of Perth and a nice enough spot to live. Albany, that is. Green and cool. Like Europe. You'd like it. They're always looking for hands at the stations. Hard work, no doubt about that, but the wages are pretty decent.' He nodded in the direction of the hatch. 'The guys in there, they're all heading for the gold finds over East because that's all they know about. But the West's something special. Best-kept secret or Bob's not me uncle. Mull it over.'

Simon nodded, but it was not something he needed to think about. However good the money, he would always be repelled by the idea of killing.

But Jack wasn't one to give up so easily.

'Thought it through?' he asked the next time he came across Simon on deck.

'Yes, I have. But no. Not for me.'

'Can't take the sight of blood?' Jack grinned. But, in fact, Simon thought, he was not far wrong.

'Not so good.'

'But you're a farmer!'

'Yes. But dairy milk – good milk. To drink. I don't kill – no killing.'

'Well, at least you're honest. Must admit it's never been something that worried me.' He tapped out his pipe on the railing. 'What are you going to do in the new country? Any plans?'

No. He had no plans – still, after all these weeks. He had thought no further than following the crowds to the goldfields. But he had to admit that panning for gold didn't really attract him any more than Jack's proposition. As for Moses's comment about his music: he knew he could fiddle all day, every day, but a bare living would be all it would make. He shrugged.

Jack took his time filling his pipe, drew at it in silence. After quite some time, he spoke again.

'Look, mate. Most of these guys – and there must be some five hundred of them on this boat alone – are heading for the goldfields. And this is one ship – just one. Ships are arriving every day; the place is overrun with Brits and Chinks, blokes from all over. Pouring in. Some strike it lucky, but from what I hear, a whole lot more don't. I've been away for nearly two years, so you could say I'm out of touch, but then again, you hear as much from those who have returned home broke, and I don't think things have changed too much.

'The smart ones, however, are those who supply the fields. Nothing complicated. Food, clothing, dishes and stuff to eat from – that sort of thing. Get me, Simon?

'Because most are, with respect, like you – they haven't thought things through. They head out like hounds on a hunt with nothing in their heads but the scent of wealth, not giving a thought to how they are going to live meanwhile. Gold is crude. You can't eat it and you can't wear it. And you can't buy food and clothing from a man who has only gold to give.

'If it was me going there, I'd buy a good horse and a wagon, load it up in town with the stuff people need – being on this tub for the past three months should've given you a good idea of that – and head off.' He scratched the back of his head. 'Where commodities are scarce, prices are sweet.' He grinned. 'But the offer to come with me still holds.'

Shutting off his sense of smell had become a habit and so the peculiar pungency in the air might have been there some time before Simon became aware of it. Something unlikely, like spicy flowers or crushed herbs, hay even, and he caught himself tilting his head to follow it like a dog with its nose up, searching. Turning back to sea, his eyes narrowed at first with concentration and then widened. He had become so used to staring at the dark thread between sea and sky that he hadn't noticed how the line was a line no more, but a thickening strip.

He nudged the young boy at his side and pointed.

'Look. Land, yes? Maybe even Australia?'

For half an instant they had it to themselves until far above them a sleepy sailor saw the same thing. He let out a shout, a cry that echoed first in voices heavy with hope and doubt and then in the mad rush of people to the railing.

Night was settling like dark snow. About half a mile from the shoreline, the *Black Swan* paused and swivelled, and a moment later there came a clanking rush of chain.

Simon had never heard a sound so sweet. He strained his eyes, but there was little that grew out of the dark save a white building on a hilltop and a line of tall dark shapes like well-padded giants guarding the land.

The next morning, he saw they were anchored at the mouth of an estuary. The large building on the hilltop was a convict prison, he was told, and the shapes he had seen the night before turned out to be not unlike the fir trees at home from this distance, although they were top-heavy and unwieldy looking. Apart from a few buildings placed some distance apart and a great deal of clean white sand, that was all there was to it. No natives clad in war paint, no convicts in stripes and chains, no kangaroos. In fact, not very much at all. It couldn't have contrasted more with his last sight of land.

So this was Fremantle? A port with no other ships? With not much of anything but a prison. This was Australia? White sand hills, inappropriate trees. Hardly worth digging for, was it, brother? He grinned suddenly as Marks's grimy young face popped into his mind. Where was he now? He shook his head.

Fresh supplies were brought on board, and the supply boat was to ferry departing passengers to shore. But the only person to leave at Fremantle was Jack.

He stood opposite Simon, a small wiry man with a mouth too wide for glumness although right now it seemed quite set.

'You sure you don't want to change your mind, mate?'

'Yes, I'm sure. But thanks. And thank you, you know, for…for everything.' For a man whose tongue rolled so glibly when he was lying with a woman, Simon felt remarkably awkward. In this case, his thanks had to stand for so much.

While he was surer than he had ever been that he didn't want to be a whaler or to have, for that matter, anything to do with the business of whaling, it didn't stop the emptiness that settled over him as his friend turned away to lower himself down the side. As he was rowed towards the shore, Jack waved back big looping circles with both arms until his action changed and he began beckoning with his fingers. *Come, Simon, come. You won't regret it.*

Simon wondered whether the darkness settling over him as the boat headed towards the landing was anything akin to what Moses might have felt when they hugged goodbye. He had been so conscious of his own pain that he had been oblivious to his father's. But it was possible that there was as much emptiness in staying as leaving. As he strained to see, there was only Jack's thumb. Upright. He waved back. But his wave was slow, only a wave, and he wondered whether all the thoughts in him had made it across the space. Not much more than a speck, the boat beached. The sand was white and bright. Did Jack turn again? Simon screwed up his eyes.

The ship breathed and took on fresh water, meat and biscuits, and readied itself for its home run. There was no damage, no threat of quarantine. The voyage was nearly over and Port Phillip was next.

There was a slight breeze and a suggestion of damp in the air on that gentle day in October, 1856, when Simon saw land again. He had been at sea for one hundred days when he stepped onto the steamer that was to take him to shore.

Finally on land, despite himself, he smiled. And then his smile broke into a wide grin. The landing stage was busy and full, but not so crowded that he didn't spot the glint of a gold sovereign half-covered with sand not five paces away. Unbelieving, he picked it up and, holding it aloft, looked around for its owner.

When no one came forth, he slipped it in his pocket.

It was an omen. A good sign. Melbourne would be a lucky town. He hitched his fiddle higher and picked up his bags. But he could not help looking back towards the rocky outcrops they called the Heads to where the sea turned colour. His smile faded.

Two minutes later, he was surrounded. There were touts everywhere – one man came right up to him, blocking his path; another, older, put a hand on his arm. The breeze of earlier had disappeared to be replaced with a day that was hot, dusty and rank with sweat. The older man tugged at Simon's sleeve.

'Reliable transport to the goldfields, sir? Only five pounds. Guaranteed. Real steal. Includes food. I'll give you a hand with your stuff.'

'You'd be mad to go with him,' another warned, his breath hot on Simon's face. 'Take you a month of Sundays to get a mile out of town. Here – take my card. I'm cheaper and faster, and you'll actually get there!'

'Ballarat. Best fare and stockman's equipment thrown in makes it the best deal this side o' the black stump.'

Simon shook them off, and tried to make his way through the crowd.

'Not today, sir? Tomorrow perhaps? Do you want to see the town? I know where you can get a good time. Clean. Good prices.' A man with a wall-eye gestured in the direction of the fiddle. 'Or do you want work, mister? I know a place where they pay good money for music. Come with me.'

The older man put his arm through the strap of one of Simon's bags. 'You don't want to take any notice of him, sir,' he muttered. 'You'll start off with a good dose of the clap, that's all that'd be good about it. Safer on the fields, believe me. Let's go, mate.'

'Hey!' Simon cried, tugging free. He pushed through the mob again, no idea where he was going, knowing only that to appear indecisive would be fatal. Move, he told himself, in the direction of the tallest part of the town and there you might find somewhere to wash, to eat and to sleep in that order. After that, he would plan.

Apart from his brief and uncomfortable acquaintance with the port cities of Gdansk and Liverpool, the only city Simon had ever visited was Łódz, in the centre of Prussia. On the face of it, Łódz and Melbourne couldn't have been more different: one with tall buildings lining busy streets, the other short and, for the most part, squat. Łódz was old and mellowed, too, with narrow, paved streets, while Melbourne was barely fledged, with streets broad and rutted and inclined to either mud or dust.

But it was with Łódz, he decided, that Melbourne had the potential to show a sort of similarity. Maybe it was because, in spite of the strange crowds and the rawness of the town, he felt at home from the start. But Simon suspected it was more than just a feeling he had that Melbourne would grow to be a city of some consequence – and knowledge breathed in from somewhere whispered that he was destined to be part of it.

A BREAK IN THE CHAIN

The orderliness of its streetscape pleased him. It was laid to a plan and, alongside humble weatherboard dwellings and plain, purposeful structures, there were already a few buildings of some height and grace. For the first time since his father had startled him from his fantasies on the hillside in Raoskow, Simon felt a faint tickle of excitement nudge away the homesickness and horror of the voyage. Maybe, just maybe, Melbourne was a city young enough to grow with.

But first he had to battle the touts. When he stepped outside his lodgings the next morning, refreshed and as eager for exercise as a loosed panther, there they were, lined up along the street. Simon was determined to ignore them again. He had yet to understand that these professional hustlers knew what he didn't: where to find anything he wanted. Eventually, he would have to turn to them, and so they would be patient; they'd met his stubborn sort before.

All the same, Simon refused to be drawn into conversation as they sidled alongside. He practised regarding them in a calculatedly unseeing way, from time to time shaking his head. Mostly they were young, barely out of boyhood. Some dropped away, lured by easier prospects; others persisted all morning. Certainly there were plenty of opportunities in the milling crowd. Newly arrived Chinese with their dark baggy trousers and black pigtails, men back from the mines, roistering, swaggering, drunk on good brandy and gold fever, women and children, and from time to time, a gentleman in a top hat and tails. There was a thrill in the town running end to end.

A BREAK IN THE CHAIN

Since nothing else had occurred to him except unresolved thoughts about dairying, Simon decided to investigate Jack's suggestion. From the comparative lack of grown men he saw on the streets compared to the boatloads dumped on shore, it was quite possible most headed straight for the fields without even stopping in town for provisions.

That being the case, what Simon needed first was a good horse. One capable of pulling a cart as well as being a reliable hack. On his way to his lodgings, he'd passed a number of stables and liveries tucked in among the jumble of hotels, warehouses, shipping offices and shops. Eagerly he retraced his steps, going from place to likely place in an attempt to price a horse and cart. But each of his enquiries was met with a shrug.

'Nothing for sale.'

'Nothing available.'

'Sold out.'

'Nothing doing, mate.'

'Try me tomorrow – I might have something then. Or the day after, or the day after that.'

He searched all day, his determined stride of the morning a trudge by late afternoon. It was as the sun reached its highest point in the sky that Simon noticed a small boy trotting like a dog at his heels, two strides to his every one, two strides to every one. It became a frustrating rhythm. In the end, he rounded on the little fellow.

'Go away,' he hissed. 'Don't follow!'

The boy blinked, stepped back. But when Simon turned the next corner, he was still following, his thin legs flashing. And Simon, tired from the fruitlessness of the afternoon, didn't have the energy to send him away.

A BREAK IN THE CHAIN

There was a cold bite to the late afternoon breeze when he gave up his search for the day. Any suggestion of spirit he'd had the day before had been flattened. But it would return after a good night's sleep; he knew that with certainty. Because another quality was slowly forming in Simon, a measure of persistence that was at this moment as fragile as an ephemeral whiff of excitement. It manifested itself in the necessity to think laterally. Maybe, he considered, as he trudged along the streets, he didn't have to join the queue for the goldfields after all. A horse would be a hindrance, and there was plenty of transport going up there. Cost a good bit to feed, too. Perhaps he should search for work here in town. There must be something he could do other than fiddle for his supper.

'Mister?'

He looked down. The annoying child was still at his side. He was about to send him packing with a clap to his ear when something in the boy's plea stopped him.

'Mister,' the boy said. 'You want a horse? I know where to find one. A good one. Come with me?' He saw the light in Simon's eyes and pressed his advantage. 'Only one penny.'

'One penny!'

The boy's grin was instant. His fingers knotted together; he was younger than Simon had first thought. Skinny as a runt with hair slicked back in an effort, Simon guessed, to look older.

'All right,' Simon sighed. He was getting nowhere on his own. 'Show me.'

A BREAK IN THE CHAIN

He expected the boy to bound off happily, but he remained in his place.

'Eh? Let's go.'

Instead, the boy held out a grubby hand. 'Up-front,' he said.

'I beg pardon?'

'Up-front. Payment. Payment up-front.'

Simon laughed. 'I am not so stupid. I give penny and you run!' But even as he spoke, he knew the boy wouldn't.

'Cross my heart and swear to God.' Solemnly the boy performed the ritual and hastily pocketed the coin. 'Quick now, mister. Before it gets taken. We have to hurry.' He started off.

'Wait!' Simon called. 'Wait.' He held out his hand. The boy's face fell and he angrily reached for the coin from his pocket. 'No,' Simon laughed. 'No.' He took the boy's hand in his and shook it. 'My name Simon Kosmanske,' he said.

The boy smiled suddenly. 'Pleased to meet you, mister. I'm Ted.'

Ted headed away from the city, sprinting now. Simon, whose muscles had grown soft, struggled to keep up. When Ted turned off the track and stopped, it was not at a stable but a smithy, with the blacksmith flattening out a twisted shoe.

The conversation between Ted and the blacksmith was too fast for Simon, but after another critical look at the shoe he was working on, the blacksmith threw down his tools, wiped his apron and silently disappeared around the corner.

A BREAK IN THE CHAIN

The boy beckoned to Simon.

'Come on. We got to follow him.'

Behind the smithy was a shed serving as a stable with three or four stalls. From here the blacksmith emerged with a horse. At first, Simon was relieved: he hadn't been tricked. But as the blacksmith led her into the light, Simon grew angry. In all his time around stock he had never seen a sadder animal. She would make neither carthorse nor hack – and it would be cruel to subject her to either. The mare was well past middle-age, her neck sunken, her sides tucked and gaunt, and from the way she hung her head, her spirit quite gone.

She was no use to him, but he couldn't help running his hands over her rough coat. It was the first animal he'd petted in months.

'How much?' he asked.

The blacksmith looked at him keenly, eyed his neatly trimmed beard and fresh shirt.

'Twenty pound.'

'Twenty!' For that price he could get himself shipped back to Prussia and put an end to all this.

'Twenty pound,' the blacksmith sniffed. 'Take it or leave it. If you leave it, she'll end up on someone's platter tomorrow. Can't afford to feed her no more.'

Ted stood to one side watching the exchange carefully. Simon dropped his hands from the horse's coat, and shook his head. 'Too old to work,' he muttered. 'Kinder to shoot her.'

He marched out of the stable, unable to shake the feeling he'd just pulled the trigger. Ted followed after him.

'Don't worry, mister,' he said. 'She was too old for you. But I know a better one. Want to see it?'

'All right,' Simon sighed.

Ted nodded and again held out his hand. 'One penny,' he said.

So, this was his game. Simon had been tricked. Then he remembered that this trick was also a living. It may not have been honest, but the boy was working his trade the only way he knew how. He threw Ted a penny.

'Okay,' he said. 'But only good horse, yes?'

Five pennies and a day later, Simon found the mare he was looking for, a bright bay no longer young, but in good condition with a pleasant temperament.

'She was trained to be a trotter,' the dealer explained, 'so she'll trot everywhere. Perfect for a cart and you'll find she can get up quite a speed on level going. Tell you up front, though: only problem with this mare is that it's pretty much impossible to get shoes on her. Being shod freaks her out... Best bet'd be to keep off the stonier tracks and then you can dispense with shoes altogether.'

Simon paid three pounds. The dealer agreed to keep the horse until Simon had assembled the rest of the equipment he needed.

'You have cart?' Simon asked.

The dealer's gaze shot sideways to Ted who had suddenly stepped forward. 'Don't rightly know, sir. Ted here might be able to help you. He's a good lad. Knows his way pretty well around the traps.'

And Ted did indeed know of a cart. In fact, he knew of three that might be suitable.

'How much?' asked Simon.

'A penny each for the two closest to here. If they're not right, tuppence for the other.'

'Oh, tuppence now?' It was Simon's turn to fold his arms.

'Yes. It's quite far away – it'll take us two hours each way.'

Simon knew enough now of the way Ted operated to know that the first two carts would be no good. So he decided against bringing the horse – he could collect her in the morning. It was a wise choice in the end: the first two carts were indeed unsuitable, while the third, a good solid-looking cart, had been sold by the time they arrived.

Ted smiled through Simon's disappointment. 'It's all right, mister. Tomorrow, I'll find you one for sure. And food, I know where to get cheap fodder for the horse and you'll need supplies for yourself. And entertainment. For the evenings. Cards?' He used his two hands in a shuffling action so innocent that Simon laughed.

Ted had done his homework. The next morning, Simon found that the boy had used one of his pennies to hold a cart for his inspection. It had no springs which would be hard on the horse, but on the other hand it moved quite freely and evenly. Good enough, he decided. With the essentials of transport, tackle and horse fodder taken care of, Ted led him to a shed at the far end of a narrow alley, and the boy rubbed his hands and dimpled when he saw the slow smile spread over Simon's face.

'Good prices, eh? Used, but still okay. This is what you'll need.' Eagerly Ted sorted through the pile and brought out a tin can.

Simon shook his head. 'Don't need.'

A BREAK IN THE CHAIN

'You need this for your tea, mister. Everyone has a billy. And a hook. You'll need a hook to hang it from poles over your fire.'

At another store, Ted insisted on suet for frying, tins of bully beef, a sack of flour, salt and tea. At the counter, Simon reached into a small pocket he had sewn into his waistband for yet another sovereign. He kept the sovereigns and the smaller change separate, but at this rate the purse in his waistband was going to be very light by the time he reached the fields.

'You need flour for your damper,' Ted explained. 'And you should buy it here, you can't get much up there. But you can fish. They say there's plenty of eels in the rivers, easy to catch and taste like rabbit. And you'll need a firearm, of course.' Ted brightened at the thought of another commission.

'Fire. Arm?'

'Firearm. Rifle. Like this.' Stretching out his arm, Ted sighted along an imaginary barrel, sweeping it up into the dim rafters, jerking horribly with each shot. 'Pow. Pow. Powpow-pow-pow...'

'No gun.'

'No gun! But then how are you going to get fresh meat? Plenty kangaroos up there – I can tell you how to make kangaroo tail soup. But you need a gun to get them.'

'No gun,' Simon repeated firmly. 'No killing kangaroos. No killing any animals.'

'But there's bushrangers on the track, sir! Ruthless men. They rob...'

'No gun!'

A BREAK IN THE CHAIN

Now that Simon was nearly ready to move, he was surprised at how reluctant he was to leave Melbourne. The three days he had spent with Ted had been profitable for both, but there was something else holding him. The young boy had trotted at his side, nudging him in one direction and then another, always in good spirits and with a knowledge of the town beyond his years. Was he to leave yet another friendship?

Back in the seconds shed, he picked up a billy, dented and blackened, and asked hesitantly, 'Buy these. Or new ones?'

'For a living, you mean?' Ted regarded him with his old-man eyes.

Simon nodded. He felt foolish seeking the advice of a boy, but he trusted Ted, and trust was a commodity in itself, rare any place in the world – rarer still in a mining town.

Ted squatted, rested back on his heels, and looked into the hard-dried mud of the floor as if he were reading a fortune. 'You don't have much money, do you, mister?' he said, slowly. 'You know what I'd do? There's a choice, you see. You could buy these and sell on. Folks are so keen to get up there, they forget they've got to live while they're seeking their fortune, so there's always a need.' He paused, his forehead creased.

'But for you, I reckon a better bet is to be a jobbing carter.'

'Jobbing carter?'

'Yep. You've got the horse now. And the cart and all. My old man always said the best way to make money is to make money out of other folks wanting to make money. Most of the diggers don't have transport and have to pay to get their stuff moved from one place to the next.' Ted scratched his nose, thinking. 'You could make a thousand pounds a year by jobbing, depending on how many hours you work. That way, your bad English won't hold you back. And you'd only be moving stuff from one goldfield to another, or even around the same dig. Means you don't have to tire the horse to death by coming back and forth to Melbourne. Them roads aren't too good.'

Simon's heart skittered with the possibility. This would be one way to earn a living without spending the rest of his savings, a way of matching the hours he wanted to work with the money he wanted to make. 'Many people need this… jobbing?'

'They sure do. I hear them talk every which way around the diggings. And you won't need a licence like you would for hawking. But later, if you want to hawk from town to town, come and see me again and I'll show you how to go about it.'

The sudden light in Simon's eyes earned an answering flicker from Ted's. They both smiled. Simon reached out and shook the boy's hand warmly.

'Thank you, Ted. But how will I find you? When I come back?'

Ted chuckled. 'Don't you worry, mister. I'll find you. Folks from out of town are dead easy to spot. So long.' With a quick wave, he was gone.

Simon sighed. He kicked out at a rut of dried mud and gazed at the uneven streetscape where a weatherboard cottage sheltered in the lee of two taller buildings. He would miss Ted – Melbourne, too. Was it only his fancy, or in his guided meandering had there been a secret exchange, a small piece of himself swapped for a footprint on the city?

It wasn't until later that day that Simon reached into his coin pocket and found it empty. Ted? Nothing wipes out sentimentality as fast as suspecting you've been robbed. His mouth twisted. And if he'd felt friendless before, he felt worse now.

Next morning, back at the horse yard, Simon took his time saddling up the mare. Before going for the dray, he would take her for a ride, get to know her, see how she handled and actually run his hands over a satin coat.

'What is her name?' Simon asked the dealer as he slipped his foot into the stirrup. At what he judged was a fraction under fifteen hands, she was a good height. Chewing at her bit, she danced a little.

'Something-or-other-Vitesse was her racing name,' the dealer told him. 'She was bred by a Frog and the word means speed, quick, that sort of thing. You get the picture? Except I guess she didn't quite live up to her name, else she wouldn't have ended up here. But she'll do you proud for what you want. If you want a run, take her through the back way and you'll find a bit of bush.' The dealer slapped her on the neck and she shot off at a sharp trot.

Simon quickly learned that trotting was in fact her only gait. She walked only reluctantly, constantly breaking into a crablike jog. When he tightened the reins, urged her into a canter, she responded with increased speed, but her rumbling action was something one could neither rise to, nor sit at – she was quite the most uncomfortable ride he'd ever had. But for a horse that had been raced, she had a good mouth and she was not overly skittish. By the time Simon brought her back to the yard, he realised that Vitesse was too difficult a name for them both. He would call her Tess.

Paying the balance of what he owed reminded him of the stolen money.

'You know the young boy, Ted?' he asked the dealer.

The dealer lifted an eyebrow. 'Not so young, our Ted. But yes, I know him.'

'You know him good?'

'Why do you want to know, sir?'

'I think he...' Simon threaded his hand quickly in and out of his pocket.

The man laughed. 'Doesn't sound like our Ted. Drives a hard bargain, but he's no thief. I'd recommend him myself.'

Simon frowned. 'He is young?'

'Good Lord no. Try fifteen going on thirty. Ted's finished with school, not that he learned anything life hadn't already taught him. Bit of a runt for some reason, but what he lacks in height he makes up for in guts. He's kept his mum, who's poorly, and his kid sisters for years now since the father shot through. Wears his shoe leather thin keeping that lot in bread and milk. No, Ted's a good lad – even if he's somewhat rough here and there.

'For all its posh buildings, this is still a village here, mate, and it's not worth a person's while to muck up. Over the years I've seen all types come and go, and Ted's one of the better ones.' He sensed Simon was still unconvinced, and added: 'Maybe you spent it without noticing? Stocking up with all the gear is an expensive business. Retrace your steps. If I was you, that's what I would do.'

A BREAK IN THE CHAIN

If, as a ride, Tess disappointed, she made up for it between the shafts. She backed up happily to the dray and stood patiently enough while he loaded up at his various stops. While the boy's suggestion of working as a jobbing carter was a good one, on overnight reflection Simon decided he would combine Jack's advice with Ted's. It made sense to load the cart – for the outward journey, at least – with as many bags of flour, tea, sugar and tins of bully beef as he could reasonably afford.

'Glad to see you again, sir,' said the storekeeper. He reached into a drawer and brought out a scant handful of coin. 'Thought you might be missing something. I found this back of that stack there. Must've fell out of your pocket when you was in the store.'

Simon took it slowly. He leaned hard against the counter. What was it about money that it had the potential to spoil something of real value – something that could not be bought.

3

Leaving town was easy. Simon only had to join the weird throng moving south-west towards Geelong. From there, he figured, he would turn north to Ballarat, sixty miles in total. An easy day's travel.

So far his only problem had been Tess. The tractable mare that had waited quietly at each stop while he loaded up with goods turned into a demon once she joined the others on the road. With teeth clamped tight on the bit, neck extended, she single-mindedly set out to pass everything in her way. Fighting for control as the wheels bumped and thumped over the deep-gouged clay, he was thankful that the journey was generally upslope, the load holding the dray down. In winter, he could only imagine the depth of churned-up mud, something to bear in mind if he were to work this route on any regular basis.

For Tess, it was a mysterious trotting track where the walkers and wagons and long chains of yoked bullocks presented no real competition at all. She was unperturbed by the long snaking whips that rang out across the backs of the animals with a sound like the smack-crack of thunder in a cloudless sky. She understood whips. The carts, too, she could cope with; they were but a form of gig. Ears laid flat back, her shoulders slick with foaming sweat, she relished the challenge presented by each, passing every animal and vehicle in the never-ending queue one by one like the star she was. It was only when she was outstripped by a horse and rider that she exploded into a fury, pulling, dancing, fretting, fighting for her head.

Struggling to hold her on some sort of course, Simon wondered which of them would tire first. A tipped cart could mean he lost all before he started.

When the mob's mood changed, Simon knew the end of the journey was in sight. All at once drivers and riders alike shook off all signs of weariness, pushing forward like men headed towards early-closing at the local pub. This unsettled Tess again and in the minutes it took to bring her under control, Simon found they had joined one of the groups peeling off from the main crowd and that this was the end of any kind of rutted track.

In fact, here was a kind of end altogether, he thought, as the carts spread out into the wasted landscape. Tess, heeding his mood rather than the reins, slowed and stopped. Simon clambered down to stand at her head, disbelieving of what lay in front of him.

Once, he imagined, it would have resembled the bushland he had been passing through for most of the trip: forests of gums with a tangled undergrowth of spiky grasses and the small, stunted trees covered with flowers like furry yellow balls that the bees loved. Once it would have been bush inhabited by the strange bear-like animals, more curious than timid that scampered like badgers, or the small kangaroos he heard described as wallabies. As he led Tess further into the waste, Simon could see that the original watercourse had been partially diverted to make a stream – now dry and scraped flat – and that the trickling creek left behind would not last out the season.

And so now, nothing would live here; nothing *could* live in a place where all that was left was the curious grey harshness of the felled trees lying with their roots pointing at the sun, where the soil was trampled to fine dust, where the flies still hovered over piles of cans, flour bags and torn cardboard boxes, and all the water was gone. Just as on the voyage, Simon thought, it was man against nature – and to see this destruction it would seem that man had won. Was this the goldfields? Was this what it was going to be like?

Simon imagined Ted kneeling before him holding out the shovel, a serious smile on his puckish face, 'To keep it neat, mister,' and he wondered what the boy would say if he were here. Had Ted ever left the town? Simon's gaze swept across the iron-grey of the dead trees. Even a hunter uses what he kills. Tess thrust her head hard into his body to rub off the flies beading at the edges of her eyes, and Simon almost fell. He curled his fingers tight into his horse's mane and pressed his head hard into her sopping neck.

When he arrived at the diggings – a hilly desertscape of tents and make-shift shelters – the enormity of his task grew clearer. There was an alien uniformity about the figures dressed in shirts of blue or red, moleskin trousers and Californian banana hats – he felt as out of place as if he'd landed on an ice flow populated by penguins. Looping the reins over his arm, he went to the mare's head.

'Ah Tess,' he murmured scratching between her ears. 'What to do next?'

A twisted, anxious feeling tore at his gut. His knowledge of English was shaky at best, and it was only now that he recognised the value of Ted's negotiations on his behalf. No doubt he spoke well enough to make his needs known, but he suspected it would be inadequate for conducting business of any kind. He had supplies to sell and enough food to feed his horse and himself for a few days, but he had very little money left. Suddenly, he felt as sick as he had that first day at sea. And then Jack's words came back to him: *Because most are, with respect, like you – they haven't thought things through.* In a strange way, it made it easier that at least he had this in common with everyone else.

Animals had always communicated with Simon, and when his mare answered him by breathing hard through her nostrils and lowering her head, Simon knew that, first, he had to care for her. She was, after all, the only living thing close to him. And now the race was over, this extraordinarily ugly environment was as strange to her as it was to him. Talking quietly all the while, he shook her free of her traces and led her about the diggings, purring, murmuring, waiting for her to cool before he fed and watered her. His words were private, staggered, animal-talk.

He settled them both by leading her back and forth, up and down the hill and around the tents and the bark-roofed huts. As he calmed, his mind began to work again. What he had before him, he realised, was a set of problems that had to be solved. It was like being back in the tunnel to Australia with Marks, only this time he couldn't just clamber out and walk away. He had to make it work. If he had to, he'd dig his way out. And this time he wouldn't give up. Moses would be proud of him all right.

Searching for the odd tussock of grass, Tess snorted into the yellow dust. It was time to give her a drink.

Late evening turned the spring air snapping cool. He had finished with the horse and his tent was stretched tight over the poles just off to the side of the main settlement. All around him, campfires lit and the aroma of sweet milky tea in the air. Further up the hill, a baby crying, and from a tent nearby snatches of a tuneless song reached him.

With the fiddle on his lap and Tess tethered close by, Simon took stock. Around was both good and bad. If it were possible to make this venture work, he would do it.

If anything, his arrival at the diggings only confirmed his reluctance for panning gold. The men worked with a focused intensity he didn't wish to understand. Easy money, it may be. But that was not always the case from what he heard. So what then to do with the raging fever of an addiction that remained just out of reach? That was something he couldn't afford to think about. Not for now would he face the niggling worry that if ever he were introduced to great wealth he might become as dependent on it as the next man. It was simply a comfortable life he was after, he told himself, not much different from the one he'd had in Prussia. But then, he remembered, he had been living off someone else's money all his life until now, the unfortunate consequences of which were framed in dusty outline through the triangle of his tent opening.

It was clear he needed to earn his own way, stand alone, preferably with a living that couldn't again be wrenched from him, and something told him that to try to make money from music was in many ways like digging for gold. For a while he might strike it lucky, but it wouldn't last for long.

Again, Simon thought how easy it was for someone like Marks. He had an open smile which spelt out uncomplicated friendliness: people were drawn to him. What would Marks do in similar circumstances? The Californian fields couldn't be much different from this. What would he have done with his new-fangled camera? Just simply walked up to people and asked whether they wanted a likeness of themselves? To have as a souvenir, perhaps, or to send to the folks back home? Marks had a camera where Simon had a fiddle – but Marks had something else, too: a sense of team spirit. Where Simon would thrill between the shafts of a dray, Marks was like one of the oxen that pulled the huge loads. One might not necessarily achieve more than the other, but they went about it differently.

Now he was here, Simon could see there was indeed a need for carting – a jobbing carter, Ted had called it. But how to go about it? Accustomed to offering his services from a young age, it was easy enough for Ted to suggest, but the idea of soliciting business by tapping on the shoulder of a complete stranger made Simon curl up inside. This was a living that would last as long as the gold it fed off. When the seams ran out, so too would the work, and he would have to start from the beginning.

And then there was the problem of his English. He spoke Yiddish and Polish and a little Russian, but though it had improved, English had him confounded with its many contradictions and complexity. His vocabulary was still scant, his knowledge of grammar non-existent, and he knew from the expressions that flitted over people's faces that his pronunciation was something of a joke.

It was difficult to fit his character to an honest living, but out of his dilemma one certainty was emerging. Like his father and like Marks with his camera, Simon wanted to work for himself.

He would be his own master and, in that way, he would at least retain some say over his own fate. Never again, he swore to himself, would he put himself in a position where he was told to pack his bags. Never again would he set himself up to be forced to leave his home. Never, never again.

Overlaid with the spicy smell of salt spray mingled with ephemeral whiffs of pipe tobacco, again a snippet of Jack's advice came back to him – about buying a horse and wagon and loading it up with necessary supplies. *When commodities are scarce, prices are sweet.* Jack wasn't wrong: every dray and wagon from Melbourne to here was piled with bags of flour, sugar and tea among the chaff and oats. But that too, he figured, would last just as long as it took some enterprising person to build a flour mill to service the acres of wheat he had seen on his way.

As the night drew in, the tuneless singing grew louder and Simon hoped the voice would eventually run dry and go to sleep. He checked the tether holding Tess and, dropping the tent flap, turned in for the night. Tomorrow was another day. But the singing went on and on.

He started out of his sleep suddenly. The soft outline of a light moved across the outside of the canvas. For a moment, he thought he was dreaming and this was the

Angel Gabriel himself come to kneel by his side. Then he heard Tess nicker softly. Instantly alert, he sprang for the opening.

Outside was a man stripped to his moleskins bending to the tether knot. In the brief moment before the fellow stepped back in shock, dropping his lantern as he fell over his own feet, Simon caught a glimpse of golden curls chopped short over shoulders bronzed as a sailor's and wet with sweat despite the cold night. The mare backed away in fright and Simon grasped the rope.

'What you doing?' he cried.

The man struggled in the sand, scrabbling for the lantern before lurching to his feet.

'What the bloody hell d'you t'ink I'm doing, buddy, but looking after your bleeding horse. She won't last a minute here with t'em t'ieving Chinks about. Know what I'm saying?'

'No,' said Simon shortly. He stared at the man's attempts to relight the lantern and when it flared it lit a face so handsome that even the sweated alcohol on the forehead and the rough-clipped growth about his chin couldn't disguise.

'You take my advice: you sell her before she gets stolen. Can't trust anyone round here further than you can t'row t'em, filthy t'ieving lot, if you know what I'm saying. There's method in the black gear they wear – can't see 'em in the dark.'

'Not for sale.'

'Jesus, Sweet Mary, Mother o' God, not another one of t'em inarticulates. Tell you what: come to my tent and we'll have a drink. Become buddies. How 'bout that?'

'Buddies?'

A BREAK IN THE CHAIN

The man stepped closer, swayed on feet planted wide, raised his lantern so the gold of a chain glinted against the hair of his broad chest. Simon winced as the stench of cheap liquor reached his nostrils. He thought for a moment the man was going to put an arm around his shoulder.

'Buddies, brothers. Friends, mates. You know, mate? Exchange stories.' He hiccupped. 'New here, aren't you? Just came in today? This is Australia, matey. One for all and all for one. No differences. All equal, un'erstand? 'Cept the place's rapidly going to t'em teetotalling dogs – that's what we have here. Bloody pussyfooting sleazes'll overrun the place before you know it. Before we all know it. Come and have a drink and I'll inish…inish… Oh well, come an' have a drink anyway. Nothing to pay – which doesn't mean it'll be free, by the way. I know what your type is like.'

Holding tight to Tess's halter, Simon shook his head.

The man's mood changed. 'Have it your own way.' Stepping forward suddenly he thrust the lantern into Simon's face, so the heat burned at his cheek and the mare reared to one side. 'Some people have to learn it all the hard way. You might just find it doesn't pay to turn down an offer o' friendship from Mick O'Malley.' Sneering over his shoulder, he staggered in short rushes down the hill until, stumbling into a guy rope, he finished his journey head over heels.

As the sun dissolved the moisture of the night and lit the fields with its own particular brand of gold, Simon indulged in a round of invective of his own. Although the tarpaulin was still roped tight, the cart beneath its cover was empty. He cursed himself for not checking earlier, although there was little he could have done save guard it all night in this derelict desolation of a space filled side to side with strangers, tents and ugly mullock heaps.

Hatred is a poison that etches the psyche, as indelible and silent as acid on marble. But it was not the Chinese passing quietly by – a line of black-clothed figures with pickaxes across their shoulders and tin dishes under their arms – that made Simon's temper rise. He was no stranger to prejudice and recognised it for the fear that fuelled it, and in this case he suspected O'Malley's bias had ripened as the liquor sapped his strength and will to work. It could have been anyone, but Simon suspected O'Malley. He was tempted to confront the Irishman, but to what avail? Altercations with drunks he didn't need. O'Malley's head would be sore, no doubt, and his pride sorer. The best he could do would be to move camp to the opposite side of the hill.

As for the missing goods, a glance at the vastness of the waking camp showed there was no more sense in speculating over their whereabouts than mourning a spilt pail of milk. Perhaps, too, there was a degree of relief in the deep breath he took. At least the horse wasn't stolen. And the dray was still there. Now he had no choice but to become a jobbing carter. And from now on, he decided, he would sleep with the mare's tether rope tied to his foot.

As it turned out, carting wasn't as difficult as he had feared. He had determined to spend the better part of the morning investigating the site, sorting and storing information and familiarising himself with the business of gold mining at the margin. But reluctant to leave Tess or the dray unattended, he decided to drive.

A BREAK IN THE CHAIN

As the field and its inhabitants grew more familiar, patterns began to emerge. He soon learned that the teamsters always stopped their wagons at the same place and that there was plenty of work for the scant number of drays carting flour and produce to the larger tents. And he learned that there was nothing intimidating in standing by Tess's head to wait until he was approached.

At first he understood only that he was needed to carry something from one place to another, for which he decided his fee would be a shilling a run. But as his confidence grew, he realised that Melbourne prices were no guide as to what he could charge in the goldfields and that money was not the only currency up here. Sometimes they paid him in gold, other times with food for himself or fodder for Tess. Occasionally he was asked to accept a note of credit or a promise, and he gained skill in assessing risk.

4

One thing was certain. The bone-weary work of jobbing was not something Simon wanted to do for long. But Ted was right; there was money in it and little risk. And it gave him a chance to travel over a good half of the new colony. Sometimes he merely helped a digger move camp from one find to another. Other times he serviced the longer and more profitable runs, driving between fields to pick up one load as he dropped off another. He reckoned Tess had done the run so many times between Ballarat and Ararat that she could make it blindfolded. The trip down to Melbourne through Geelong became progressively easier; each time he went the road gangs were widening and reinforcing the tracks.

On his frequent trips to Melbourne, Ted often found him. 'How do you know I'm here?' Simon would ask. But Ted only shrugged.

'You stand out like a sore thumb, mister. You can tell a stranger just by how he walks.'

Now that he needed supplies in quantity, Ted led him to the warehouses in the Lane, the huge go-downs piled to the rafters with goods from all over the world. Chests of tea from China, the fresh and delicate scents finding their way into the very clothes you wore. From

A BREAK IN THE CHAIN

Manchester came massive rolls of cambric for sheeting and pillowcases. And from the Near and Far East: carpets and silk hangings, bowls and urns of brass and copper. Sacks of oats from Britain. Closer to home, great stacks of bagged flour, too, grown in some of the reaches he travelled through, brought down to be processed in the city only to be trekked back out again.

But it was the textile houses with their bolts of cloth that fascinated him. He was thrilled by the sheer variety of the stiff linens, the luscious brocades and vibrant satins, the muslins and delicate laces, and the lengths of embroidered silks from India, edged sometimes in silver, sometimes in gold. In one particular store he stood for a long while in front of a wall of small drawers filled with all manner of frills and feathers and cheeky furbelows for ladies' hats, and with ribbons, threads, bindings and buttons of every size and colour. One day, he thought, he would have his own store where such merchandise could be displayed in a manner that would do it justice.

Ted's awareness of the emotions and needs of his customers was keenly honed and he found it easy to gauge Simon's excitement as he ran his fingers lightly over one piece of cloth, a creamy silk.

'Fit for the Guv's wife, that one there,' he said. 'Think you might take up some materials, clothes, hats, as well as food this time? Stop off at one of the towns on the way?' Seeing the store merchant hovering close by, he rapped out. 'Get the counting glass.'

'No, not yet, Ted. Not yet,' said Simon hastily. 'One day, maybe.' He turned away, willing himself to work harder, faster.

Another time, Ted met him at the door to his lodgings, glowing. 'There's a good opportunity come up to buy a store, mister.'

'I'm not ready. One day, perhaps. Not now.'

'Opportunities like this – they don't come every day. It's not far from here. Do you want to take a quick look? No harm can come of taking a look…'

'Not today, Ted.' Simon's voice was firm.

But the following day, delicately flicking his whip at the flies on Tess's rump as he drove back up to the fields, Ted's suggestion resurfaced. As the lad had said, there was no harm in taking a look, even if he had no intention just yet of moving down to the city. It would be in the nature of investigating how much he would have to spend to get a good business site. Something that ultimately had to be done.

What had stopped him? Was it that he was afraid he would discover it so expensive that it would be forever beyond his reach? Or was it simply that he was enjoying the country and felt, for the moment, content to polish his skills on his own customers who were starting to get to know and like him? As his savings gradually increased, so did his respect for money. He found some of his previously held convictions about the stuff changing. Money was power, he began to understand. It had a language all its own.

It was at this point that he realised uncomfortably that as his new world grew more real his memories of the past were fading. It was as if the two views were attached to one another by some sort of pulley system and he couldn't have both in sight at the same time. The faces of the folks at home grew filmy, like a dream that refused to come into focus. The more he tried, the hazier it became. Even the pain was dulled – no longer even an ache. He began to wonder now who he was trying to make proud: his father or himself?

The thought set up a little panic inside him. He wasn't sure he was ready to let go of his imagined homecoming. His vision had been, to that point, simple and constant, his line of sight leading straight back to Moses and the farm. He saw clear through the centre of the earth and imagined himself arriving home in style, unannounced, in a carriage pulled by twin greys, himself in fine clothes with the manners of a gentleman, a wife at his side, his purse fat and full.

'See,' he would say to his astounded father. 'See how well I have done. You didn't think I would be any good and now I have all this.' He would hand his father money, enough for the rest of his life, and he would buy the farm next door, surround himself with sons and sit on the side of a hill and play music to his cattle.

If he let this picture slide, what would take its place? What would drive him then? A store of his own? In the country or in the city? That would be the end to his dream of sitting on the grassy slope of the hill back home – and he wasn't quite ready to let the other image go. Maybe that was the reason he had shied away from taking a look at the store.

On another longer run, this time with a commission of goods for a storekeeper up at the Ovens fields to the north, Simon wondered about what drove the human psyche beyond its simplest needs to a place where desire became a disease of the spirit. Among all the begetting of the first book of the Pentateuch, the writers omitted the simple fact that obsession begets obsession. It was impossible to be in the business of gold-digging with its single-minded rinsing and puddling, channelling and tunnelling, without becoming infected. If you arrived bewildered, then bewitched you became by simply breathing the air. If this giddiness was the fever they said it was, then it was an extreme disorder, a space beyond the margin of reason.

Simon learned quickly that among the codes and symbols embedded in this new life, mateship ranked well down the list. Men, women too, went there for one purpose – to arrive home richer than when they'd left – and friendship only got in the way. The purity of this single aim could only be sustained by bloody-mindedness, a capacity for hard work and by keeping to yourself.

But there was something else he observed. There was a type of grit the diggers possessed that somehow overcame the extremes of heat and cold that scorched and blistered or numbed in turn, that survived the wind storms that swallowed the air and turned it yellower than any reef, that barely recognised the audacity of the flies that settled and sucked at the corners of the eyes and the mouth, and clustered thickly on backs sticky with sweat.

But was it grit or something else that made men, used to sheets soft and thick and smelling of soapy wash, roll into a hessian sack still reeking of chaff only to fall straight asleep? Was it grit that made it so easy for them to forget the bone china with the succulent roasts when they dipped their damper into a stew and stared unseeing at the rats sifting for morsels among the piles of slop and rubbish? Or was it an oversupply of both grit and greed that encouraged them to tough it out with barely enough clean water to drink and none in which to bathe, and food only when there was gold to exchange?

Finally, individual characteristics – like discrepancies of sex or clothing – became unimportant. After a while there was a sameness about the diggers he'd noticed when he first arrived. Only now, the broken fingernails, hard-centred palms and eyes turned inward all spoke the same story: a tale of hope gone sour as old milk.

But they kept arriving, of course, because their ears were closed to all but the happy stories. The one about Paolo – called Iti on the fields – who built a stuccoed mansion with chandeliers out of real crystal when he arrived back in Tuscany. Or Anthony Geddes who went back to England, bought a title, wed an heiress and played golf for the rest of his life. Or Rowan Hardy who decided to put the gold back where it came from when he joined the squattocracy and built one of the country's finest studs. But you never heard about the ones who didn't make it – the other 99.99 per cent.

Perhaps it was as simple as the carrot-and-stick principle. Despite their pomp and pretence, humans weren't so very different from other animals. You just had to make them want something enough. Then they wouldn't give up until the prize was won or they were lost. And if they wanted it enough, they wouldn't question the price.

Although he wasn't aware of the changes he was making to his own trade, he found his philosophising gradually became part of his business practice in that his method of charging his customers differentiated in line with his discernment of their level of need or desire. He quickly learned to judge those who could afford to pay more and, for a while, he balanced his conscience by allowing these to subsidise the needier and less wealthy.

For the most part, Simon enjoyed the living he made alternating his trades of jobbing and hawking. He grew to have a sense of what he might charge for a job, a knowledge of what his time and goods were worth. He learned when to press his advantage in a sale, and when to withdraw and found his customers starting to trust him. He had his favourite stopping places along the way: sometimes it was a share wattle-and-daub hut, other times he would unroll his tent. And then there were times when he could afford a bed in one of the lodging houses along the way, others when the nights were warm enough for him to unroll his swag and sleep under the cart.

When he counted backwards, he was surprised to find it was seven years since he had been ferried to the Melbourne docks from the *Black Swan*. Time had passed almost without his noticing. But while it was suddenly 1863, it was less the fact of time passing and more the change in his mood from happy to despondent each time he returned to the goldfields and the surrounding sad and desecrated land that set Simon thinking that perhaps it was time to settle somewhere.

In the end it was Tess and not his emerging discontent that provided the catalyst for change. Over the past few weeks, she had developed a limp he thought might be a strained tendon, not altogether surprising given the state of the roads.

A BREAK IN THE CHAIN

Although she wasn't in pain and it seemed to worry him more than it did her, with a little shock he realised she had been working steadily since he had been in the country and it was clear she deserved a rest. But, of course, to do that he, too, would have to stop work or change tack, at least for a time. Perhaps it hadn't been a bad thing after all that Ted had started him thinking about a place to buy. Maybe the time had come to start a small business. But perhaps up here rather than down in Melbourne. It would be infinitely easier to keep more than one horse in the country than in the city with its high stabling fees.

If the bigger picture was simply too large for his imagination, he would concentrate on the immediacies.

He had enough money now and a small experience of shopkeeping with Brown at Woolshed to run his own store. He would find some place away from all this. Set up for himself. He would start asking around.

5

Simon smiled a peculiar smile when he saw the flour mill with its canvas sails wide-open and softly circling. For some years now there'd been flourishing fields of wheat and barley lining the tracks. He'd known all along that once the gold became more difficult to get out of the ground they'd tilt at the land from a different angle, start settling down to produce crops – particularly wheat for the essential flour. And that sooner or later the raw product would be processed where it grew rather than being hauled down to the city and back again. He had often wondered at the general lag in foresight. Why weren't the mills a regular sight on his travels? He had perceived a need and more than once had thought of going into partnership to build his own mill.

He'd kicked at the heavy lifeless sacks as often as he'd hefted them and he knew from long experience that nothing was heavier than a hundredweight of flour. He'd come close to breaking the third commandment one time when a station owner's wife inspected the neatly piled sacks in her storeroom only to declare one and all full of weevils and stating flatly that they'd have to go back.

Simon was riding Tess gently now. He had taken to wrapping a poultice of hot linseed around her leg each evening and for the moment she was not limping. But knowing her fetlock would always hold a weakness, he had sold the cart and was riding her slowly south. If there was one worry Simon had on that sunny winter day he rode into Mortlake, it was Tess. He didn't want to work her anymore and she had never been a comfortable ride. But she was his closest friend and he had confided many a secret to her flickering ears.

But for now, it was enough to be away from the goldfields. It was clear to him that he should settle and having finally made the decision, he wondered at his own obsession, travelling ceaselessly through the years as though the tracks were tramlines, never diverting from the trails, stopping in a town only to sell his wares. He felt strangely light, as if something heavier than a sack of flour had been lifted from his shoulders.

For some time now he had been riding alongside the base of a large hill, so like the tapering slopes in Raoskow that it was easy to imagine he was back there with Marks, his mother holding out glasses of milk and slices of bread thick with fresh-churned butter and cream and the jam she made with the small, sweet strawberries, still whole so you could pick them off with your tongue...

It's only a hill, he told himself, and Raoskow a memory fast becoming distant. But all the same, his mood was such he was unable to avoid swinging off the track towards the small mountain with the black spots on the slopes that turned into cattle as he grew nearer. He breathed in the air. Damp. No dust. Good cattle country. And the juicy green of the grass was the right shade for a rich yield of creamy milk. All this travel and it was not until now he had happened to pass through this particular area. Even before he'd seen the glint of metal roofs snuggling at the base of the mountain, he knew this was where he would live.

As he rode into Mortlake, Simon could see there was enough settlement to make a trade. The essentials were all there. A couple of hotels, a general store, a post office, a courthouse, a butcher shop with sheep carcasses hanging outside in the sunshine and a group of men smoking in the shade of the verandah. It was big enough to have the makings of a good-sized town, but not so big there wouldn't be gaps of opportunity. Thought had been put in here. The main street was lined with saplings and built three-chain wide for the bullock carts to turn. A grove of tall pines shaded a group of well-built bluestone buildings off to one side.

There was a new feeling in Simon – not quite a thrill, something both more and less than that. Maybe he was just tired and looking for a reason to stop for a while. But still, this place had a plan, something lasting about it, absent from most of the places he had travelled in and out of over the last few years.

He decided he would stay for the night in the hotel with the gables that looked like a bit of Europe and called itself Mt Shadwell. As for Tess: tonight it would be a stable strewn extra-deep with straw and a hot barley mash. He jumped down, swung the reins over her head and stood for some time looking up and down the dusty street.

He started as he was hailed. 'Hey. Hey! Simon! Is it Simon? Simon Kosmanske? Here!'

Brows tight, Simon's head swung towards the voice. His hand light on his horse's rein he gazed about him while, as slow as hand-drawn frames, the full picture of the town slip-slipped by.

But behind him, there was a scuffling, a sound not quite right, a sudden snapping weight on his grip that wrenched his shoulder. He turned to see Tess side-on to the ground, her head moving, trying with all her stubborn will to right the heaviness of her body, tremors like an incoming tide rippling across the shine of her damp coat. Her leg, finally, or her heart?

Nothing. Nothing to be done.

Against the tide of knowing in him, he shouted at her. Bending, he slapped at her withers, tugged at the nose strap, trying with something that was more than strength to help her lift her heavy head.

'Up! Get up! You, Tess, get up.'

'Simon? Simon?'

Nothing to be done.

'What is it? What's up?' A voice somewhere. Not here.

Other voices. Surrounded. Surrounded by dusty shoes.

Nothing to be done.

His own voice unreal. Coming from someone else. Saying things he didn't believe. 'She's not young. She's an old horse. It is okay, okay...' Lies, all lies, the words lost in a common language as he knelt, his hands firm and strong on her face.

Not Tess. Please, not Tess.

The sound of blood in his brain. Or was it the ocean still? Endlessly battering, swishing, rushing, folding-in and folding-out? Perhaps he was still at sea standing at the deck rail, his eyesight blurred with loneliness and sleeting rain, and it was this – this horror in front of him – that was not real?

Tess, far too quickly, still. A hand with long fingers, fine like his own, gently nudging him, holding a pea-jacket to his shoulder. He looked up, swept his hands across his eyes to clear his sight.

'Here,' said Marks gently. 'Put this over her for a moment. I'm afraid there's not much that can be done for her right now. Come and have a drink while we work out what to do. Come, we'll return later.'

Marks waited until they were seated at the bar in the Mt Shadwell Hotel before he started talking. He had arrived at the Port of Melbourne from Liverpool on the *Red Jacket*, the fastest clipper in the world. He told of how on her maiden run between New York and Liverpool in 1854, she had defied ferocious winds and the weather of the North Atlantic by running under full sail, smashing records by arriving in Liverpool in just over thirteen days.

'Of course,' Marks mused, 'it took a great deal longer to get to Melbourne. But all the same, she's still the fastest there is – and such a beautiful ship.'

Simon took a sip of ale, winced at the bitterness, willed himself to concentrate. His brother's stories droned on through a fog he couldn't seem to shift. '*Red Jacket*?' he said. 'Strange name for ship.'

'Named after a Red Indian, Sagoyewatha, a chieftain who was donated a red jacket by the departing British.' Marks reached for the buckle of his knapsack. 'Here, I have a photograph.'

He held it out proudly. The photograph was of only part of the ship, a fine-carved figurehead of the chief himself, reclining with his hands folded over his beaded buckskins and a halo of feathers framing his grim face. He was indeed wearing a jacket, the red colour of which could only be imagined.

'Your photograph?'

'Of course.' Marks leant forward, his eyes shining. 'Plenty of opportunities on the fields. And you know what they are charging in Melbourne for a studio? One thousand pounds a year, and that's not even on the ground floor. One thousand pounds! Or two thousand for the whole shop.' He shook his head. 'I started off that way because on the ship they told me that was the easiest way to get known. But it's not.

'In towns with some pride, Simon, like Mortlake for instance, they're keen for a likeness and so there are always opportunities. Not overwhelming, but consistent. And on the goldfields it's different again. If they find a nugget, such excitement – you can't imagine. It's like hooking the big fish: they need proof of the occasion.' His eyes lit up. 'It's just like a wedding, Simon. They go off, get fresh clothes – clean – from somewhere, anywhere. If there's anything fancy to be borrowed, on it goes. And they want photograph after photograph and pay good money for them, too. Pay anything, sometimes. Yes, plenty of opportunities,' he repeated. He stopped for a moment, fingered his glass. 'So far, between California and here, I've saved seventy pounds. It wouldn't go far in Melbourne, but out here.' He shrugged. 'That's what I was doing when I saw you, photographing outside that shop.'

He was silent for a moment and then another thought occurred to him. He looked more closely at Simon. 'Are you still Kosmanske?' And when Simon nodded uncertainly he said, 'Some years ago I changed to Kozminsky. Easier for them to pronounce. Better for business, you know.'

Traces of an American accent overlaid his thicker European tones. In the seven – or was it eight? – years since he had last seen him, Marks was a different person. His little brother was now a man, someone he would have to get to know all over again. Simon had changed, too. There was a lot to discuss. But before they talked, he wanted to bury Tess.

'Bury her?' Marks looked doubtful. 'Wouldn't it be easier...?' The look on Simon's face silenced him.

'We bury her,' Simon said tersely, 'just outside the town.'

But the long night came first, and once Simon was alone the anaesthesia of shock was gradually replaced by a pain pressing in on him from all sides. He told himself that she was only a horse, an animal, that she was easily replaced. 'She was old, she was old,' he kept repeating. Time and again he clapped his hands fiercely to his head, berating himself for working her too hard and too long, searching for a reason – something, anything – to stem the hurt, to stop the slow burn that seared his body. He thought it stemmed from guilt, this relentless punishment, and perhaps it did in part, but because such affection was not part of his experience he was unable to acknowledge that he had loved her, too, and that his grief was the natural result of loss.

As night gave way to a cold, clear morning, he resolved to block Tess from his memory, much as one might tie a tourniquet. And he tugged the knot tight, not understanding that such a savage clamp on his emotions would be, in the fullness of time, irrevocable. Sitting on the edge of the iron bedstead, staring grimly at the scratched floorboards, he laid out a plan.

He was tired of the road. He must settle somewhere, if only for a few years, and Mortlake was as good a place as any he'd visited. He would combine his trading skills with his Melbourne wholesale contacts and open a store. He would become a storekeeper, a merchant. Perhaps a draper. He would change his name, like Marks. Call himself Kozminsky. K.o.z.m.i.n.s.k.y. He rolled it around on his tongue, practised saying it aloud. He sounded less foreign already. With Ted acting on his behalf in the city, it might work. It would work.

And Marks? He sensed that Marks had not yet arrived at the stage he had. His brother still had photographic contracts to fill and wanderlust to satisfy, but he would be back.

Part Two

Simon and Emma

1869

6

With two clippers and a cargo ship unloading, Station Pier was an incoherent jumble of sight and sound, of people, animals and possessions which grew and dispersed, divided and joined like a restless set of assorted cells. With a band enthusiastically adding another layer of confusion to the shouting and sobbing – with people grasping, gripping, hugging and kissing – the air was charged like an electric storm, full of panic and relief, excitement and apprehension.

Leaning against his jinker, idly smoking while he waited out the usual customs delay, Simon was distracted by an added commotion at the passenger-end of the quayside, where a lady had come close to be being toppled when two sheep charged from the folds of her billowing skirt. At first he laughed out loud at the astonishment on her face; the next moment he had tapped out his pipe and quickly threaded his way towards her.

She was smoothing her skirts and adjusting her hat just as Simon reached her. He retrieved her dropped parasol, raised his voice above the clatter.

'This is a poor welcome to a new country,' he said with a smile and a small bow. 'It can be rough...'

With a nod of thanks, she returned his smile, and looked away. He felt dismissed, empty as a pot that had served its purpose. But it gave him the chance to observe her more carefully, and he saw she had a greater composure up close. Although, not a beauty. Her gown might be fashionable – the garment cut well and the sheen of the silver-blue satin subtle enough – and her bonnet tasteful, with just the right amount of ribbon, yet the face under the wide brim was a little too long, the eyes severe. But he liked the fullness of her mouth, he decided, and her straight nose, and what he could see of her figure was shapely enough.

He hadn't realised he had been staring until she frowned. 'Thank you,' she said firmly.

It was not polite, he thought, to give a lady his card, but the struggle in him was lost before it started. After a moment, he withdrew a card from his pocketbook and, with another small bow, presented it to her.

'Allow me to introduce myself, please. Simon Kozminsky of Kozminsky's here in the city. I have a store in the country, too.' How silly it sounded. Kozminsky of Kozminsky's. Like some sort of tavern in the town. He wanted all of a sudden to tell her about the store. But he lacked the words to describe it in its present state – somewhere between the coin and curio shop he had originally bought and the watchmaker's den that dealt with Marks's imports – while at the same time readying itself for its next iteration as the elite jewellery and antique store that it would one day be. She would hear the pride in his voice, but the words themselves would let him down, or worse: let down his dream by being imprecise.

A BREAK IN THE CHAIN

The young woman hesitated. Simon was unsure if she would offer her own name or turn away altogether, but she did neither. A little resignedly she took the card, placed it in the reticule hanging from her wrist, nodded once more. Rather too cold, this one, he thought, touching his hat and moving off. Not rude exactly, but overly contained. How different from Tola! And then he realised it was many years since he'd thought of Tola. How could two women so different link themselves in his brain? Annoyed with himself, Simon made his way back through the scramble to wait for the customs all clear.

The flies were bothering the horses, sailing in and out of their whisking tails, rising from their legs when they stamped only to settle again. Tempted himself to stamp, he lit another pipe to keep them from his face. From time to time he glanced towards the woman, who looked as bored as he was himself. She couldn't see him from there, in any case. Even if she was curious. She was framed by a towering load of luggage against which she leant from time to time. As he watched, another figure, smaller, less well-dressed – her maid, perhaps – approached her, a small dog squirming in her arms. An argument followed, some altercation between the two until they were both upset in different ways. When the second figure ran off, the first raised her hand to her forehead and leaned more heavily into the pile which, slowly and quite deliberately, started to collapse about her.

And so for the second time that morning, Simon found himself at her side. 'Steady,' he said. 'There now, much better to sit.' He dragged forward a metal trunk. 'Sit, please, just here. You are unused to the sun.' He bent to cover his own surprise when she obeyed, while he restacked the spilled baggage, unable to stop himself running his hands lightly over the fine calfskin of a carry bag.

But with the luggage sorted, he stood undecided. He didn't want to risk another rejection, nor did he want to bow and retreat. This was starting to have the makings of a pantomime. The day was so warm he could feel his collar starting to soften, knew that before long the grey silk of his necktie would grow dark at the edges. He coughed, and just as he was about to offer her the use of his transport, a rather dumpy little man hurried up and pushed himself between them. Ignoring Simon, he bowed deeply to the woman.

'Miss Solomon? Miss Emma Solomon? Lamport at your service, Madam. Albert Lamport. My apologies for the delay. Quite beyond my control, I do assure you. I hope you have not been too inconvenienced?'

Simon cursed his shyness, his poor English, his lack of sophistication, his clumsiness. He felt invisible – or certainly of little consequence. He turned away.

But she stopped him. 'Mr Kozminsky?'

Rising, her sense of balance apparently restored, she turned from one man to the other. With a smile that made the day warmer still, she added, 'Mr Lamport. Allow me to introduce Mr Kozminsky. And Mr Kozminsky, this is Mr Lamport, manager of the English, Scottish and Australian Bank.' She smiled at the bank manager. 'We, that is I, had an...incident just now. And Mr Kozminsky was very kind indeed.'

After bending briefly over her outstretched hand, Simon moved off hurriedly, anxious to cover his delight. Perhaps saying his name twice hadn't been such a bad move, after all? At least she had remembered. He knew he would see her again. Emma Solomon. It was the second time Simon Kozminsky had stumbled across gold at the Melbourne dock.

It was only two weeks later that Simon arrived at the colonnaded entrance of the bank chambers in a smart brougham drawn by a well-matched pair of greys. It was fortunate, he reflected, that he had placed the account of S. Kozminsky with the ES&A Bank the year before. And perhaps it also furthered his case that he had recently been introduced to the manager, although given the particular circumstances, he couldn't think he had made a particularly favourable impression. That is, if Lamport remembered him at all.

But he had a chance to remedy that. Conscious always of his dress, today Simon had taken special care and the dark grey wool of his suit emphasised his starched white shirt. Tucked into the folds of his cravat was a star-ruby pin, the facets of the stone polished smooth to better show the five points of the star which glinted like a spill of moonshine. The pin was one of Kozminsky's first purchases during Simon's tentative move from coins to jewellery, one he had decided to keep back from sale for his own use. He touched it now for luck.

He planned to ask for a small increase in his loan, a perfectly reasonable request considering the wealth flowing into the city, the clientele the business was attracting and his recent decision to start specialising in pearls and gemstones. The discussion regarding Miss Solomon would be almost incidental, he had decided earlier. But now sitting in the scarlet velvet-covered chair outside Lamport's suite, his ivory-handled cane and his hat resting on his knees, his mind was as dry as his mouth.

When he was ushered through, Albert Lamport greeted him with a shake of his hand, frowning slightly as if he were trying to remember him. He waved at a chair and seated himself behind his grand oak desk leaving Simon to stare into the exaggerated gap between them. And then, for no reason at all, Simon remembered Tess, the mare that had pulled him so willingly for so many years up and down the country roads. The loss of Tess still hurt when it came across him unexpectedly like this.

The clock on the wall started to tick. Lamport was waiting for him to speak. Simon gritted his teeth, gripped hard at the brim of his hat, made himself a promise. He would, he vowed, accept no further loss in his life without a fight. Too often he had moved aside purely for others' convenience. Willing his eyes away from the clock to the implacable face half a room away, he breathed deeply, once, twice, and began to speak.

'I beg your pardon, Mr Lamport. Sometimes the language, you know... I come to you on two matters. My first request concerns my businesses: both accounts at your bank, both profitable. The turnover in my city store increases at a most satisfactory rate. I now wish to buy and sell gemstones, pearls. Selling, in some cases, for future payment. Like this.' From his pocket, he withdrew a wallet from which he took a piece of folded paper. 'You see, I have here a promise for payment due in one month. I would therefore be grateful for a sum of fifty pounds to be added to my loan. This I will of course pay off within the next four weeks.'

Lamport was taking notes. Simon breathed deeply. The manager looked up. 'Fine,' he said. 'Four weeks. And the other matter?'

Simon coloured. 'Yes, sir. More difficult. Perhaps you may remember?' He coughed, sat taller. 'Some weeks ago... The young lady at Station Pier? Her luggage collapsed. I was able to lend her some assistance... '

Lamport held his pen quite still in one hand, with the other he stroked his moustache. He nodded slowly. 'That was you, was it?'

Simon nodded, pressed his jaws together hard.

'And what is your interest in this young lady, Mr Kozminsky? I should add that the lady in question could be regarded as my protégé. In other words, I am responsible for her welfare.'

Simon felt a trickle of sweat reach his collar. 'I thought as much, sir. That is why I was hoping...' He sighed, raised his eyes to Lamport. 'I would like to meet her,' he said, finally. 'Very much.'

The two men regarded each other uncertainly. Lamport hadn't expected Kozminsky's second request, but he was no fool. He knew that the man was going about this in a right and proper manner. Melbourne was still a young city, rough enough and small enough for a man to further an acquaintance with a young lady in quite a different way. He was impressed that Simon had decided to approach him for an introduction.

Lamport was a thorough manager. He might have forgotten the face of the man before him, but prior to their appointment he had taken the time to check out the books of the two stores and the Kozminsky credentials. There were two Kozminskys in Victoria, he found – Simon and a brother, Marks – both currently storekeepers, both well-regarded.

While the figures didn't quite convince him that Simon was a particularly astute businessman, there was nothing to indicate that he was other than honest and hardworking, and it was clear that he'd had the initiative to start – and the staying power to successfully run – two businesses over the last five or so years. That could not be denied. With a comparatively minor loan, he operated out of a store in Mortlake that provided a steady source of income and for the last few years he had owned a curio business in the city, about which Lamport was less confident. The shop had been vacant for some time with the stock gathering dust before Kozminsky had revived it. Still, the annual balance sheets were all heading in the right direction. Kozminsky's collateral was sound.

Lamport drummed his fingers on his blotter. And if, despite his efforts, his earnings were a pittance compared to Emma's small fortune, that wasn't surprising. By any standards Emma Solomon was an extremely wealthy young woman and if her remittance were husbanded wisely over the next few years she would be in a position to buy and sell Kozminsky's businesses ten times over. He dressed well, too, although Lamport suspected that the care Kozminsky took in this regard masked a somewhat plain chap underneath.

There was perhaps only one negative. Still looking rather absently at the doodles on his blotter, Lamport balanced his pen across the knuckle of one finger. Kozminsky's chosen transport and the cut of his clothes suggested he spent his money rather too freely. Lamport had seen him arrive that morning by carriage, doubtless hired but possibly his own. In either circumstance an unnecessary extravagance. But that was a small thing to hold against him. After all, the man was of a marrying age and attractive unmarried women were not abundant in the colony. Then, too, a good match for Emma would prevent any difficulties from arising that he might be required to sort out. As that woman's nominal protector, he might do worse than introduce her to an eligible young man evidently already predisposed to like her. And then, of course, there was the religious thing. Given her family name, no one would know that she was not a Jew. Since she had been brought up in a Jewish family, he doubted she would object. And as the only person in the know outside England, Lamport was bound to secrecy. Kozminsky appeared so keen it wouldn't make much difference to him. It would be a good outcome for all, Lamport suspected.

Gazing across at the poorly concealed dread on Kozminsky's face, Lamport knew he had to say one thing, and one thing only, to seal the deal.

'You need to know, however, that Miss Solomon is an extremely wealthy woman. And that she is clever enough to spend her wealth wisely. Each month she receives a remittance, a payment.'

Simon's fingers went to the stone in his cravat.

'Who pays?' he asked.

'Her family. Her family pays.' Rising with a smile on his face, Lamport held out his hand.

'Yes, on both counts then, Mr Kozminsky. Four weeks for the first. As for the second: give Miss Solomon a little time to settle to life in the colony? And so, let's say a dinner party at my house in eight weeks' time? Dinner dress. Eight o'clock.'

7

Back in the country, Simon worked quickly. There was no doubt in his mind that Emma would marry him and that they would live in Mortlake. The settlement he had chosen as his home with its wide main street and graceful peppermint trees had attracted him from the first. Although he was proud of what he was doing with his city store, he was more comfortable in the country. He was greeted by name all the way down Dunlop Street. He exhilarated in a fast ride on a good horse through the surrounding districts, the pastures and woodlands, up and down the hills and valleys to visit Marks's new home at Buangor. He breathed in the scent of the green grass that surrounded the town. He belonged. And he was convinced Emma would feel the same.

Now that the two shops were well-established he was able to entrust the Elizabeth Street store to a manager while – with Ted's continued help – he concentrated on the buying for the two outlets, managing the Mortlake general store and commuting between the two. It would, he realised, mean that his new wife would be on her own for regular periods, but hopefully these would be short, only a matter of days, and on the fragile evidence of his one meeting with Emma, he was convinced of her ability to rise to, and above, any occasion.

One of his first actions was to exchange his old weatherboard cottage for a bluestone house. Staring at it for the first time from the road, it had looked adequate enough, but once inside he was doubtful.

All rooms led off a central passage. While spacious enough, they were dark and unfriendly and there was an overriding mustiness and smell of something foul that he couldn't quite identify, a dead animal or decay of some sort, he guessed. The damp clung to the mildewed walls and the cold streamed up through the cracks in the floorboards. At one end of the sitting room the boards had been eaten away, by termites quite likely, and would have to be replaced.

Gingerly he opened another door to find a smaller room that looked as though it had been designed to function as either a dressing room or a nursery. A thought occurred to him. He knew where he might purchase a cast-iron bath and there would be enough space on the other side for a washstand and basin.

Rubbing his hands to counteract the chill – and the sudden vision of his future wife lying back in the bath in clouds of steam – he moved on through to the kitchen at the rear where the wood-burning stove brought to mind that other kitchen and where, for an instant, the mustiness was overpowered by the smell of fresh-baked biscuits and creamy milk... But the past was the past, he reminded himself, as he thrust the thought aside.

He bought the house the next day and a week later he had moved in, stacking his belongings in the front room while he repaired the damage to the rest of the dwelling.

Each evening after he'd closed the store, he worked to fix up his new home. He started with the bigger jobs like re-stumping the worst section of the floorboards, patching the iron roof and filling gaps bigger than his fist in the lathe-and-plaster walls. Then he painted the ceilings and the walls, fixed window sashes and replaced glass, fitted shelves and door locks.

Too restless to sleep one night, he wondered whether he could still play a good tune. It was so long since he'd had cause to think of his old fiddle that it was a few moments before he remembered where it might be. But when finally he unearthed it from the bottom of the weathered chest at the foot of his bed, he was astonished at how small and insignificant it had become. He picked it up, studying it incredulously.

Even by the light of the lamp it was a sad sight, and it was difficult to believe that this scratched and battered instrument was once the glossy golden-brown music-maker that he had lofted and played with such pride and passion in the tavern back home. He had had it restrung since the accident, but still the life was missing from it.

Sitting on the edge of the bedstead, he tuned it carefully until, finally, drawing it to his chin he tried to recapture the strains and layers of melancholy it had once offered up. But to his critical ear, it was wrong. No matter how he stroked and coaxed, the soul of the music eluded him. Perhaps it was that his hands moved too clumsily over the fingerboard? Or was it the angle of the bow, its weight somehow wrong against the strings? With a small grunt he put it back in the chest, alongside the remnants of the old album and the knotted handkerchief that contained the gold sovereign. He was, at least for now, out of step with music.

On another impulse, early one Sunday he saddled up a new horse, a chestnut filly, relishing the liveliness under him as she danced out of the township. Turning her towards Buangor, he shortened the reins, bent low over her neck and let her run. He raced across the pastureland and through the long kangaroo grass reaching halfway up the horse's flanks, threaded his way through the stands of red gums and honeysuckle trees, skirted the swamps, and thundered along at such a speed that his shouts of jubilance were scattered by the wind as soon as they left his mouth.

Marks opened the door with a hoot of joy.

'Hey! Hey! Simon! Come in, come in. Somewhere I have some good brandy. Sit down. Let me get organised. What brings you? Are the businesses going well? Tell me everything! Everything.' He spun away. 'Get talking, brother!'

Simon smiled. Standing still in the centre of the small room, he spoke to Marks's back.

'I'm getting married,' he said simply. Saying it aloud somehow made it more real.

'Married,' Marks repeated. 'You?' He stared at Simon, brandy bottle tipped and still pouring into the glass. 'My brother married? Whoo! I think I am the one who is going to have to sit down!'

Simon laughed outright at his expression as Marks bounded across the room, punched him on the shoulder, hugged him hard. He was fairly dancing.

'Well, this is a huge surprise. Wonderful. But simply wonderful. Tell me everything. Where did you find this woman? What does she look like? How long have you been courting her? Is she Jewish? Of course she's Jewish...' He stopped for breath. 'Simon, this is so exciting. To think of you, my brother, married. I'm so happy for you.'

'Whoa, whoa. Slower.'

'All right. One question at a time. Is she ... you know?' Marks shaped the air with his hands.

Simon laughed. 'Yes, of course, she is a very shapely woman. As far as I can tell.'

'As far as you can tell! You've been seeing this lady for some time?'

'Well, no. Actually, I've seen her once only.'

'Once? My God, brother. I know you move fast. But this fast?' The expression on Marks's face was so comical that Simon was unable to bring the glass to his lips for laughter.

But then a thought came to Marks. 'She's not a, you know...?'

'No, of course not. Nothing like that! She's a lady. A real lady, Marks. Quite refined, I suppose you would say. An Englishwoman. Nice soft voice.'

Marks finally took a sip. 'Simon, I think this is a story you had better start from the beginning.'

'There's not much to tell. Just that I met her at the pier. I was waiting for some goods when something for her went wrong. I was able to assist. That's really all.' He looked at his brother intently. 'It sounds strange, I know. But she is different from the others. I like her...I can't explain. '

'What happened after that?'

'I traced her through her banker – we share the same bank. We are to be formally introduced next week at dinner.'

'You mean you have literally only seen this woman once, that you haven't even stepped out with her, and that you are going to marry her? Simon, don't you think this is somewhat strange, I mean, how do you know she'll even have you?'

Simon shrugged. 'I know, that's all. I can't say why. I just know.'

'And, by any good chance, is she Jewish?'

'I think so. Her family name is Solomon.' He stopped. 'And yet, I'm not so sure. Let's say there is a good possibility.'

'Well, that's promising,' said Marks, relieved. 'Good, good. I think there's a synagogue in East Melbourne now.'

'But something else.' Simon reached into his bag, drew forth the damaged album and handed it to his brother.

'What's this?' Marks feigned surprise – but Simon knew he knew. Marks turned the few pages that weren't stuck together with salt.

'So,' he said softly.

'Yes,' said Simon. 'So.' Thrusting his hands deep into his pockets, he got up and walked to the window. He stood for a while looking out, his back turned. 'Have you heard from home?' he asked.

'No. I've written, but not heard. Not for a long time.' Marks let out his breath, shook his head. 'But your marriage, big brother. Phew. You certainly know how to surprise a man.'

A BREAK IN THE CHAIN

Just as, for Simon, other more profitable pursuits had taken the place of music, photography was no longer Marks's main source of income. For some years, he had made a living by hawking to and from the goldfields, but as the miners began to leave the fields and take up selections, he began to supply his goods to the country towns. In many respects these towns were self-sufficient, but the brothers knew well that basics like flour, tea, sugar, tobacco and brandy would always be in demand and that if you found the right supplier, the mark-up on alcohol could be particularly profitable.

Since he and Simon had dissolved their formal partnership, the small village of Buangor had become part of Marks's run.

He, too, had a talent for making money and Buangor was in his estimate growing as a centre of importance. There was a sense of proprietorship in his conversation – and something else, too. A sense of need, a needing to belong perhaps, just as Simon had experienced many years before as he rode into Mortlake. It had taken Marks longer than Simon had expected to reach that point.

'I was getting tired,' Marks settled back on his chair, stretched out his legs. 'Tired of the travel. You know how it is. But the good thing about selling is that I got to know the towns and their people. Something like you did. Buangor suits me. People are arriving by the day and I think it has a future. It's right on the main route between Ballarat and Beaufort, and Cobb & Co. have just built a fancy changing station here. We've got a pub now, butcher, blacksmiths, schoolmaster, even a policeman! And…' He gazed out towards the red gum forest. 'And I have plans,' he went on. 'Just as you found with Mortlake, this town also lacks a good store. I have the contacts and I know I can supply that. But at the same time, there's also another opportunity.'

He paused before turning back to Simon.

'There's a possibility to go into partnership in a sawmill operation on Mount Cole. The timber is beautiful around here, straight and clean with a close grain.' He jumped up, came back with a piece of milled timber, ran his fingers lightly along the wood. 'Look. See how this is. Beautiful. Good solid wood. Look at the grain. Tight, eh? Hard. There's talk of using this stuff for the streets down in Melbourne. If that's the case, there's a lot of money to be made milling.' He was quiet for a while, staring at the wood, stroking it lightly with his fingers. 'So I must admit that this possibility is appealing, too. Just have to flick a coin and choose, eh? Or figure how I can do both at the same time.'

Their talk got lighter as the stars came and went and soon the dawn was unrolling, turning the sky into a canopy of pink and orange silk. As the sun rose, Marks flung another empty bottle into a sack hanging from the doorknob.

'Women, Simon. They love curtains. Remember that. Very bright with patterns. Flapping like this. Fill this house with frilly curtains!'

It was time for Simon to leave. They clasped each other hard. Simon saddled the chestnut and made his way, quite soberly but just a little more slowly, back to the town that lay in the shadow of Mount Shadwell.

A BREAK IN THE CHAIN

Simon and Emma were married in a private ceremony at the East Melbourne Hebrew Congregational School on the 13th of October, 1869.

The date isn't as important as the one particular moment that occurred just after the short ceremony when Rabbi Moses Rintel was filling in the marriage certificate in his elegant copperplate handwriting.

'Now, names of parents,' he said, his eyes swivelling from one to the other. 'Your father's first and then mother's maiden names. Mr Kozminsky?'

'Moses – that is, Moritz – Kozminsky is my father. My mother: Hendel Sternberg.'

The rabbi turned to face Emma. 'And yours, Mrs Kozminsky.'

'Michael Solomon,' she said. She stopped. Her eyes flickered to one side. She bit her lip.

'And your mother's name? Before her marriage?' The cleric's pen hovered over the page of creamy parchment.

She sensed Simon move restlessly. 'Frances,' she said, slowly. 'Frances Cohen.'

It was November in Mortlake and cold enough for Raoskow. Or so Simon told himself as he pulled the door to the store closed. He needed to walk and smoke. He stepped into the lee of the next doorway to light his pipe, cupped his hand around the flare, welcomed the brief heat. He walked quickly, his thoughts sliding one into the other. He would have liked a ride. Saddle up the mare and head for Buangor and Marks. But he was a married man now, with a home to go to – and this was where his thoughts should be directed, not on scurrying out of town. He made an effort to slow his steps. Married less than a month and already he felt like this: the gloom of that front room, another night of watching his wife watch the ceiling.

Something was wrong with Emma. She was still a young woman, but in some lights the tight line of her lips made her look old. She did not turn from him, but neither was there joy in her. At first he had thought she was homesick, and he tried to remember how he'd felt when he first arrived. But his memories were unreliable and choppy, and all that remained of that time was a haze of uncertainty, where only the big things stood out, like his shock at the rape of the country or events like losing Tess and finding Marks in the same moment. He could chase them further back to the day of his father's confrontation in the pasture, but they were dim and cobwebby and devoid of feeling. He knew that the voyage for Emma and her subsequent landing were substantially more comfortable than his own, and so the sickness must stem from either before or after.

But she rarely mentioned London, and if she did she spoke of her father with fondness, of her mother not at all. There was no clue as to whether she was transported against her will, or what shape any persuasion might have taken. Lamport knew, he suspected, but the banker was bound to secrecy. Perhaps Simon wasn't the only one who felt they'd been too hasty in marrying. While he preferred the country, he guessed she would be happier in the city. But he had been open with her from the start. And fair, he believed. Mortlake for now, he had said. After that, we will decide.

He stopped by the swamp in the centre of the town, leaned for a moment against a paperbark. This was the swamp they were talking of deepening, of making into a lake with a surrounding park, a sort of centre for the town. It was possible that this was what Emma needed too: a focus. Last night she had told him she was expecting their first child; perhaps this would help. But there was still no gladness in her when she told him, no joy.

'I wish,' he'd said, 'you would try to meet people. Take a walk down Dunlop Street. With me or by yourself, if you prefer. Nice people. Or drive. The countryside, I think, is very beautiful. I will make the jinker ready. You only have to ask.'

Impatiently, he swung back towards home. It was dark by the time he let himself in through the front door. He heard sounds of the maid banging saucepans in her usual manner at the rear of the house. It surprised him when Emma rose as he entered, moved towards him to turn on the light, take his coat. For a moment, he wondered whether she had been concerned because of the lateness of the hour. But it was something else. He could feel it in her concentration as she poured the tea.

'Simon, there is something I have to tell you.' He looked at her closely, something in her tone causing him to frown. 'That marriage certificate,' she went on, quietly. 'Our certificate, that is, contains an error. My fault. My mother's maiden name... It's Coaten, not Cohen.'

The fire crackled. It seemed to him to burn more brightly tonight. He stretched his feet towards it. 'But at our wedding, you said Cohen. Frances Cohen? What is this Coaten suddenly?'

'It was a mistake on my part. I was taken by surprise. It didn't occur to me that he, that is the minister, would need details. Of my mother's past. All that part of my life, our lives, contained so many... difficulties. It's impossible to go into...'

'Coaten?' Simon repeated. 'This is important?' He stared up at her, spread his hands, his confusion deepening. But for a moment he welcomed even this agitation – better by far than the lifeless dummy.

Emma looked down at her hands. 'What I'm trying to say is that my mother was not Jewish and that I felt – on the spur of the moment – that something might go wrong with the ceremony if I revealed it at that particular time. That it – that is, our marriage – might be annulled or cancelled or something. So I gave my mother a Jewish surname.' She raised her chin. 'It changes nothing. It was just something I felt I should tell you. I'm afraid we have never spoken frankly.'

'What do you mean it changes nothing?' Simon shouted. He rose to his feet. 'You are telling me that you are not Jewish? That is what you are saying?' His fists clenched, he strode to the window and stared out. When he turned back, there was a thin line to his mouth that was not there before.

'And Solomon? Your father?'

'My foster father. My father, too. It's complicated.' She bit her lip. She could hear his angry breathing from across the room and it was some time before he trusted himself to speak.

'Then, I suppose, it can't be helped, but I have to say I am disappointed. You were happy enough to be married in a Jewish ceremony and with your father's name and so on and so on. There was no sign, and I assumed... But now there is an added difficulty. We have lied on the document.'

A BREAK IN THE CHAIN

'A slip of the tongue, not a premeditated lie...'

'But still a lie.' He turned away, spun back again. 'I have this to ask. Would you be prepared to convert to the Jewish faith?'

'I was brought up as a Jew. I am married to a Jew. If you want me to formally convert, naturally I'll do so.'

The window pane trembled as he let his head drop against the glass. And when next he turned he was alone.

A package addressed to Simon arrived from London in the middle of the following year. It was a small Jewish prayer book carefully inscribed on the flyleaf in black ink:

Presented by M. Solomon to his Son-in-Law
S. Kozminsky Feb 1870

Part Three

Israel

1875

8

If, as Israel later became convinced, there was no such thing as chance and that it was by the intention of a greater force that he was born in Mortlake at the foot of the olivine mountain under the sun sign of Virgo on 26 August 1870, then perhaps it was also no coincidence that the gemstone most often connected with a Virgo birth date is chrysolite or peridot, also known as olivine. It could therefore be said that it was not fate, but design, that decreed that gems were to form such a large and important part of his life.

And so perhaps it was not chance either that his other great love came from his first memories of the stars viewed from his perch behind the pommel of his father's saddle as the horse picked her way up the mountainside on those nights when the moon goddess showed herself as no more than a sliver of silver. Or that the Milky Way viewed from the dark slopes of this mountain was the brightest he would ever see.

Whether the nights were warm or cold, sinking back into the heat of his father's body, he was always shivery with the delight of the treat, aware too of other riders, invisible to his father, shadowy bodies detectable only as patches of a denser darkness and whose presence gave him a delicate tremble of something that wasn't quite fear, more like a wet leaf brushing lightly against his neck.

'You see that star,' his father would say gently in his uncertain English, one strong hand holding him tight, the other loose but watchful on the rein. 'The brightest. Can you see that, eh?' He raised his bearded chin. 'Do you remember what that is called?'

Israel nodded, wriggled with the importance of it. 'Yes. Venus.'

'And what is that?'

'It is the evening star.'

'And that kite shape over there?' His horse swung round as he tightened one rein.

'Southern Cross.'

'More, Israel, more. Some description, please.'

'Four bright stars. But really five.' He made a star of his hand. 'But it's the four that make the kite. And it's seen in the south – so that makes it southern…' He leaned into his father's chest, twisted his head upwards to see Simon's eyes shining in the starlight.

'Exactly. Just so. And now…'

This was the part Israel liked best. As the boy clapped his hands together, the horse jerked her head. 'And now I can make a wish on the brightest star.'

His father stepped the horse around again so they could see the lights of the small hamlet that was home, flickering in the darkness way below them. 'Yes, but quietly now. To yourself. Wishes have to be secret. Or else they won't come true.'

His wish was always the same, but no less fervent for that. He wished to know more about the mysterious world with its pinpricks of light hanging above them. More about the moon and the stars – and the sun, too. And about the earth and how it contained the gold his father said men killed for, and whether all mountains were full of green stone that could be cut out of the cliff side and made into polished gems for the rich and famous people who came to his father's city store.

He wanted to know not only what the stars were called, but how they stayed up there in the sky. He wanted to know why they twinkled, and how. And *if* those stars were other worlds as his father said, he wanted to know for sure and what sort of worlds these were and who lived in them. He needed to know the answers to the questions that were beyond the knowledge of his father who cared mainly about his shops and the daily bread and butter. He wished with all his heart that the universe would share its most precious secrets with him.

But tonight, as well as the wish, he had a question for God. Under his breath he asked politely why the moon was such a changeable thing, from the sickle shape it was this evening to the full moon which changed colour on its path through the sky – from orange to a ghostly white – turning night into day, making dogs howl with terror and sending some people quite mad.

It was possible that his wish for learning started to take effect that very night because after he had answered as many questions as he was able, his father sighed.

'You get too clever for me, Israel,' Simon laughed. 'So many questions. Your mother is right. It is time, I think for *shul*.'

'For *shool*?'

'Yeh, *shul*. But school, too. Between these two, you will learn the answers to it all.'

'*Shul* or school. What's the best?'

'There is no best. One is one and the other is the other.'

'What's the difference, then?'

'One is where you learn about God and how to be a good person, and the other is about things like reading and sums.'

'But Mother teaches me that.'

'Yes, your mother is a very clever woman. She teaches me, too. But school is necessary as well.' For a minute or two, there was only the sound of their breathing and the mare snuffling as she went about making her choice of grass. His father sighed. 'You will, however, have many books, as many as you like. In there you will find the answers to your questions. If you study hard, you will one day become very clever. Clever enough to provide answers to your own questions.'

Why was it that even though the horse quickened her pace, it still seemed to take forever to get home? And why was it that Israel couldn't sleep that night, but watched the silvery moon until it was outshone by the rising sun? Well into the night, he heard his parents talking quietly and he didn't have to hear the words to know the wish at last was underway.

But the wish took time. More than one January was to come and go while Simon commuted between the two businesses, readying the city shop 'for expansion' and preparing to sell the store in Mortlake. In the end, Israel gave up asking, but his father seemed to know the question hung between them anyway.

A BREAK IN THE CHAIN

'Be patient,' he snapped as he tidied drawers, sorted buttons, flung out and refolded huge bolts of fabric. 'These things take time. Time, Israel! Have faith, for goodness' sake. We will go when everything is ready. Always questions, questions, questions.'

Time and faith. As if a person should just accept a fact without knowing the exact outline of that fact. And the essence of the matter was that time was not linked to clocks or calendars, but rather to whether someone was looking forward to something or not. The time stretching ahead that he wished away was soft without real edges – an endless middle. On the other hand, if he was busy, it bent back on itself so that things like going to bed and getting up in the morning always came too soon. Time was therefore unreliable and couldn't be trusted. And faith might mean something different, but he suspected it came down to the same thing in the end: giving your power over to someone else.

The irritable positioning of his father's eyebrows fascinated him. It would not be difficult to imitate Simon. He tried it out in front of his mother's dressing-table mirror. Kneeling on the stool for extra height, he placed one hand on his hip. With the other he alternately thumped the air before him and clasped his forehead, drawing his brows together and then lifting one just a fraction higher than the other.

'Eh, Israel. Why do you keep asking me the same thing time and time again. I ask you. Why? All these questions. What is it with you that you never stop? Eh? Eh?'

Through his fingers he eyed the pots laid out on the table. To do the thing properly he needed a beard and there was a brown crayon he could use. He licked his lips, reached for it.

'Israel! What on earth are you up to now?'

His mother was framed in the mirror behind him. He thought quickly. Brought both hands over his eyes and peeped at her from between his fingers. Sometimes he was able to deflect her wrath or make her smile with his play-acting, but a glance at her face suggested that this wasn't one of those times. He folded his hands behind his back.

'I was only acting.'

'Oh for goodness' sake! The sooner you go to school the better. And what have you got in your hands? Show me.'

In this, by the Grace of God, he was still innocent. He lifted up his hands for inspection. She sniffed.

'Off you go then. You've no business being in here.'

Israel climbed slowly from the stool, only letting out a sigh of relief once he was safely out of the door. His parents were so different from one another. Although both were preoccupied, his mother's thoughts were taken up with something inside that bothered her, whereas his father's attention was absorbed in the day-to-day.

In his mother he sensed a reflection of his own impatience. He wasn't sure why, but this move to Melbourne had made them partners in some sort of way. When he started to ask his father how long now, even if he was not looking in his mother's direction he'd know her eyes would be narrowing just a little and her head shaking almost imperceptibly, a sign he should press his lips together. It was almost as if she were saying, I too am eager to leave, but do you hear me complaining? We will leave when your father is ready. Until then, we have to wait patiently. Pray even.

'It wouldn't hurt you to start saying your prayers, young man,' she'd said a few months ago. And then every night since: 'Have you said your prayers?'

Maybe that was what being patient meant: not saying or doing what you wanted, but kneeling on the floor and praying about it instead. Even if you felt you would blow up inside with the unfairness of it all, patience meant you had to balance that feeling with another just as strong.

If ever there was a treat that could rival his evenings under the stars on the slopes of the mountain, it was riding out in the trap with his mother, tripping through the forest on one of those afternoons when the sun slanted through the trees in a way that made you feel you were the only people in the world. Israel could tell his mother was enjoying herself by the way she sat up high and proud, the whip flicking lightly at the flies on Jessie's hindquarters, her eyes softer looking than usual. It was as good a time as any to ask about faith.

'And what is it you would ask me about faith, Izzy?'

'Because he said I had to have it.'

Her brows knitted. 'He?' she snapped. 'Who's he? People have names, Israel.'

'Father,' he said hastily.

'Oh yes, of course. Naturally you have to have it.' She answered quickly, her whip still tickling the pony's rump. And then she was quiet so long he thought she had forgotten his question. Finally, she countered with a question of her own. 'What does faith mean to you?'

He shrugged. 'Not much, I suppose. Nothing really. It's only that Father said it's something I have to have. For wishes to come true.'

'Nothing? To you it means simply nothing?' She backed into her silence again.

'Mama?'

She looked at him. 'I'm wondering whether I've done a good thing,' she murmured.

'What do you mean?'

She was making no sense – but then his parents often didn't. They had a tendency to make two worlds out of one without a boat to link the two. Again she was silent for so long that he thought she wasn't going to answer, and when she spoke her voice was quite quiet and measured.

'Faith is just a name for believing, Izzy, and it's all tied up with trust. For example, when your father asks you to have faith, he is asking you to believe in him and to trust that he will keep his word. He has said that we will move to Melbourne, but he has a great deal to do to make that happen properly.' She paused. 'I have not spoken to you enough about God, Israel, but here again you have to have faith. You have to believe there is a God who is responsible for you, for all the beauty and wonderful things we see around us. That is the same faith as trusting in your father's promise.'

Israel nodded. He knew that God was there – there was no need for her to look at him strangely because most of the time he could see him as clearly as he could see his own face in the shiny paint of a carriage door. God was there all right. It was just that, like the stars, he was not visible every minute of every day. Israel had to go somewhere quiet, like into the soft shadow at the base of a tree and look up through the leaves to see him. Sometimes he could catch him floating across the bedroom ceiling, checking on Israel as he went to sleep. He could never feel he was particularly present during prayers, but he knew he was there all the same. What his mother said was true: it was trust. God appeared when he stopped wanting and reaching out and just let himself be in a stillness. She had taught him more about God than she knew.

They came to a quiet part of the woods. It was autumn, and very warm and lazy with the shadows of the leaves playing tag on Jessie's back. Emma let the reins lie loose in her strong hands.

'All this soul-searching!' She turned to look at her son closely. A note of suspicion entered her voice. 'This is not about school again, is it?'

To have such an extended conversation with his mother was rare. To preserve her mood, he said quickly, 'And he – Father that is – said I had to have patience, too.'

'That's good,' she said in a stern, isolated voice. 'Necessary, in fact. Something you have to have in life. You won't get far in this world without it.'

'But what exactly is it? What's patience?'

'Patience? Oh my God. What is it about you, Israel? You ask what patience is?'

Quite suddenly, a question he had thought rather small and ordinary became large and uncomfortable. He wished he hadn't asked because her shoulders lost some of their straightness as she started fighting something he was unable to see. The eyes she finally turned towards him burned bright before huge drops of water squeezed out and ran in silly staggers down her face and into her mouth. He gripped the side of the trap as she dropped the reins to look in her purse for a handkerchief while the pony clattered on regardless. It was some time, a very great long time it seemed, before she said in a quiet, firm voice.

'Israel, patience is something you will have to learn for yourself. Sometimes life doesn't quite turn out as you plan. Or wish, for that matter. So that means waiting. Waiting sometimes for a very long time. In this case – in the case of going down to school in Melbourne – like me, you will have to wait. Learn to wait. Wait for things to turn out the way you'd like them to be, or better maybe than you ever imagined.'

'But that's patience?'

'Yes. It's actually that simple. Simple to understand, sometimes very difficult to achieve. Patience is just another word for waiting for something that is hidden or not clear to us, to make itself known. Not everything is clear from the start. Sometimes life becomes clearer in the living of it.' She gave up looking for her handkerchief and wiped her eyes and her nose on her sleeve, which surprised him since it was something he was never allowed to do. He pretended not to notice because he had upset her enough already, so much so that maybe their partnership was spoiled. 'And don't let me hear you ever again refer to your father as "he". Do you hear? Show respect, young man.'

The shadows cast by the clouds and the trees were fuzzier than before, and Israel saw a small shiver pass across her shoulders. She was about to gather up the reins when a grey wombat wandered across the track.

A BREAK IN THE CHAIN

The mare saw it before either of them. As if they were one, both her ears swung back smooth as a key in an oiled lock. As she lunged, first sideways and then forward, the trap lurched and the reins ripped from his mother's grasp. The rutted track was not made for a vehicle drawn by a galloping horse increasingly stricken by its own terror, and they both tipped backwards. Emma dragged herself upright, hauled on the reins, but the trap rocked from side to side, each pitch wilder than the one before.

A second passed so slowly that it felt to Israel as if heaven was holding its breath. Then his mother leaned over and, smothering his protests, folded her arms tightly around him. Throwing her wide skirts up around them both, she gave a sound like a cat in pain as she jumped from the cart. Suddenly they were both rolling off the track and down the bank while the trap disappeared with a great rush around the bend.

They could be forgiven for wondering whether they were dead for when they came to a halt and the leaves and twigs stopped rustling and crackling, they held their breath in a silence that was thick and other-worldly. From the distance came a whinny and then a crash, the echoes passing like bush telegraph along the tops of the red gums to where they lay curled, still as sleeping possums, at the base of a tree.

9

The wind snuck in from the southern pole with such a rush up the city streets that the storekeepers opening up for the day were glad to get through their doors. It was January, with the heat until now turned up unusually high even for mid-summer. But this morning was an awful mess of a day, thought Israel, as he dropped his brand-new satchel to do battle with the front door. Indeed, it could have been spring, winter even, with the shutters banging and clattering as they were. Playful as kites, scraps of paper ducked and dived in the littered streets, the cab horses stamped their feet as they chewed on their metal bits and women wrapped their shawls snugly about their shoulders as they hurried across the street.

Israel had played his first day at school over and over in his mind. So often, in fact, that when the reality of it finally arrived, it felt weird and a little ghostly, like the first time he remembered seeing himself in a long mirror, the image more real somehow than he was himself.

But the day had finally arrived and with it the glory of getting into school uniform for the first time – the finale of a string of smaller thrills that began with the clothing list and Emma's patient sewing-on of name-tapes. Along the way they had overcome all sorts of impossibilities, not the least the purchase of shoes that were rather too roomy for comfort.

'If they rub at the beginning, you can wear two pairs of socks, young sir. But believe me, it won't be long before you're growing out of them.' Turning to his mother, the saleswoman had sucked in her cheeks. 'You'll thank me for this, madam.'

But the topmost achievement of it all was his name in letters in dark blue script on the name tags. Israel Kozminsky. He glowed. Such a name!

This first day, too grown up now to hold his mother's hand, he set out with Emma for the walk through the city. Despite the inclement morning, he was so flushed with excitement that his new sweater was unnecessary, but he put up with it for the emblem of honour it sported. His dark brown hair had been damped and combed until it competed with his shoes for shine, and he was sure that everyone they passed could not help noticing the badge with the strange curling letters over his heart or the flashy white bands on his navy socks. All he lacked was a cap and that, he was promised, was a treat he could claim on entering big school.

They were city folk now, his mother had told him, since all the family was living, working or studying in the city block. So much time had gone by that his sister Minnie and even baby brother Michael were now part of the family. So much time spent waiting with faith and trust and patience – and then all this happening at once.

As the impressive building beyond its scrolled gates came into view he bit his lip a little and almost imperceptibly his steps became a little less lively and his satchel dropped lower. Flowing from all directions and fast gathering on the pavement in front of the school was a maelstrom of hesitant mothers and children, and by the time Israel and Emma had navigated a way to the gate, his excitement was turning into something quite unfamiliar. But just as he turned towards his mother, a young woman in a flowery dress and cardigan arrived at his side. She winked at his mother as she went to take his hand.

'Thank you,' she said firmly to Emma. 'We'll see you at three o'clock.'

His mother nodded. As usual, she said so little, but there were some things one didn't have to say. All at once he felt let down like bathwater disappearing down a plug hole. He wasn't quite sure what to do. He looked about him. Some of the smaller boys were trying not to cry, one clinging to his mother's hand and demanding to be taken home, another hanging off his father's belt. He fought the treacherous wobbly feeling, turned back to his mother, forced a sort of smile.

'Have a good day, Mama. I'll see you later on.' There was a burst of light in his mother's eyes and she nodded as he hitched his satchel higher. He gave a little salute, declined his teacher's hand and walked beside her up the long driveway. Not looking back once. He knew she would be there long after he turned the corner and disappeared into the puzzle of corridors, doors and windows.

Israel learned a lot of lessons that first day, none of them the reading, writing and arithmetic he had anticipated, but all of which he was to reflect on for the rest of his life. He learned the meaning of conditioning, and that here it was applied by means of a bell. When it rang, it demanded action on his part, whether it was assembly and prayers or class or break or lunch or afternoon rest or going-home time.

He learned the power of being a teacher. When one of them came into a room, all the students rose together to chant 'Good morning Mr Brimblecombe' in chorus, sat down or stood up when and where ordered. He learned that the teachers who didn't smile tended to receive the loudest welcome. He learned that all school desks were scarred, even though no one was ever caught in the act of writing his own name, initials, the shape of a heart or even a bad word. He learned that stars weren't only fascinating pinpricks of light in a darkened sky but also shapes made out of paper with sticky backs, and that they came in reds and blues and yellows as well as gold and silver. And that although gold was awarded for the highest mark, for reasons he kept to himself he always preferred the silver. He learned that the school was divided into groups of students who met in different rooms to study the same God in different ways.

He learned that prep stood for preparatory and that he was being prepared for big school where the real learning would start and where he would have homework, which everyone said he would hate because it was compulsory and boring. He learned that each day there was something termed roll call where he had to wait for his name to be called out and then say 'Present' in a dull sort of voice. He learned that those big boys who were bound to bully little boys did so in response to their own demons. He learned the rudiments of games played out in the streets of the city, like snakes-and-ladders and chess. But most of all, he learned the cost of a name.

A BREAK IN THE CHAIN

They had been dismissed early from the final class as a special dispensation for the first day, but told to stay within the school grounds until the final bell sounded. Israel collected his satchel and waited in the shadow of an enormous oak, in sight of the gates and near to the administration building.

Three boys from the big school were standing close by, alternately snorting with laughter and whispering, and he wondered whether they would come up to him and start a conversation. He hoped not, because he was what his mother would call 'bone-tired'; he just wanted to go somewhere quiet to think things through. He kept his face turned away, but their voices grew louder.

One boy had something cupped in his hands which he brought up to his face, turning away from Israel as he did so, before passing it to the next, and all three were laughing so hard their shoulders were shaking. After a few minutes, when whatever they had been sharing was either finished or had lost their interest, they looked around for another source of fun. Seeing a young boy hot and flushed in his sweater from the heat that had reinstated itself during the day, one grinned at the other two. They put their hands in their pockets and strolled over.

'Hello. First day?'

He nodded, his mouth suddenly dry; they were so grown-up and knowing.

'Good day, was it?'

Again he nodded, but didn't speak.

'What's the matter? Cat got your tongue?'

He shook his head and the boy asking the questions looked at the other two, raised his eyebrows, and made clicking sounds with his tongue. 'Don't know what the school's coming to.' The boy sighed. 'Obviously we've got a consignment of mutes this time.' His friends threw back their heads and laughed as if they hadn't had this much fun in a long time.

Israel shifted his feet, the strap of his satchel biting into his shoulder.

'Do you think you're going to like school?'

He was tempted to nod, but a type of fear was taking over. 'Yes, I hope so,' he said politely.

'That's better.' The interrogator glanced at his chums and back at Israel. 'You see, we can do it if we try.'

It must be nearly home time. Where was the bell? He could walk off down the drive, but he didn't quite know how to extricate himself.

'What's your name, sonny?'

He straightened his shoulders. 'My name is Israel. Israel Kozminsky.'

They shuffled their feet as they digested this, thrusting their hands more deeply into their pockets, looking up into the tree and about the schoolyard. One started to whistle. Israel let out his breath. Deciding to wait no longer for the bell, he moved off in the direction of the gate, but the leader stepped forward and tapped him on the shoulder. He was smiling broadly, but with his mouth turned down at the corners as if he'd eaten something bad. He bent over Israel.

'Not so fast. We haven't quite finished making your acquaintance.' He stood back, hands on hips. 'Lord above – has the establishment gone mad? Just who *are* they letting into the school these days. Israel? What sort of a name is that? The Israel of the Bible? Are you a Jew?' No one was laughing now and Israel had begun to shake with anger or fear or both.

He couldn't wait – he felt sick, frightened of these boys, of what they could do to him. And suddenly, as he turned to leave, he felt the horrible sensation of his urine leaking down his legs.

The boys rocked with hilarity. After him they yelled: 'Better tuck a nappy into your satchel tomorrow. Make it a big one. And ask your father what he has in his trousers!' Their laughter followed him for the next few years.

He did not greet his mother and was unable to speak to her on the way home. He refused a cup of tea and ginger cake and shut himself in his bedroom. Kicking off the shoes and tearing off his soggy shorts and socks, he threw them into a corner.

He heard the front door open when his father came home, the muted sound of voices. When he heard Simon's steps on the stairs, he pretended to be asleep. He didn't want to talk to anyone. And he certainly didn't want to set foot in the school grounds ever again.

Simon knocked and entered his room, his eyes glancing over the pile of damp clothing and his son's still form.

'Israel?'

When no answer came, he sat on the edge of his bed, put his head in his hands and waited.

'Israel?'

This brought a red and crumpled face writhing out of the pillow.

'Don't call me that!'

'Don't call you by your name? Why all this suddenly, eh? Are you so grand that you are Mr Kozminsky now?'

A BREAK IN THE CHAIN

It was the gentleness in his father's tone that set off the tears he had fought all day to stop. Israel buried his head back in the pillow. After some time, Simon put his hand on his shoulder.

'What's so bad?' he asked.

'I hate school. And I hate my name.'

'Hmm. The first day of anything is always difficult. New school, new job, new country. It makes no difference. By its very nature, newness is strange. But what is this about your name, Israel?'

'I hate it.'

'You hate school and you hate your name. That is a lot of hate grown out of just one day.'

His face still turned away, Israel shook his head.

'All of a sudden my son hates his name and hates his school. The school I can understand because it takes a little time for the strangeness to wear off. But the name is one to be proud of.'

'I hate it,' repeated Israel savagely.

'What really happened, son?' asked Simon. 'One moment you are so proud, the next you are like this...' He pushed his handkerchief into the hot clenched fist and rose from the bed. 'When you are feeling better, come down. After dinner, if you're not hungry. We will talk together – your mother, you and me – to see what can be done about the school and about your name. We will find the problem and talk it through.'

Israel waited until the sounds of dinner had subsided when he knew his mother would be sitting in her tall armchair, her fingers busy with her tapestry, his father at his desk. He had been given permission to miss dinner, but he knew he would have to face his parents sometime.

A BREAK IN THE CHAIN

He wasn't sure how to raise the subject, but if he didn't, there would be no question that he would have to go to school the following day. Anything but that.

He sat at the big table with the silver candlesticks looming over him and before long he was joined by his mother and father. His father pushed the candlesticks to one end and they sat around the other, his parents talking about business until cook arrived with coffee and hot chocolate.

'So?' said Simon finally.

Israel looked down at his hands, hot and sticky with the waiting. There was no avoiding it. Keeping his head down, he took a deep breath.

'What's a jew and why is it so bad?'

'Ah, I see. I see,' said his father slowly. Even with his head down, he knew his parents were looking at each other. 'So that's the matter, is it?'

Israel looked up now because he had no idea what his father meant. 'I don't know,' he said. 'I mean, I don't know whether that's the matter because I don't know what being a jew is.'

There was silence until his father started muttering while his mother continued to stare at the lace of light and dark the candles cast on the opposite wall. Finally Simon found some words.

'Let me tell you a story. Once there was a small boy who wanted very much to go to school.' Israel started to speak and Simon raised his hand. 'No, first you listen.'

And so Israel had to sit back and listen to his father's pretend story about a boy so desperate to go to school, where he'd been promised he would find out all there was to know about the world, and more, and about the universe too, with all its stars and planets. He would find out, too, that his father was not a tutored man, that he hadn't been to a proper school, and that he knew few answers to these important questions, and that his son would have to learn to read and study to find the answers for himself. The boy had thought it would be simple, that all he had to do was to build on the alphabet his mother had taught him. But that is so simple, it is impossible. To become a learned scholar, one first has to know the ways of the world because the world is an everlasting schoolroom.

Israel had heard so much of this before that his attention kept wandering. One of the candles guttered, a spray of wax settled across the table and his fingers itched to pick at it. But then his father's tone changed.

'I am guessing that at school today you came across a no-goodnick – a bully, coward, same thing. More than one, eh? These people are seldom alone.' He took his eyes from his son for a moment and met his wife's gaze.

Israel nodded. 'There were three of them,' he whispered.

Again Simon and Emma exchanged glances.

'So. They make themselves feel important this way. Because they are small. In mind. And not only in school. The only way to deal with these people is to stand up to them. But quietly. Do you see? Hold up your head. Like so.' His father lifted his own head, his beard pointing straight at the wall. 'That's all. No fighting, no yelling. Just ignore them if possible. And if that's not possible, tell the teacher. Don't let them scare you. Tomorrow, you'll find them and do things differently from today.'

Israel shook his head. 'No. I'm not going to school tomorrow.'

'Yes you are, Israel. I am quite sure that things will be different from today. Do you think I have never been bullied? That your mother, too, has escaped? That the world is not full of people who are jealous of other people, who need to climb on the shoulders of other people? Who need to hurt other people in order to feel good about themselves? There are bullies all over... Everywhere. Trust me – stand tall. That is the only way.'

'It's not fair.'

Simon leaned forward. 'I don't want to hear you say that again...ever,' he said evenly. 'Life is life. Neither fair, nor unfair. You succeed; you fail. Win some battles, lose others. No one has promised you fairness from the world we live in. You find fair in fairyland only. Have you ever heard me complain that life is not fair? Your mother? And now this sudden dislike of your name...' Simon sighed, scratching his beard. 'Well, the only way we can fix that is to know the whole story.'

'You can't fix it! They laughed because it is a stupid name and I wish I didn't have it.'

'And?'

'They said I was a jew...'

His mother interrupted. 'I never did think...' She stopped, but his father seemed to understand what it was she was about to say.

'I blame myself,' he said. 'Not for your name, which is a fine one, but for not giving you the understanding to go with it.' He studied his hands for a long time until he quite suddenly clapped them together. 'Right now it is late,' he said, 'and you must sleep. But one further thing you must know. To be a Jew is honourable and good. We will go more deeply into this another time.' He took a deep breath and there was an unexpected edge to his voice. 'However, since your mother has not yet taken on the Jewish faith and you have not been brought up in the Jewish way, you are not, strictly speaking, a Jew. I myself am Jewish, however, and proud of it. We'll make time to sit down together, eh? Talk this through.' He saw Israel about to speak, raised his hand. 'But enough. Enough for today. When you say your prayers, pray for forgiveness for these people.'

Israel glanced at his mother for help, but she shook her head. 'Go to bed, Israel. I'll come and tuck you in soon.'

He slipped off his chair and kissed his parents goodnight.

On his way to the stairs, he turned.

'But why aren't you a Jew, Mama?'

Emma shook her head and now her voice had a jagged edge. 'That is not your business, Israel. Do as your father says and go to bed. Remember what we always say? That the past is only good for the experience it provides. Don't be tempted to look back. It's invariably a mistake. Turn the other cheek. Goodnight.'

As Israel dragged his feet up the stairs, he knew his parents would sit and talk further into the night. Turn the other cheek, his mother says, but how often he has heard his father mutter 'an eye for an eye'. The contradictions. Sometimes, grown-ups made very little sense.

He knew it was going to be impossible to sleep, but he readied himself for bed nonetheless. The clothes in the corner stank. His feelings of shame and despair, disgust even, had been replaced by an excitement which made it boring to kneel by the side of his bed. He would make it quick.

'Dear God. Please forgive those horrible boys. I don't wish them any harm. But don't forget I hate them.' Leaping up and walking backwards to the wall, he took a flying leap like a circus artist right into the centre of his bed. And then, remembering, he hopped off and fell briefly to his knees again.

'And please bless Mama and Father and Minnie and even Michael and pray he'll get big enough to play proper games with me soon.' He paused. 'But I still hate my name. Remember that.' When his mother crept into the room later, he pretended to be asleep.

Once she had left, he got out of bed again. He went to his bedroom window. The fierce wind of the morning had drawn back into itself and the city was almost asleep. Some windows still were lit and occasionally a cab would rattle by, the rhythmic drumming of hoof beats and the jingling of harness soothing, but not enough to make him sleepy. A man and a woman walked by, leaning into each other, foreshortened like dwarves from this height. He liked living in the city. It was much more alive than Mortlake and he regretted only that his view of the night sky was limited to a rectangle instead of the huge shallow pudding bowl of stars that had hung over his last home.

He sat at the window through the night, watching the city fade as his own thoughts grew. As usual, his father had not even begun to satisfy the questions bubbling up inside. He still had no idea what a Jew was, only that to be a Jew could be viewed as either good or bad depending on whether the person's viewpoint was Jewish or that of someone caught in between, like his mother. And why his name should be a source of laughter was still unclear. It was all very well to have pride – that he could understand – but there were difficulties that lay just below the surface that still needed explanation. And his calm and elegant mother. What long story could she possibly be keeping from him? His father knew. His mind started to frame the thought that it wasn't fair, but he stopped himself. No point.

The house and the streets were so quiet now he could hear his own breath. His stomach started to clench and he whispered out loud to himself in his father's deep, stern voice.

'Courage, Israel. We will play-act, if necessary. But we will not let them see they scare us.'

As the dawn seeped colour into the surrounding buildings and candles began to flicker behind the curtained windows of the buildings opposite, Israel formulated two strategies. One, he determined, would be put into place immediately; the other would take some time, but would in the end be done.

10

Simon slept soundly, but all through that night Emma moved restlessly in the big bed. Although last evening her husband had taken full responsibility both for his son's name and lack of Jewish education, she knew she was also guilty.

It was true she hadn't wanted to name the baby Israel, but Simon, perhaps feeling pangs at his lack of observance these many years, had persuaded her that it would in some way redress the balance – make peace with God was the way he put it. He had knelt by her tall chair one evening when their son was a few weeks old and she was rocking him to sleep. Propping his elbow on the arm of the chair and resting his chin on his hands, he'd spoken more gently than in recent times.

'I am guessing that Israel might not be your preferred name for the baby, Emma, but I would be proud. It has an honest sound. And strong, too. Israel Kozminsky. Eh? What do you think? Are we agreed? This child is Israel. And then perhaps the next Michael, after your father. He would be well-pleased.'

Emma's face was guarded. For Simon, her father was a shadowy figure over the other side of the world he was not likely ever to meet. She suspected that the two men had formed this paper bond because they were of the same religious leaning. Or perhaps because of the emotional letter that had accompanied the little Jewish prayer book Michael Solomon had sent Simon, both of which were safely tucked away in the small chest at the end of the bed.

Hungry for any contact from back home, she remembered the flowing copperplate and heavy punctuation stroke by stroke:

Dear Mr Kozminsky

You do me a great honour by taking the trouble to write from such a vast distance to ask for Emma's hand in marriage –
I have, of course, no hesitation in giving my permission and I wish you a long and productive marriage. Please accept my most cordial congratulations –
I regret only that I will not be there to share in the occasion of your wedding day –

Yours faithfully

Michael Solomon

Postscript: Please keep me up-to-date with events as they transpire in that big new country of yours –

Simon rarely asked for anything she was unwilling to give. In fact, Simon rarely asked. And yet Emma knew his doggedness when he felt himself to be in the right.

'Yes, my father will be pleased.' Reluctantly, her own guilt at delaying conversion coming to the fore, she had agreed to the bargain. 'Although I suspect he would be even more pleased if we were to name this child for him. But yes, you are right, God-willing, there will be a second and therefore we can agree on both counts.'

But now she wondered whether she had given way too easily. Since she was not a Jew, technically her son could choose his faith when he was old enough to understand. But Israel was such an obviously Jewish name, surely it made things more difficult should he decide not to convert. It was not impossible, not too late – never too late, she supposed – to change a name. But she would have spared Israel the loss of self that accompanied the discarding of one name and the adopting of another – a loss she knew only too well. But at least Israel had parents who were concerned, who cared whether he was one thing or another. Refusing to give way to the heat building behind her eyelids, she moved impatiently onto her other side.

'Don't look backwards,' she had cautioned her son that very evening. The words reverberated through the mattress. She would do well to listen to her own advice. It didn't do to dwell on the past – but that was hard when she wasn't looking forward to tomorrow, either.

But the next morning, with his chin lifted at such an angle that she was surprised he could still see where he was going, Israel strode by her side as if the day before had never happened. He has grown, she thought, my son. Grown years in just a day. At the top of the driveway, he turned back to give her a small wave. I shouldn't be surprised, she told herself. He is, after all, my child.

Since Israel now had the advantage of knowing what it felt like to be brought so rapidly low from a feeling of pride, the first strategy that had come out of his night's resolves was not to allow a lack of confidence to sneak up on him again. If the world was indeed so uncertain, it was best to approach it on those terms. It was, after all, only words he had allowed to hurt him; there had been no actual physical threat. He decided, however, that he would stay away from the large oak tree and remain well within the boundaries of the prep school. And if he ran into the boys again, he would try out the soundness of his first strategy.

He clamped his teeth hard together at roll call, but as it turned out, many of the names attracted sniggers and his was no more exceptional.

Unlike yesterday, there were proper classes. Emma had taught him well; his letters were well-formed and his reading progressed. In numbers, he could count to one hundred. It was all so familiar he became impatient. He began to wonder what they knew that he didn't. The others were still bent over the task of moving wooden blocks with large coloured numbers from one group to another to equal three thirds. The clock in front of him showed him it was nearly time for the bell. He had completed the exercise and was balancing his ruler on one finger when his teacher loomed above him.

'Would you mind staying behind for a minute – Israel, isn't it? I'd like to have a word with you after class,' he said.

The bell began its tinny beat and his lack of certainty returned. The rest of the class poured out amid banging desk lids and whoops of glee. The teacher waited until the sound subsided and then smiled at him, a determined-to-be-happy look on his face.

A BREAK IN THE CHAIN

But once he'd spoken to him, Israel was pretty happy, too. He was to be moved to Junior School. After only one day in prep. How delighted his parents would be! He moved off in a bubble of warmth that even the boredom of rest time couldn't quash. This, after all, would be the last rest before he joined the bigger boys.

Still elated by the news at the home bell, he was making his way down the drive when he was hailed.

'Hey. Jew-boy. Over here. We've something to ask you.'

He had a choice: to ignore them and continue his path as his father had suggested, or turn and confront them in line with his plan. But the night spent preparing for this moment shouldn't be wasted. Almost instantly he made up his mind. He swung slowly round to face them, shrugging his satchel from his shoulder. Never mind that his head was buzzing like a dying fly, that his legs had the strength of a shortbread biscuit and that his eyes had temporarily lost the power to focus. Never mind that home time was here and he had so much to tell his mother. All that mattered was that yesterday was yesterday. And that here was an opportunity to set things for the future.

'Yes?' he said politely.

'Ah ha! Baby's found his voice at last. Come here. Have you had a good day so far, Jew-boy?' The same boy was doing the talking.

'Actually,' said Israel. 'I have something to ask *you*.'

'Oh?' Smiling and raising his eyebrows, the youth looked round at his friends, but their eyes were on the new interrogator. His mouth curling further, he rammed his hands into his pockets. 'Go ahead.'

'What's *your* name?'

A BREAK IN THE CHAIN

'*My* name?' repeated the youth, giving a snort. He shifted his feet. He looked younger than he had yesterday. Not quite so tall either.

'Yes, your name,' Israel said. 'I'd like to know.'

The boy started to laugh and looked around at his friends for support, but so far they hadn't found Israel quite as funny as they had yesterday. The boy's snigger died away and he took his hands out of his pocket, inspected them carefully and rubbed them on the sides of his trousers.

'I can't see that it's your business to ask, but my name's George, if you must know. George Cartwright. Although I can't imagine what it's to you.'

One of the other boys moved restlessly. 'Come on, Georgie, let's go.'

Israel's eyes lit up. 'Georgie?' he asked. 'Georgie Porgie, like in the nursery rhyme?'

George's eyes flashed angrily. He tightened his fists.

'Why you young...' His friend jabbed him in the ribs.

'The worm turns. He got you this time, George. Leave the kid alone. He's not worth the trouble.'

Israel hitched his satchel back over his shoulder. At the gates, his mother was waiting.

Like the Melbourne weather, change too has its seasons. It can arrive swift as the fall of a chef's cleaver or it can work away underground like a rhizome, small signals barely noticed, hidden and trodden over, but growing nonetheless.

They would say later that the metropolis of Melbourne sprang up overnight – that even after the height of the gold rush few buildings of note shadowed the humble dwellings that ranged each side of its broad streets until, all of a sudden, it was a city with its own St Paul's and one hundred banks.

But was its transformation really so rapid or was it just that in the years leading up to the golden land boom of the 1880s its residents failed to notice the particular quality and quantity of the fur trim on ladies' bonnets, the mounting numbers of plush pearl-grey top hats, the horse jinkers getting fewer as the broughams multiplied? And that these indicators in themselves fuelled the establishment of such businesses as milliners, dressmakers and livery stables all with a need to advertise their services, which in turn led to the founding of any number of news sheets and journals alongside the great newspapers of the day: *The Age* and its arch-enemy *The Argus*.

Perhaps they also failed to observe that down at the docks, alongside the daily arrival of passenger ships, the number of cargo ships unloading towering consignments of polished marble. And that the rolls of carpet that spilled and sprawled so brightly over the wharf were woven from some of the finest silks and wools of Persia, and that the tea chests filled with Sheffield plate and cut crystal were destined for the heavy oak sideboards in the increasingly lavish suburban villas? And while they may have wondered at the deep trenches gradually appearing along the middle of the main thoroughfares, if they had been asked, most would have guessed these were storm drains until one day the paperboys on the street corners sang out the news, 'Cable trams for Melbourne, cable trams for Melbourne'.

A BREAK IN THE CHAIN

For many, the boom arrived with all the subtlety of an explosion, feeding and growing on its own excitement, but there were others whose lives to this point had depended on keeping their wits sharp, who had read the signals and were quietly anticipating. Among them were Simon and Emma.

Simon's move from Mortlake to Melbourne was timely. Awaiting the arrival of a second child and accurately forecasting the future land boom, Simon and Emma had purchased the floor above her original long, narrow apartment at 25 Bourke Street West, combining the two by means of an inner staircase. The lower floor would continue as a living area and kitchen – at the back of which, despite Simon's loudly voiced opposition, the maid would have her quarters. The upper floor would be rearranged to accommodate bedrooms, dressing rooms, a bathroom and a nursery.

The small curio shop on the corner of Elizabeth and Bourke Streets was well-situated to take advantage of the growing wealth of a city where collections of such things as rare coins, paintings and *objets d'art* or unusual pieces of jewellery were testimony to the status of being somebody.

The coins Simon had inherited with the shop. It was something he knew nothing about, but that had never stopped him before and it didn't now. The art of selling he had already mastered: he worked on the well-known principle that after love and fear, the greatest motivator is greed. For the rest, he learned the way he'd always learned: by observing. He got to know the hawkers and their sources. He scrutinised the body language and the dress of his customers. Most of the stock from the

A BREAK IN THE CHAIN

Mortlake store had been taken over by the new owners, and would be compatible with city trends. As the wealth around him begged for display, he started specialising in gemstones – tentatively at first – knowing that he would make mistakes, but knowing too that he had a knack of instinctively judging good from bad. In time, he grew so adept at handpicking the best that he surprised even himself with his growing reputation for dealing in only the finest. If you wanted a gem to catch both the light and the eye from its perch in the fold of a silk cravat, a jewelled brooch, a necklace of matched sea pearls or a simple gold pin for a lapel, the store to visit was Kozminsky's.

Almost from the start, Simon had bought his pearls unstrung, checking each for authenticity by placing it between his teeth and biting gently to uncover any telltale chalkiness. Next, he examined each for perfect roundness, for the glow that has to come from deep within and for its ability to adorn even the scrawniest neck with distinction. He had glass cabinets built for the gems and lined the trays inside with coloured velvets: scarlet for the pearls, royal blue for the diamonds, cream for the coloured stones, black or purple for the coin collections. Traders soon learned not to try to pass off an imitation to Kozminsky's and, in turn, customers knew that to buy their ropes and chokers there was a guarantee in itself.

Emma, too, was busy. She gave birth to two children in Bourke Street. The Michael she had been expecting turned out to be a daughter they called Minnie. Michael was born two years later.

Finding she had a liking and a skill for figures that Simon lacked, Emma gradually took over the accounts.

A BREAK IN THE CHAIN

Because the merchandise was pricey, the problem with a firm like Kozminsky's was the number of promissory notes that accumulated. Promises were all very fine and, in writing, acceptable, but Simon disliked calling in his debts. He prided himself on his ability to judge human character, and while he was more often right than otherwise, there was the occasional purchase for which he was never paid and many of his more loyal customers stretched their credit beyond reasonable limit before he reluctantly asked for settlement of their account.

But there was another talent that Emma discovered she possessed and that was a flair for real estate. The land boom had arrived. And she bought and held.

11

The way the morning started, Israel wasn't sure anything would work out very well that day. Uncle Abraham was coming to town, all the way from Prussia – or was it London? No one knew for certain, and he found it hard to believe that something that had caused so much speculation and discussion was now overshadowed by the fuss involved in getting to the quay on time. His father was more preoccupied than ever, which meant that he spent a lot of time frowning and not really getting on with things. He had pricked his finger putting in his stud, which led to a drop of blood on the cream silk of his cravat, which in turn led to all sorts of complications because he didn't have a spare laundered one.

Clara, the maid, was red-faced; she'd just finished dressing baby Michael in his velveteen jacket and frilly shirt when he rewarded her by messing his nappy. And Minnie, like the cry-baby she was, decided that she wasn't getting enough attention so she fell over her own feet and started crying.

Only his mother remained cool. She had sponged off the speckle of blood and, ignoring his father's protests, arranged the pin among the folds in such a way that the gem snuggled and sparkled all at the same time.

A BREAK IN THE CHAIN

'You go and finish getting ready. I'll see to this,' she said to Clara, taking Michael from her and disappearing into the nursery with the howling Minnie at her heels. He heard his mother say, 'For goodness' sake. What's the matter now?' She never was taken in by Minnie's wiles. Nor his, for that matter. Israel sat on the arm of her favourite chair, swinging his legs, wishing that they were at the docks already.

Strictly speaking, Uncle Abraham wasn't really a full uncle. Because he had a different mother from his father Simon and Uncle Marks, he was only their half-brother. But whether that made him a half-uncle or not was the question. Half-brother sounded right, but half-uncle didn't somehow. Perhaps it was as simple as using a lower case initial letter in his mind. Israel tried it out aloud – *uncle Abraham* – and it did have a sort of downgraded sound to it. He wondered whether he would look at all like his father or Uncle Marks. Would they recognise each other? How did people recognise those they'd never seen grown up?

His parents had sat up late the night the telegram arrived. It was past bedtime, but if he held his breath, he could hear clearly from the top of the stairs. They were at the table with the candles trimmed so the light was dimmer than it would otherwise have been. His mother sat quietly, her eyes alive with questions, but his father had his head in his hands and was having trouble coming to terms with something.

'Abraham. After all this time. He was only a baby – about the same age as Michael is now – when I left Raoskow.' The candlelight flickered for a minute in his eyes as he looked up at Emma. 'He must be over twenty now. Twenty-two, perhaps. Maybe more. A young man. Is it possible that all that time passed? It seems to me quite impossible. And now he is coming out to Australia.' He picked up the yellow page in front of him. 'Not from Prussia, it would seem. But it's not clear. From London, perhaps.' He waved the paper. 'So little information after so long!'

Over the next weeks Israel often heard his father muttering to himself. He was more absent than usual, with a crease between his eyebrows that was becoming permanent, as if he were remembering things from the past and not everything was pleasant. Meanwhile, his mother tackled the practicalities of such things as extending the house and bringing the water closet inside to make another bathroom.

'That way he can stay as long as he likes and be out of the way of the main household,' she said firmly.

Discussions of this nature that so absorbed grownups bored Israel and he had tiptoed off to bed, wondering how long they would have to put up with this man called Abraham.

That night he dreamt of uncle Abraham, a huge man with a bushy beard and eyes the colour of his father's, reflections of a summer sky. They were alone in a small boat in the middle of the open sea and Abraham's strong arms were rowing them smoothly towards the safety of the shore. Then he stopped rowing and looked out through the tangle of his curling hair at Israel.

'Time for you to take over,' he said, passing the oars to the boy. But as Israel rowed, the tide began to go out, and no matter how hard and fast he pulled, the boat was sucked further and further into the vast ocean. He looked to his uncle for help, but the man was unconcerned. 'Row the boat, boy,' was all he said. 'Row the boat.' In the end, Israel's chin collapsed on his chest and by the time he rallied, his uncle was nowhere to be seen. He woke cold with sweat and shivering.

'That's a nightmare and best forgotten,' said his mother when he told her. 'I don't know what gets into your mind sometimes, Izzy. You have too active an imagination for your own good.'

'But where did he go?'

'He went back into dream space.'

'What do you think he looks like? In my dream...'

Emma interrupted him. 'Israel, stop! None of us have any idea. Not even your father. You will just have to wait and see.'

And now the day had arrived. His mother came back into the room with Michael in her arms smelling of baby powder, and Minnie hanging on to her skirt with one hand and biting the nails of the other.

'Are you ready, Simon? Clara? Don't kick the chair, Israel,' Emma said in one breath and at last they were out and on their way.

After all that, they were early. So much rushing about only to be forced to stand and wait felt like being in a glass bottle with the stopper on. That is, until he spied the ship approaching the port.

The wind was such that with her huge spread of canvas the clipper was out-sailing the two tugs wallowing in the foam behind her. Beyond the tall and graceful ship, the painted ocean stretched over the edge of the world. Israel's senses roiled. He gazed sideways at his father and for once he knew that Simon had guessed his thoughts.

A BREAK IN THE CHAIN

'Yes, it is beautiful,' his father said. 'Quite beautiful. There are few things in the world, save gemstones perhaps – and your mother, certainly – that are more striking.'

The crowd thrilled as the ship came at an angle towards them, her sharp bow dancing. As her sails were taken in, she slowed and wavered. A sleek white bird coming to rest after a long flight. When she rounded up to a buoy, it looked at first as if she was going to anchor offshore. The crowd was so quiet he could hear his own breath and even Minnie seemed to have some understanding of the occasion. But as she was furling her sails, one of the tugs steamed past her, and not long after that the wind filled her remaining canvas and she drifted gently to the wharf. Even at rest, with the most of her sails packed, she was more graceful than anything Israel had ever seen.

People crowded at the rails, waving and calling, and somewhere among them was his uncle Abraham. But Israel was content, for once, to allow events to unfold without pushing. He stood among his siblings, secure in the knowledge that however fast they grew they would never catch him up. Watching every movement as the lines were dropped over huge bollards, he was still lost in the magic of it all when there was a loud shout.

'Simon? Ah, Simon!'

Israel spun around just in time to see his uncle with his hands on his father's shoulders. From the back, all he could see was a frock coat of fine dark wool stretched across well-shaped shoulders, and trousers with fine white stripes. The man removed his hat and bowed to his mother.

A BREAK IN THE CHAIN

'My wife, Emma. And here...' said Simon, with pride or something even stronger furring the edges of his voice, '...here are my three children.'

As Abraham turned and stood alongside Simon, the discrepancy in their ages was such that he looked more like his father's son than his brother, thought Israel with a little shock. There was a resemblance in the shape of his face and in his long fingers, but his lips were fuller and despite his youthful look his hair was already thinning. And although he had a moustache and beard, Israel was relieved to find that Abraham had none of the hugeness and hairiness of the dream uncle. In fact, his eyebrows were quite fine and arched. Israel suddenly became aware of his mother shuffling her feet and knew he was about to get into trouble for staring. But after wondering for so long, it was difficult to look away.

'Ah, Israel. A worthy name, young lad. The very best!' Abraham stretched out a hand to Israel and his own came out to meet it. For a moment longer, as his uncle pressed something into his hand, Israel held his gaze and the eyes that stared back were strongly lidded just as Simon's were, and blue. But it was a hue of blue paler than a watercolour wash. He tried to remember the colour of the eyes of the man in the dream boat, but the image faded as he groped for it.

He sensed his mother was about to nudge him, but as Abraham withdrew his hand, something crackled in Israel's grip. He opened his hand to find a wrapped toffee.

Abraham's gaze flickered down at him and Israel grinned. Forgotten, all at once, was the small 'u' for uncle; the dream was ancient history. His mother prodded. 'Thank you, sir.'

'I want one,' said Minnie.

His mother rounded on her swiftly. 'I beg your pardon?'

'Please,' said Minnie, linking her hands behind her back and wriggling in the way she usually reserved for Simon.

There was no trusting Minnie.

At first the household fluttered about Abraham, but after a few days things settled down and his uncle was out of the house more and more often, meeting first this man and then another.

Whenever possible, Simon engaged his brother in long discussions about Raoskow. Israel hadn't realised how hungry his father was for news of the place he still oddly called home – though surely Melbourne was his home? The two brothers sat up late each night and sometimes well into the morning, with the tea-coloured liquid in the cut-crystal decanter disappearing as fast as the melting candles. When his mother went to bed early, which was more often than not, it was all the more risky, and therefore more fun, to snoop from the top of the stairs.

That was the only way he found out that his father's father – his own grandfather – was dead. There was an uneasiness in the exact centre of his stomach which suggested that he should perhaps be sad, or at least show sadness, about such an event. But he couldn't really see where it came from, or why he should be sad about someone he had never seen and hardly heard about.

Clinging tight to a stair post, he slid his bottom one stair lower. He had learned that the lower the level in the decanter, the more intense the discussion which decreased the risk of discovery. He rested his head against the wood.

A BREAK IN THE CHAIN

Abraham's fingers strayed briefly to touch the shining silver of the candlesticks. 'I note you do not observe?' he asked. It was said like a fact that he hoped was not true.

Was he imagining it, or was his father's colour rising?

He edged down another step.

'No strict observance. We were married in the synagogue in East Melbourne and naturally I attend. But I don't take the boys. Not yet. Michael's still a baby and Israel... Well, Israel...'

'And your wife?'

'She was raised in the Jewish tradition, but she is not Jewish.'

Israel could almost hear Abraham raising his fine eyebrows. He pressed his face tightly against the banister.

'Raised in the faith, but not Jewish? How can that be?' The tone of his voice increased. 'But then how was it you married in the faith? Did she convert?'

Israel bent closer as his father shifted in his chair. He could tell Simon was uncomfortable by the way he raised his hand as if to steady the other man.

'She will convert. In time. It was...it is important to me, not so much to her. She is knowledgeable about the culture and caring of my views in the tradition. As in all things.' Bending closer to his brother, Simon changed the subject. 'But your upbringing, I think, was a little different from mine. Your mother Sarah more observant than mine, perhaps?'

'The family was observant. Always,' said Abraham, and Israel detected an edge to his voice. 'For me, it is a natural and important way of life. I am sorry that it hasn't yet become so with you.'

A BREAK IN THE CHAIN

Simon drew in his breath sharply. He was gazing into his drink, rolling the bowl of his glass gently between his hands. It was a little while before he replied.

'You see only this.' He swept the air with his hand. 'But at the beginning it was a question of survival. It is hard to describe. In fact, even now, looking back, it's like a dream – mostly a bad dream. What you see here...' Again Simon gestured. 'All this is new. Due to my wife. And, of course, her money. For many years I lived plainly. In such places you can't begin to imagine... It's not an excuse, Abraham. It's just how it was.' His father leant over to splash a little more of the decanter into the two glasses and the brothers sipped in silence for some time. When Abraham spoke again, his voice was gruff.

'But the boy, your eldest child. I'm glad you called him Israel. He has the makings of a good lad. And I'm seldom wrong about character.'

On the stairs, Israel drew in a long breath and straightened his back. But just then he saw Abraham's chair tilt back and he knew it teetered on the edge of the scraping sound that he needed to cover the traces of his departure. He edged back quickly into the shadows, backing up the stairs. To bed, but not to sleep. How could his mother have been brought up as a Jew, he wondered again, but not be Jewish? How could a person be a Jew and not be a Jew?

When he had asked her, she had looked grim and said that she would tell him one day but that the time was not quite right. His face had flushed and she had placed her hand under his chin so he was forced to look up. He always hated that.

'I repeat: when the time is right, Israel, I will tell you. There is nothing bad and nothing that you have to worry about. It is my business for the moment, but one day I'll tell you. You have to trust me. Promise.' Her eyes were deep and fluid.

'I promise.'

In bed, finally, where despite the crisp-cold night, he threw off the covers. His mother was wrong in this. It was not only her business; it affected him too. That was what his father had said. It wouldn't keep cropping up in his life unless it was important. That being so, he had a right to be in on whatever the secret was. And if there was nothing bad, why did it have to be a secret in the first place?

The sounds filtered down the passage from his parents' bedroom. 'What do you mean, things have changed? Nothing has changed. I suggest only that we humour him by observing some of the traditions. Ah, Emma, no argument. We have too much that's good in our lives to argue. Besides…'

His mother had interrupted and Israel could tell she was angry by the way her words erupted with little hissing sounds impossible to interpret. Not so, the still measured tones of his father.

'I realise that. But that the boys at least go to *shul*? You can see that's important, surely? We agreed, Emma. Remember. We did agree.'

His mother's reply echoed like a gunshot. Hiding deep in the impartial snow of the feathered pillow and sticking his fingers in his ears, Israel set up a small humming sound in the back of his throat so he would hear no more.

He hated this. *Shul*. *Shul*. He wanted to go, anyway, and so the whole argument was pointless.

When he went downstairs that Saturday morning, breakfast looked just as nice as always. The oak sideboard was set with as much care for the family as it ever was for visitors. His mother didn't believe in keeping the silver and cut-glass for best.

'Life is too short,' she said. 'Besides, what good are they in the cupboard? Beautiful things should be displayed. And used.'

As usual the fine glass jug was filled to the brim with foaming orange juice. The autumn sunlight streaming through the breakfast room cast a rainbow across his favourite serving dish, a cut-crystal bowl with edges so sharp that if you weren't careful it could slice open your hand. This fine morning it was filled with cubes of apricot, peach, plum and melon steeping in honey-sweetened lemon juice. In winter this fruit would be replaced by slices of orange, apple and pear and segments of mandarin and grapefruit. Or on the coldest days, when the sun failed entirely, there might be a bowl of porridge with steam that rose so strong and pungent around the thick cream centre that you would be instantly cheered. Or sometimes pancakes light and fluffy with brown sugar for sprinkles and lemon quarters for the brave.

Next came a row of tureens, and under the first lid Israel knew he would find a choice of buttery fish smoked golden on the outside, flaking firm and white on the plate. In the others would be creamy scrambled eggs, crisp curls of bacon, lightly grilled tomatoes and mushrooms. And under the last silver lid there was usually a dish they called devilled kidneys in a creamy gold sauce, which was as wicked as it sounded – or so his mother said.

But the bacon, both a signal and an incentive to get out of bed, was missing this morning. He had thought something was lost on the air when he awoke. His parents were already at the table, his mother eating carefully, his father with a full plate before him as yet untouched as he glanced through the morning paper before heading off to the store. Uncle Abraham had not yet appeared and Minnie and Michael still had breakfast in the nursery.

'No bacon?' he asked.

'Good morning,' replied his mother. She had that rather straight line to her mouth that warned him to rephrase his question.

'Good morning, Mama,' he said hurriedly. 'There is no bacon,' he pointed out again.

'There is no bacon,' agreed his mother and father in unison. Israel looked at one and then the other. His parents were acting very strangely these days. He shrugged, turned back to the row of dishes. There were no devilled kidneys, either. He had poured his orange juice and was about to help himself to the fish when the double doors to the dining room opened wide and Uncle Abraham strode in. In each hand he held a lightly wrapped loaf of bread, still steaming, which he placed proudly in the centre of the table. He rubbed his hands.

'*Gut Shabbos*. Good morning, Simon. Emma. Young Israel. Ah, the usual good meal, I see.' He lifted his nose into the air and Israel wondered whether he, too, would miss the aroma of bacon. 'Ah, excellent. A beautiful day,' he announced happily. He reached for a loaf and tore off the paper wrapping to expose shiny twisted bread of a type that Israel had not seen before. Drawing his napkin from its silver ring, he spread it over the bread.

Israel's father nodded; his mother exchanged greetings, but continued to peer at the wall as if she could see through it into the next room. Uncle Abraham had a particular skill of only seeing what he wanted to see. He went to pull out his chair and then hesitated, one hand resting on the table as he looked from one to the other.

'We're doing all this back to front, I know, but I was out early and passed the bread shop. I couldn't resist...' He gestured to the loaves. 'Shall we? Simon, do you wish to partake?'

His father wobbled like a man trying to walk two paths at once. He vacillated briefly, but he knew he had to make a choice.

'Ah yes. Come, Israel. Come. I'll show you. This is part of the *Shabbat* ceremony. Customary on Friday night, but today we introduce tradition and depart from custom.'

He rose from the table and turned to his wife. 'Emma?'

She shook her head, her hands in her lap and her chin very defined.

Israel set down the spoon he had been about to use and got up from the table. 'What's *Shabbat*?' he asked of his father, but Simon was already out of the room.

Abraham answered. 'You could say, Israel, that *Shabbat* has arisen as a tradition where we celebrate the successful creation of the world. From your Bible studies, you'll know that on the seventh day God rested. This seventh day of no work is Saturday or the Sabbath, but it is customary for the celebration to start on Friday night before sunset. It ends on Saturday, when it is just dark enough for three stars to show up in the sky. There are certain rituals to be observed. It's very particular and very special. Come. We follow your father.' He held out his hand to Israel.

'Why three stars? Which stars?' And if Saturday was a day of rest, why did his father work on Saturday and rest on Sunday? Abraham was about to answer, but by this time they had arrived without warning in the kitchen where Cook was in the process of sitting down to relax over a mug of milky tea. She leapt up so abruptly that the drink spilled, and was even more surprised when Simon growled at her, demanding a clean towel and a small jug.

Israel wondered whether his mother was listening. He knew she preferred to instruct the servants herself. Around him, tension mingled with the excitement of what was about to happen next.

Turning on the tap, Simon filled a jug carefully with water and handed it to his brother.

'Abraham. This is your idea. You show the boy.'

Israel watched as his uncle ceremoniously pushed up his sleeves and then, taking the jug, poured a little water over the right and then the left hand. He closed his eyes and started to pray in a slow murmur.

'But what's it for?' Israel asked as his father passed the towel to Abraham and stepped up to the sink. He could see that his uncle was bursting to answer, but for some reason was holding himself back.

'It is ritual, Israel,' said Simon. 'To cleanse. A way of appreciating what we are about to eat. But once the water has been poured on, we are not supposed to talk before we break the *Challah*. When I have finished, it will be your turn. Copy, eh.'

A BREAK IN THE CHAIN

His father had refilled the jug, poured the water, muttered a blessing and was silent. After he had dried his hands, it was Israel's turn. The seriousness of this occasion demanded an equivalent degree of ceremony from himself. In a way, it was a little like becoming a member of a secret society. Solemnly he stood on tiptoe to reach the sink. His father filled the jug and handed it to him, and carefully he poured the liquid over his hands. He then lifted his hands slowly in the air. Closing his eyes and murmuring under his breath just as he had heard the others do, he reached for the towel.

By the time they returned to the dining room, Emma had finished her breakfast and left the table, her starched napkin crumbled over her plate. Israel felt just a little light in the head. *Shabbat* had changed Saturday into something quite different; the bacon and kidneys were missing, which was a pity in one way, but he felt older, wiser – as if he were learning something important.

Abraham uncovered the plaited loaf, looked at the table as if something were missing, muttered and tore off chunks of the bread. The brothers each took a piece and then it was offered to Israel. He was about to eat to release the silence when he noticed they had bowed their heads and that his uncle was saying a prayer. With their eyes still closed, they took a bite of bread, chewing it reverently. To his surprise it was different from any bread he'd had before: sweet with a fragrance that was as much taste as smell, and which lingered on his tongue long after he'd chewed and swallowed.

A moment later it was all over, like the lights being turned on after the school play. The two brothers opened their eyes, rose from the table, talking, heaping their plates with steaming food. But by now, the candles were burned low under the dishes and to Israel the food wasn't as tasty as usual. He wondered where his mother was.

Something heavy slid across the polished wood of the dining table, and if Israel hadn't snapped his hand over it, it would have tumbled over the edge. He opened his fingers. In the centre of his palm lay a pocket watch so splendid he gasped. The edges of the bright gold were chased with a scrolled decoration; the marks that he knew as Roman numerals surrounded a small round window through which he could see tiny wheels of different metals and sizes. He looked up to see his uncle smiling.

'Open it,' said Abraham. 'Go on, open it up.'

A small clip at the side opened both front and back. When he pressed it, the casing sprung open, the numbers repeated now on a white background and the mechanism visible from both sides. With the case open, the ticking was loud, fairly throbbing in his hand. Was this for him – a present? All he could do was stare.

'See the jewels?'

'Jewels?'

'Yes. Look carefully. See the jewels in the movement?'

Israel swallowed. It was beautiful. But was it his or should he hand it back? Perhaps that was the polite thing to do. He rubbed his fingers over the chasing in the gold. It was smooth and cold. He felt his face flushing. There was only one way to find out and that was to ask. 'Is it for me?'

Abraham laughed and nodded. 'Yes, lad. It's for you. A growing boy needs a reliable timepiece.' His father also seemed surprised. He shook his head.

A BREAK IN THE CHAIN

'One of my best watches. You spoil the boy, Abe.'

'He's a good lad. Make you proud one day. You mark my words, Simon, he'll make us both proud.'

Determined to help this prediction along as best he could, Israel was bent over his letters one rainy afternoon. It was what his parents called 'a typical Melbourne day', the sun playing hide-and-seek with the clouds, creating a gloom that the three lit candles on his desk did little to diminish. He was so focused on what he was doing that some time had passed before he heard stifled sounds from down the corridor.

The sound was coming from his parents' room where he found the door partly ajar. He hesitated briefly, figuring that it was only when it was closed he was not allowed in. But once he stepped inside he wanted to leave again just as quickly.

His mother was lying over the big bed, her head under a pillow, heaving like a galley ship in a tempest. Could the feathers absorb that degree of grief? Israel stood there for a moment wondering what to do. He had seen his mother upset, but never like this.

His father was still at the store and the only other grown-up in the house was Clara. He was about to start down the stairs when he stopped. Would his mother want Clara to know she was upset? She always made a point of appearing kind and in control of things in front of the servants. Perhaps he should walk away? On the other hand, if she was this upset, she might need understanding more than any other sort of help. And what if she was sick?

He wavered for what seemed longer than his own life, his feet as ready to take him backwards as forwards, but the storm in front of him was worsening. Her suffocated sobs fed into gurgling streams. She sounded as if she was dying.

'Mama.' He took a step forward and having started it was natural to progress. He crept up beside her. Put his hand softly on her shoulder. 'Mama, please don't.'

To his alarm she cried harder and, it seemed to him, with even more passion than before. He wondered what had happened to cause her so much pain. Perhaps he was the reason for her distress.

Maybe it was accepting the present from Uncle Abraham? He knew his mother was wary of his uncle, who was so generous and kind on the one hand, but who – or so he had heard her say – placed *expectations* on them. But the watch was really lovely. Maybe it was that Israel wasn't as nice to Minnie as he could be, though she was a silly girl. Or maybe he wasn't doing well enough at school. Or perhaps he shouldn't have gone to the *shul* with all the men in their black caps and loopy beards. All sorts of things he could have done to make his mother so unhappy.

'Mama,' he said again. 'What's wrong?'

Shockingly, she reared up and grasped him about the shoulders. Her eyes, large and dark in a face streaming wet with tears, showed her attempts to fight a battle clearly too big for her.

'I'm so sorry,' she gasped. 'I didn't know what to do.'

Israel stepped backwards, his hands palm upwards as if help might come from somewhere high.

A BREAK IN THE CHAIN

She gulped, tried to swallow her tears. He stared at her. So unlike Mama.

'It's all right,' she managed at last. She took deep breaths and blew her nose with a sound like a horse on a cold day. He sat on the edge of her bed and after a while she seemed better.

'Go down and see Cook,' she said. 'Ask her to make us a big pot of tea.' She smiled crookedly. 'Ask her to make a fresh batch of scones, too. The big ones. With lots of strawberry jam and cream. Set it on the big table. I'll be down in a minute. And, Israel... Please don't worry. I'm sorry you've seen me like this. But it'll all be all right. Everything will be all right.'

A lazy sun peeked through the western window setting the silver on fire and turning the steam from the freshly baked scones to curls of smoke. A warm glow came from the logs in the huge grate that a moment before had fizzed and hissed bright red and gold.

His mother was more herself but her face was still swollen and blotchy and Israel wondered whether his father would notice. It was not long before he was due home and he didn't like it when anyone was upset, particularly Emma. Israel reached out. Scones were a treat.

'Just wait, will you, while I pour your tea. And then offer the plate to me first,' his mother snapped.

He sighed with some relief. Things were back to normal. When at last he was allowed to fill his mouth with buttery scone oozing strawberry jam and thick cream, she took a sip of tea and sat straighter than ever.

'Israel. I have something to tell you.'

A BREAK IN THE CHAIN

This was it! At last she was going to let him in on her secret. He closed his mouth quickly before the next bite. The big table always meant something important. He put down his scone.

She sat even straighter than usual, her dark hair coiled back from her face into a heavy roll on her neck, her long fingers threaded through each other as they rested on the lace cloth.

He put his hand in his pocket and felt his gold watch for luck. Now he was going to find out why she had been brought up Jewish, but wasn't a Jew.

'Israel,' said his mother. 'Your uncle is coming out for a visit. A quick visit.'

'My uncle!' Oh dear God, not another uncle. 'But I already have an uncle,' he said. 'In fact, more than one.'

She almost laughed. 'That's so. But it's quite usual to have several. You have, let's see – three. Your fathers' brothers – Uncle Marks and Uncle Abraham – and, now, *my* brother, who is your third uncle.'

'What's his name?' He didn't really count Uncle Marks, whom he'd only met only once long ago in Mortlake. He remembered him as like his father to look at, with the same kind smile and crinkly eyes as both his brothers, but with a different sort of energy – all the time wanting to do something with his hands. I certainly don't need another uncle, Israel thought.

Emma bit her lip, looked down at her plate for a moment. 'Let's just call him Uncle, shall we?'

'But why's he coming? Where's he coming from? Does it mean that we get to visit the port again?'

'He's coming out to see me. To see us all, really. From London. He won't stay long. Only as long as the ship is here, two, perhaps three, days. And no,' she added, 'I don't think we'll go to meet him. He would prefer to come straight here.'

'But why's he coming all this way just to see us?'

She shrugged. 'Maybe he wants to see if we're all right.'

He drew the warmth of the room, of his mother and the smell of hot sugary tea and jam close around him. At this particular moment, he had to admit, most things were fine.

'Well, we are, aren't we?'

She did laugh this time, put out her hand to his cheek.

'Yes, we are, son. We were a little shocked at the suddenness of things, but we really are quite all right.'

12

Luckily it wasn't raining the day his new uncle was due to arrive because his mother asked Clara to take them all into the garden. Israel resented being lumped together with his siblings. It was somehow demeaning, and they were always going to be too young to play the games he enjoyed. It was bad enough that he would have to share a room with Michael and that his bed had been moved into what he still regarded as the nursery while a larger bed had been placed in his room for the uncle.

The only upside in all this was the possibility that he would be allowed to keep the new bed once the uncle had returned to London. He had asked his mother, but she had only looked at him in a puzzled sort of way as if she hadn't seen him before. She kept picking things up and putting them down somewhere else and then forgetting where they were. Maybe she was getting old.

But right now, Israel was more interested in what was going on in the house than playing ball outside with Minnie. Catching him peeking into the morning room through the lace curtains, his mother had loosened the ropes on the heavy drapes. The room was blanked out and he was well and truly consigned to childhood. It wasn't fair to treat him as a growing boy one moment, a child the next.

Pulling a lemon from the tree, he bit into it savagely and spat out the sourness over the side fence, which earned him a reprimand from Clara who was upset anyway because someone called a valet was coming with the uncle, which meant that she would have to share a room with Cook who snored. He kicked a hole in the neat lawn. Flinging himself on the grass, he folded his hands behind his head. He was too old for a nursemaid.

Clara stood over him. 'Get up off the grass, young man. You'll be ruining your best clothes and then what will your mother say?'

He got up slowly. All this fuss for two days. His mother hadn't been strictly honest with him either about the visit to the port. He knew his father had gone because he had seen the carriage calling for him. Why was it that adults had to build such mystery into everything? She still hadn't told him the story she promised.

He wasn't sure why he should have been shocked that the uncle looked like a copy of his mother with the same dark hair brushed off his face, deep eyes with heavy lashes, and a straight mouth. And they were both tall. The only real difference, he thought, was in their clothes. They even moved in the same deliberate way – often graceful, at times awkward – but always considered. He wondered whether the uncle had also been brought up as a Jew but wasn't a Jew.

His mother sat erect in her usual wing chair, her hands loose in the folds of her favourite dress of cherry red trimmed with creamy lace. His father stood next to the new uncle. Both men had discarded their coats, and while his father wore his usual dark grey satin with the star-ruby pin in his white cravat, his uncle's vest was of heavy gold and silver brocade and his cravat was of a silk so fine it draped like liquid. The small table held the tea things which meant that it was a polite occasion and not the time for serious discussion. They both held a cup and saucer in their hands and Abraham was nowhere to be seen.

'And this young man,' his mother said, 'is my elder son.'

Once again, elevated from childhood just for the occasion. It was a bit of a double-cross, Israel thought. But he walked up to the visitor and held out his hand. He was, after all, the person who was going to make his father proud one day.

'Good morning, sir.'

Setting his cup down, the uncle stooped slightly to reach his hand.

'Good morning to you, young fellow. And what, may I ask, is your name?'

The uncle's hand had a slightly spongy feel to it and very little grip. Israel avoided the impulse to wipe his hand on his trousers.

'Israel, sir.'

'Israel?'

Did he imagine it or did one of the perfectly clipped eyebrows lift just a fraction? For a moment, the boy was back in the schoolyard and his stomach roiled. He straightened his shoulders.

'Yes, sir. And what would you like me to call you, sir?'

A BREAK IN THE CHAIN

His mother's brother laughed, but it wasn't a real laugh; it was brittle as if the sound itself might break, not one that rumbled out of the belly like Uncle Abraham's or one of his father's short chuckles that made you want to join in.

'Ah. How about Uncle,' he said, with a quick look at Emma. He reached into his vest pocket, went to draw out his pipe and changed his mind. 'Just call me Uncle.'

The whole household turned upside down for two days. Then Uncle was gone. But not before Israel had met the valet.

Some days earlier, Israel had gone shopping with his mother to buy Uncle a present. And the present, she had decided, would be a pair of slippers. They were to be fine slippers she explained to Israel as they strode up Bourke Street, ones that her brother would be proud to wear with his smoking jacket.

'What's a smoking jacket?'

His mother gave his hand a little tug as if it were something to which he should have known the answer. 'A smoking jacket is something a gentleman wears when he retires to his rooms after dinner. To keep the smoke out of his clothes when he has his last pipe for the night.'

'Why does he need slippers as well? When is he going back?'

His mother didn't answer.

They reached Royal Arcade just as Gog and Magog were tolling the hour and they stopped to watch. The terrible giants were people of a great age and savage temperament, his father had told him, who came from faraway parts to live in Melbourne and guard the fortunes of the city.

A BREAK IN THE CHAIN

Royal Arcade was usually fun because the shops were very grand and not poky with curling wood staircases. But that day, Israel wished he had stayed at home, for his mother examined pair after pair of slippers, exclaiming over this one and that one and even getting the man behind the counter to try on a pair. Never, he was sure, had there been so much fuss about something to wear on your feet. In the end, even the booming gongs of Gog and Magog lost their magic and in the last shop Israel simply sat on a chair and wished himself back at his numbers. He couldn't understand why they were going to so much trouble for someone who should be thanking them for the trouble of moving so many beds to different parts of the house for such a short stay.

Now Just-Call-Me-Uncle was getting ready to leave and Emma had suddenly remembered the present. As Israel looked as the neatly wrapped and sealed parcel sitting by his mother's elbow, he knew she was going to ask him to deliver it.

He squirmed as she placed it in his hands. 'What should I say?'

'I've never known you to be short on words, Israel. Don't make such a face. The wind will change and then what will you do? Be stuck with a face like that for the rest of your life. Go and find Uncle. I think he may be in his room. Wish him a good trip.'

His room. Israel's head fizzed. It certainly was not his room and the sooner he left the better for all. There were too many people in the house at the moment. He dragged his feet up the stairs just to show his mother how unhappy he was about this chore, but she had picked up her tapestry and her full attention was engaged in following the journey of the needle.

The door was closed and he was tempted to leave the parcel there, but if his mother happened to come upstairs and see it he knew he would be in trouble. Just as he raised his hand to knock, the door opened and he fell back to face the rather undernourished figure of the valet.

'And what do you think you're doing?'

Israel blushed. A task he had found distasteful from the first took on a life of its own, and all sorts of reasons for his standing outside the door flashed through his mind. Suddenly confused, he thrust out the parcel.

'This is for Uncle. Please give it to him.'

The valet took the box delicately. 'What is it?' he asked suspiciously. Israel could see he was itching to open it.

'A present.'

'Yes, I can see it's a present, boy. But what sort of present?'

'Slippers. It's a present from us to wish him a good journey back to his home...' He had an inspiration. 'To wear with his smoking jacket.'

The man's laugh was a copy of his master's. Under the thin wrapping, he slid a fingernail so long and yellow it made Israel shudder, and the tissue parted as cleanly as if he'd used a paper knife. The boy watched as he peered inside without lifting the lid quite clear of the box. He sniffed the leather and a thin, downturned smile appeared at the corners of his mouth. Poking at the tissue paper, he shook his head.

'The master is very particular about his clothes. He would never wear anything like this. You'd better take them back,' he said shortly. Letting the lid flop down, he dropped the box back into Israel's hands as though they were a receptacle for waste paper. And then wiped his own.

Israel's face was burning. He hadn't wanted to deliver the present in the first place. To make matters worse it had now been rejected and he had no idea what he could possibly do with it. He couldn't bear the thought of his mother's hurt if she discovered that the present for which she had shopped so painstakingly was spurned in such a manner. And before the person for whom it was intended had even sighted it.

He was tempted to offer the gift once more, to suggest that if the slippers were not suitable for Uncle, then perhaps someone else might have a use for them. But looking into the man's eyes, glassier than those of a dead fish, he knew there was little point. He'd have to hide them. But since he didn't currently have a room of his own, this posed a problem.

Turning on his heel with as much dignity as he could muster, Israel went down the corridor to the room he shared with Michael. Fortunately, it was empty. Clara must have taken the baby for a walk. He went quickly to the window, pushed up the sash with some difficulty and tossed the box into the garden. It hurtled through the air and landed, conveniently enough, in the shelter of a large camellia tree. He would bury it later. Meanwhile he had to allow some time to lapse in the hope that his mother would vacate her chair in the room through which he would have to pass to gain access to the back garden. He hoped she wouldn't come looking for him. His eye caught his books stacked neatly on the desk that had been moved from his room to Michael's and he decided that, should she come by, absorption in his studies would be the best way to deflect an enquiry.

With a sigh he sat down at his desk where, in a very short while, his attention was claimed by his books.

He heard the clock downstairs chime the hour, but otherwise the house was hushed. Could Uncle have left already?

Quietly he opened the door and made his way to the staircase. Down each step he crept, holding his breath. Intent on making it to the back door undiscovered, he was halfway through the sitting room before he looked up. There in front of him, so close that if he stretched out his arm he could have touched them, were his mother and Uncle with their arms around each other. For a split moment, he wondered whether his eyes were playing games with him. He froze balanced on the ball of one foot. For what seemed a long time, he wavered, unsure whether to creep past – so absorbed were they in each other – or to retrace his steps.

Erring on the safe side, he kept his gaze steadily on the sight in the centre of the room, his lungs bursting and the heat building behind his eyes. He stepped away to the stairs and began to climb them, one by one. He made it as far as Michael's room before his body exploded into a confusion of gulping breaths and hot tears. Flinging himself on the bed, he pulled the pillow over his head.

It was not until the following day that Israel remembered the slippers. Uncle and his hateful valet had finally left and after its short but turbulent upheaval the household was back to normal.

A BREAK IN THE CHAIN

Israel wandered out in the garden, only stopping to cast a quick look behind him as he closed the door. So far, so good. But there his luck ended. The slippers had gone. He cast about under the camellia. They had landed well into the shadow of the bush. He had seen that clearly. But now it was just as clear they had disappeared. No one had mentioned finding them. Certainly his mother hadn't or he would have heard about it by now. Perhaps the valet had seen them thrown from the window, had realised that they were actually of first-class quality and had had second thoughts. Whatever it was, they were gone. And good riddance, Israel thought. At least that was the end to this business and to Uncle, too. He hoped he would never see the man, his valet or the slippers again.

13

At last Abraham showed signs of moving out. His disappearances each morning – with his bag full and his days teeming with appointments – were paying off. The land boom was just around the corner and Abraham was well- placed to go with it. He made an announcement one Sabbath.

'The building is starting to look more like a house and less like a construction site. If any of you have the time, I would be delighted to show you over.'

There was a deal of excitement and discussion as to where it was and what sort of a house it was and when it would be completed. But underneath the questions Israel thought he detected a slight feeling of sadness rather than the relief they were all expecting.

After the initial disruption to their lives, and particularly after the arrival and departure of Uncle, having Abraham around had its advantages. He was more patient than Israel's father when helping with homework. While Simon was willing enough to glance at a problem sum and supply the answer, Israel was not able to make him understand that he had to arrive there in a particular manner.

'But that is ridiculous,' he would say. 'Why take the long way?'

'But we're not allowed to just show the answer. We have to show the workings.'

'But here. This is how it's done. Look…'

'No, Father. I'll get into trouble. We're not allowed to do it that way. We have to show it like this.'

Simon turned to Emma. 'I wonder about this school,' he muttered. 'They teach the boy in such a roundabout way.'

Uncle Abraham, on the other hand, took a different approach. Since the philosophy he applied to almost every facet of his life was the importance of the journey over the arrival, he would put his hands on his knees and listen intently to Israel's particular difficulty before, carefully clarifying each step of the equation, arriving at the answer.

'You see, it's not so difficult. You are treating each of these equations as different entities – as if they are all separate problems – when really they are similar in that one methodology solves all. Spend some time learning and thoroughly understanding the method and you can unravel any one of these problems. It's the journey, you must understand, not the arrival that is the point. People put too much emphasis on the target and miss all the pointers – and the enjoyment – along the way.'

Israel wondered whether he had, after all, noted Emma's absence that first Sabbath because after that he had stayed out of family matters. He continued to make his own observances, but he withheld from pressing them upon the family. They had all come to like him in different ways and one day he took Israel on a special trip to view the new house.

On the tram to St. Kilda his uncle was unusually quiet until all of a sudden he slapped his knee. He turned to Israel, his face breaking into a smile. 'I know what we'll do first. Since this drops us off in the main street, let's have some honey cake at one of my favourite shops. Would you like that?'

What was not to like about honey-cake? It turned out that the shop was just half a block down from the tram stop, in a row of identical shops all with shining glass windows displaying row on row of burnished pastries, tiny cupcakes with pastel icing and bright sprinkles, squares of fudge or chocolate, delicate custard tarts and huge cream-filled buns. Israel wondered whether his uncle had tried them all to come up with a favourite. If so, there was no wonder he was looking so prosperous these days. Israel licked his lips. Suddenly breakfast seemed a long time ago.

He was about to enter the shop, Abraham's hand on his shoulder, when Israel stopped at the sight of a man coming towards them. He was dressed from head to toe in black. Although the day was not particularly cold, he had on a round fur hat and wore a long black coat which flared out at the hem. Over the shoulders of the coat was a huge triangular woollen shawl. At the centre of his forehead was a small square box similar to the one strapped to his left arm. His beard and long hair were intricately braided. Israel stepped back. 'What's the matter?' Abraham asked quietly.

'That man. Why is he dressed like that?'

'Because he is an orthodox Jew.'

'That man's a Jew?' The boy let out his breath. He didn't look like any Jew he'd seen so far. Dressed like that, and it wasn't even cold.

Abraham was watching him closely. 'Yes, Israel. That man is a Jew. He's a Jew who is a member of a special branch of Judaism called Chasidism. Would you like to say hello to him?'

The man was getting closer. Israel was anxious to move out of his way.

'Oh no. Not really.' He repressed a shiver.

'Well, let's stop staring and have our cake. And then, if you like, I'll explain some things to you.' He was about to move on when he stooped quickly down to the boy's level. 'But only if you want me to explain. If you need to know more, you will have to ask me, Israel.'

The man passed as they entered the shop. Abraham raised his tall hat. 'Mordechai,' he said.

The other man gave an answering nod. 'Abraham.'

The shop was crowded with people coming and going, huddled around tables or perched on stools, chatting over their cake and coffee or reading quietly. There was a preponderance of men, many like those he'd seen in *shul*, with the plain black caps clipped to their hair with bobby pins. He was the only young person, but no one took any notice – so busy were they either conversing or sitting with their heads folded into their newspapers like birds tucked up for the night.

Nevertheless, Israel was uncomfortable. Again, this Jewish thing. It seemed to follow him around. And this place; it was on the one hand so close to home, and on the other so different. Both familiar and alien. He felt so unlike these people that he was appalled he had once been taken for a Jew. It was not something he particularly wanted to be. He found it a strange world with so much in it that was inexplicable.

And so, even though he felt Abraham's eyes on him from time to time, he was silent as he ate the little cake. But at last he could bear it no longer. There was no use asking his mother; she was impatient with such questions. Besides, there was already so much mystery about herself that she was guarding anyway. His father he knew would give him an explanation, but he knew also that it would be too complicated to understand. He pushed his cake around on the plate. It looked more of a treat than it actually was.

Shooting a glance at a little man alongside him reading assiduously, he shielded his mouth with his hand, bent towards his uncle.

'What actually is a Jew?' he whispered.

The man rustled his paper.

'Finish your cake,' Abraham said, smiling, 'and while we walk to the house, I'll tell you a story.'

In all circumstances of his life from then on, Israel was to look back on the walk from the St Kilda main street to Uncle Abraham's new house. The day was fine but not hot, and the way led them down streets hedged with roses and hawthorn, past houses that were neither grand nor small – comfortable-looking homesteads with their wide shady verandahs and doors with bright brass knockers flanked by window lights of coloured glass. Israel and Abraham walked in silence. His uncle seemed to be considering what he would say. Finally, he spoke.

A BREAK IN THE CHAIN

'You ask a question that has no simple straightforward answer. In other words, there is no answer that can do it justice in a mere few words of explanation.' He thrust his hands into his pockets. 'Let me start again. You see, to ask "What is a Jew?" is a very reasonable question to which there is no easy answer. Let me first tell you how a Jew behaves. Then perhaps I will give you an idea of how a Jew might view the world. And then you will begin to form your own answer to your question. Eh?'

Israel nodded.

'All right. First the story...'

'Is it a true story?'

'Yes, of course. It is a story by the great Baal Shem himself. All stories of this nature are true. Now listen. One day, not so very long ago, in a town not dissimilar to the village in which I was born, there was a *yeshiva*...'

'What's a *yeshiva*?'

'*Yeshiva* is a Hebrew word for a place of learning, where one might go to study special Hebrew subjects. Do you see? But this *yeshiva* had no dormitory attached, which meant the students had to rent lodging in houses nearby. Most of the landlords were very helpful to these young people because they were clean and tidy, quite quiet, and seldom caused any trouble. There was one landlady, however, who was a widow. You know what a widow is?'

Israel nodded. 'Someone whose husband has died?'

'Exactly. Well, although when her husband passed on this woman was left with a large house, she had no money. See?' He lifted his eyebrows, waved his forefinger at Israel. 'However, she was far from stupid: she perceived a need and decided that in order to make a living she would take in a lodger, maybe more than one. So she sent out the word and in the fullness of time quite a few young men took up accommodation in her house.

'But there was anger in her. She was very bitter at the way her life had turned out, and not having any other outlet, her anger fed on itself. Soon she was treating the students badly. She often screamed at them and made fun of them. Sometimes, she turned off the water taps, so that there was no water for bathing or for washing their clothes. Other times, she refused to allow them to use candles in their rooms to study. Naturally, before too long the boys found other accommodation. They all moved out. Save one.

'You would think that would make her change her ways, wouldn't you? But it made matters worse. She couldn't stand the fact that this one boy was not afraid of her. It made her madder than ever. One day, when she saw him coming home, the woman started to scream abuse at him. She used every nasty word she could think of to get him to pack his bags and move out, but he merely stood there looking a little sad.

'"What are you doing here? Why have you not run off like the others? Tell me that! Tell me that!" The woman was so furious that she wanted to hit him, but the young man just moved out of her way until eventually she ran out of steam. And then he started speaking.

'He told her that the reason he stayed was because he thought she would be lonely by herself. He said he was worried that she might have an accident or become frightened in which case, if no one was around, she would be in great trouble.

'After that, things were sorted very quickly. To the young man's surprise, the woman started crying. At last someone had taken the time to understand that her anger was in fact a protective barrier she had put up between herself and the world. She stopped her angry outbursts and her horrible aggression, put a guard on her tongue and on her actions and, over time and one by one, the boys returned to her house.'

'That's a good story,' said Israel, as they walked past another block, 'but I don't see what it has to do with being a Jew.'

'Let me put it this way, then – why did the last youth not run away from the angry woman like the others?'

'Because she was unhappy.'

'How do you know she was unhappy?'

'Because he, the young man, could see she was unhappy?'

'Then how is it that he knew that when the other students didn't?'

Israel shook his head.

'How?' asked Abraham again. 'By her words, by her actions? Why did she push people away if she were in fact lonely? And how would a young man work that out?'

'Perhaps he guessed.' Israel shrugged. He wasn't getting any closer to what he wanted to know and Abraham was for the first time behaving irritatingly like his father. It occurred to him that maybe they were trying to cover up their own lack of knowledge. When he grew up and had children of his own, he would make sure that he answered every possible question directly. Abraham stopped walking and, putting a hand gently on his shoulder, swung him around. 'Israel. Think of what I said at the beginning. That this would be a story about how Jews behave. These youths are all Jewish. How do they act?'

'Well, most leave and one stays.'

'Exactly. What do you think that says about Jewish behaviour?'

Israel was stumped. He hoped the house wasn't too far away. The day was getting warmer and more complicated by the minute.

'Your mind is looking at the obvious and seeing nothing special. Try to pull aside a curtain. Glimpse a little truth beyond. Row the boat, Israel. Don't just sit in it.'

Israel looked up at his uncle quickly. He had forgotten the dream, a nightmare his mother had called it, and he wondered for a moment whether she might have discussed it with Abraham.

His uncle sighed. 'All right. Let us leave it for the moment. You will work it out for yourself over time.'

'Do you know the answer?'

'I know *an* answer. Jewish scholarship doesn't insist that one is more right than another.'

'But what about that man, that man we just saw?'

Again Abraham let out his breath. For the first time, his voice was a little clipped. 'That man, Israel, has a name. You heard me greet him as Mordechai, didn't you? Because you see someone who dresses or acts differently from yourself, there is no cause to forget the manners your mother has taught you so well.'

'But all this doesn't help me. I still don't know what it's all about. You're a Jew, my father's a Jew, Mordechai's a Jew...and you're all different.'

A BREAK IN THE CHAIN

Abraham's eye crinkled as he let out one of his big rumbling laughs. 'As are all the peoples of this world! You see, this is part of why it is complicated because there are as many ways of being Jewish as there are rosehips on that bush over there. Again, you see only what is in front of you. You don't stop to consider other layers. And it is the layers that make up life. That make life interesting, too. Nothing is as straightforward as it may at first seem. Feel for the shades of grey. There are many branches of Judaism and each branch sees the world a little differently.'

Abraham stopped, and once again put his hand on the boy's shoulder. 'Mordechai and myself – we are both Jewish. We dress differently because Mordechai follows the traditional branch where they still dress as they did in Poland as long as two hundred years ago.'

Israel looked at him evenly. He was beginning to feel that nothing could surprise him now. 'And my father?'

'Your father is also Jewish because his mother was Jewish. In the Jewish law, the Talmud, it dictates that a person is only a Jew if the mother is Jewish. To a large extent, being a Jew is a matter of choice.'

'My mother isn't Jewish,' said Israel.

'No,' said Abraham after a minute. 'Technically, that would appear to be the case.'

'So,' said Israel, 'therefore I'm not.'

'As one premise follows another that would certainly seem to be so,' agreed his uncle. 'But remember, it is a matter of choice. Keep your eyes and ears open and put that keen mind of yours to work. Don't throw out your dirty water before you get new.'

A BREAK IN THE CHAIN

'Are we nearly there?' the boy asked. They had turned down another street and it was getting hot. The taste of the cake was still sticky in his mouth and he couldn't think of any reason on earth to want to be Jewish.

The sounds from the street outside his open window rose on the warm air that night, but that wasn't the only reason Israel was unable to sleep. He rolled from side to side, searching for the cool spots in the sheets. He had accepted his father's Jewishness and he knew this was something the brothers shared. It was just that it was not something that was ever discussed and somehow no one ever managed to get around to explaining it properly to him. His requests for enlightenment were always deflected in one way or another. And then someone like that Mordechai man turned up and confused things further.

Perhaps, he thought, it was because it was so obvious to themselves – such a natural state of being – that they failed to see the bewilderment it created in others. There were signs, but then he hadn't known what to look for. It was all very well for his uncle to talk about looking beyond what you saw in front of you, but how much simpler it would be if he just explained clearly, without talking in riddles.

His question had remained unanswered. But this was the first time Abraham hadn't answered directly. Was that because there was no answer? What had been the point of the story? To show that some Jews were braver than others? Or more stupid? Why would one stay when all the others were chased away? Unless there was something in it for him, perhaps? But if there was a motive of that nature, it would have had to appear in the story. Why then?

The answer – an answer, he corrected himself – might lie in the courage of the lodger who stayed. But that seemed too easy. Row the boat, Israel. He wondered about the woman herself. About what it would be like to have a home full of laughter and discussion, to have a husband who made enough money so they could live so well in the big house, to always have good food on the table and fine clothes to wear – and then quite suddenly to be alone. He supposed one would feel lost or cheated a bit by life. It certainly could give rise to so much anger that you might want to strike back. Not everyone would see that immediately, though. And so perhaps one answer lay in the understanding that the young man showed towards the woman, in that he was the only one of the bunch who saw through the ruse she put up. That would mean that a Jew was a person capable of taking the trouble to understand the real problem underneath.

For a moment, Israel thought he had it solved, but then his excitement evaporated. Since they all came from the same village and all attended the *yeshiva*, then all the others were Jews, too. And yet they had run off. Did this mean that Jews were cowards, too?

He would tackle Uncle Abraham in the morning.

But Abraham was not at breakfast the next morning so Israel sought him out in his room. He found his uncle sitting on the edge of his bed, hands on his knees, looking as if he had not slept much better than Israel himself.

'I think I've worked out an answer, Uncle Abraham,' said the boy.

'An answer to what?'

Israel frowned. 'To the story you told me.'

'Ah yes. I didn't think it would take you long,' said his uncle. 'Let's see what you have come up with. But first, I have another quandary you may be able to cast some light on.' He looked down at his feet. 'How did these come to be in the garden, I wonder?'

Israel followed the path of the point of Abraham's beard to the slippers on his feet, well, not quite on his feet because the fit was a little too snug. Israel stood and looked. And looked. He might have known he hadn't seen the last of the wretched things.

'Quite a strange thing, don't you think?' his uncle continued, turning his toes this way and that. 'I found them growing under the camellia bush. Just as well it hadn't rained else they would have been quite spoiled. Nice slippers, too.'

He looked up at his nephew. 'Any idea of their provenance?'

'Provenance, sir?'

'Provenance, Israel – where they may have sprung from, apart from up out of the ground.'

'It was me, sir.'

'You? They're yours? They do look as though they might be a little large for you, although I have to admit too small for me.' He flipped them off his feet and handed them to the boy. 'Nevertheless, if they're yours, my quandary is solved. Would you like them back?'

'No, that is, I mean that I was the person responsible for throwing them under the tree.'

'You threw them under a tree?' Abraham's eyebrows shot up. Israel didn't like him in this frame of mind. He was so different from the uncle who spent so long in explanation.

'Might I ask why?'

'I was going to bury them later.'

'Bury them? Ahem. The plot becomes more and more complicated.'

'They were meant to be a present for someone, but they were…turned down.'

'Ah, I see. I see,' said Uncle Abraham thoughtfully, although Israel was not sure how he could. 'I suppose you had a good reason for wanting to bury them instead of indulging in an explanation as to why they were rejected in the first place.'

Israel gripped his fingers. 'Yes, I'm afraid I do, sir.'

'And I'm guessing that it's a very, very good reason –like not wanting to hurt someone else,' Abraham said, slowly, 'not just to save your own skin?'

'A bit of both, to tell the truth.'

Abraham looked at him steadily. 'The truth is a good thing. That's a good answer.' He was silent for a long moment before he continued. 'Your parents are still at breakfast in there, aren't they?'

Israel nodded.

'Look, I tell you what,' said Abraham. He jumped up, rubbed his hands together. 'Grab me a spade, lad. Let's get rid of the evidence. We'll go out this door here and no one will be any the wiser.'

14

The winter air was warm, a hint of twilight about the streets as Israel stepped through the shop door early one evening. His father was doing a deal, so he settled on a stool to watch. Although they were quite different personalities, there was a definite similarity in the Kozminsky brothers' approach to the matter in hand. So intense was their focus that space outside the immediate moment or the current task did not exist. And yet he sensed that on some other level they were well aware of everything that was going on around them. Simon knew he was there even though his attention was consumed by an imminent sale.

The customer, a tall stringy man, made even taller and thinner by the droop of his moustache, was shuffling about the store, his toes nudging at the counter kickboards, fingers running through his hair. A small necklet of pearls lay before him on the counter. Simon was displaying them on the scarlet silk, Israel noted, so he would be after a good price. Several other strands were pushed to one side.

'Four hundred pounds, you say. Daylight robbery, my good man. There's no way I have that sort of money. No sirree.' His sentence ended with a whistling sound.

A BREAK IN THE CHAIN

His father's expression remained unchanged. 'I quite understand, Mr Weildon,' he said, his voice soft as a feather pillow. 'A lot of money. However, expensive items always look refined. But these are, of course, so perfect that it would be almost a crime to wear them. Better, perhaps, for investment?' Lifting the strand in one hand, he pulled the pearls gently through a pale-coloured chamois in the same leisurely manner a woman who was not quite a lady might take off her silk stockings.

'A perfect necklet of oriental pearls, each found in the flesh of the oyster, quite separate from the shell. The lustre is beautiful, eh? Definitely suited more for investment, I would say.' Quietly, so the customer had to lean towards him to catch his words, he repeated. 'Rare to find pearls of this quality that match so exactly.' He placed the necklace back on the silk and picked up another strand from among several that lay to one side.

'This, for example, is half the price and let me see...' Holding it to the lamp, he paused to fix his glass to his eye and turned it this way and that. 'Just as beautiful, yes?' He placed it on the silk beside the other. 'But for a different purpose. This, I think... Yes, this I would use as jewellery, certainly.'

The man wet his lips, stroked his moustache, passed his hands through his hair again.

'I really don't know... It's a large sum. I'll think on it. Are you sure you can't do any better, Kozminsky?'

Simon shrugged. 'Not for either of these strands, Mr Weildon. The others...yes, certainly we can discuss. But these are...different. Consider for a few days.' Gently, he returned the tray to its place under the glass countertop. Israel held his breath as the man hung over the glass, while his father, unconcerned, started to wipe the counter, readying to close for the night.

Quite suddenly the customer's body went limp. He slumped against the counter and an expression of relief passed across his face. He clasped his hands and Israel knew he'd been won over.

'Parcel them up,' he sighed. 'The investment strand. I'll take them. Put them on my bill. My credit, as you know, is good – you'll get the money within the seven days.'

Israel thought for a moment that his father was going to demur, but the hesitation was so subtle that he realised it was all part of the play. Mr Weildon must continue to believe in his reluctance to part with the goods.

As Weildon slipped the package into a pocket on the inside of his vest, he turned back. 'I'll bet you've done well out of these, Kozminsky.' The door closed behind him with a short burst of tinny chimes.

Israel slipped off his stool, his face alight. He was halfway across the room before he realised that his father hadn't moved. He was sitting, instead, with his chin in his hands, a look of infinite weariness on his face.

'Silly old bugger,' said Simon.

Israel started. His father didn't often use such terms. 'Aren't you pleased, Father? It was a good sale.'

Simon sighed. 'Yes, yes, of course. And no, not really.' He shook his head. 'The truth is that I'm sorry for those pearls. Silly old bugger Weildon and silly old bugger Kozminsky. One is no better than the other. Money is a terrible thing, Izzy. Greed tops the list of the deadly sins.'

Israel shook his head. 'I don't know what you mean.'

A BREAK IN THE CHAIN

'Yes, I'm not making much sense, am I? Sometimes not even to myself.' Simon sat heavily on the stool behind the counter. 'But the fact of the matter is that pearls live; all gems have a...' He searched in the air around him for the word he wanted. 'An energy, you could say, about them, but pearls in particular are alive. If they are not in contact with the skin, they die and are worthless.'

'So?'

Simon's eyes were glassy, his gaze turned inward. 'Don't you see?' he said. 'I made the sale, and money is always important. I am in a trade and one has to live. One's wife and children have to live. But I also condemned those beautiful pearls to death. All I said was perfectly true: they are well-matched and of a first-class grade. But the tragedy is those pearls will never know the skin of a lovely woman. Now they will die in a hole in the wall of a bank.'

Israel looked down at his father's clenched hands and saw there what he was trying to say. That there would be years between visits, years between the moments Mr Weildon held them in his hands. And when he did so, when he took them out, he would not do so to love and admire them, to roll their cool smoothness over his fingertips or to smile at the little bubble of light that moved constantly across the skin of the pearl. Instead he would do it only to be sure the bank had not cheated him by substitution. And each time, each time he visited, those pearls would look just a little more age-stained, just a little yellower and a little more lustreless.

Simon blew out a cloud of breath, brought his hand down hard on the counter. 'But I doubt he would even notice.'

Israel shook his head. 'But it was you who encouraged him to put them away.'

'Yes, but why did I say that? Why did I say that? Eh? Wasn't it because I knew he was an investor? Because I knew he would then purchase? Because I knew that in his greed he would not be able to resist? And in my own greed I have killed something very beautiful.

'Money is a wicked thing,' Simon repeated. 'But this time I was also led by another type of greed. *Selling*. I love it.' His eyes gleamed. 'The trick to sales is that people have a need to be led, Israel. They like you to do the thinking for them. From then on, it becomes a game: push here, pull there. You look for the weak spot. In this case, I had an immediate advantage in knowing Weildon's passion. He is a collector and when he asked me for a discount, I knew I had him and that it was time to back off. Making the sale was more important than anything else. And in the end too easy.'

He threw the empty red-covered board in the bottom of a cabinet and slammed the door. 'Pah,' he said. Pah!'

Closing up for the night was a ritual. Israel rubbed blotchy sets of palm prints and imagined drops of perspiration from the countertops, while Simon emptied the display window of temptation and turned the keys in drawers and cabinets, his movements gradually losing their edge of anger. Tipping the money drawer upside down, he counted out the takings in small piles of paper and coin, listed the tally in a small cotton-covered book of faded red, swept the coins and book into a leather bag and pulled the string tight. Israel knew his mother would count it all again later before carefully entering the figures into the ledger.

Simon stood up, his brow clear. 'Well, that is all past now. Let us move on. But first, I have something to say to you, Izzy. Something I have been meaning to say, but which keeps getting pushed to one side for no good reason. But it will not be long before your tenth birthday and the time has come for you to do something here in this store. Not just help out from time to time, but a regular job after school for which you will be rewarded. Minnie, too, is not too young to do the same.'

His gaze flickered to the window where the last street lamps were being lit as the rain tumbled from the gutters in spills of shot silk. He checked his watch and blinked. 'But it is nearly dinner time. I hadn't realised it was so late. Your mother will be cross.'

As he helped turn out the lamps, Israel wondered what job exactly his father had in mind. He wasn't entirely surprised; as the eldest, he had expected it. His only concern lay in the reduced time it would give him for reading between homework and bedtime. His mother was unyielding on both counts and he had just come across a translation of Ptolemy's *Tetrabiblos*. While there was a lot he didn't understand, right from the first pages of the first book he had been entranced by the astrologer's discussion of the influence of the sun and the moon and the stars on everyday life. As he had started to read, he had exclaimed out loud. He had suspected all along there was power in the heavens that most people didn't know about. That someone who lived in the second century should have a mind so open and so exploratory that he was able to unravel some of that mystery was a wonder. Here was the knowledge Israel had been seeking.

As they set out, Simon outlined his plan. He would have, his father said, a seat and small desk in an area designated as the workroom; it was part of the main shop with its collection of glass cases, but half-hidden by the wobbly spiral staircase for privacy.

'This carries, of course, a certain responsibility. You will be working in sight of the main entrance and you'll need to keep an eye on things. If the store is unattended – if I have to go to the bank, for example, or the customs house or if I am working upstairs – your job will be to attend to the customer in a general fashion. Do you understand? If they want to purchase or pay for something, they will either have to wait for me or return later. Do not unlock the glass cases or accept any money. Do you understand?'

Israel's face dropped. 'Why not? Don't you trust me?' he blurted out.

Simon stepped out of the rain into the entry of a closed shop. Furling his umbrella, he bent down so his face was level with his son's.

'Israel. Even though you live in a city, still you live what many would call a sheltered life. If you are not alert to the ways of the world, that is precisely because your life is privileged. One circumstance calls up the other. Although they say this nation is making its fortune on the sheep's back, they forget the huge wealth that has accrued from mining. You only have to look at what's happening around us. Here, in front of your eyes. Everywhere cranes, building, piles of rubble. Make no mistake: this is a city that was born on the back of the gold boom and, in some respects, still tends to hide behind a fancy front. Some of the rough and tough of a mining camp still exists. Our business is pearls and watches, antiquities, coins. Jewels, timepieces and things worth collecting are always a cause for lust and greed. Most people are honest, fortunately, but sadly not everyone. Crooks don't carry flags to shout the news. Many times, they are cool and pleasant-looking people. But as often, also, they are desperate people. That means violent. That's not a situation I want for you. Leave the money side of things to me for the time being. And be assured, it's not a question of trust. All right?' He pressed his son's shoulder lightly so that Israel had to look up to meet his eyes.

'Besides, as much as I myself love selling, you are different. Instead, for you it is books. And I am glad for that. One day, they will make your fortune. But before then, between the covers of those books you might find the type of information that will help the business.'

'What sort of information?' asked Israel.

'Oh, things like how to tell the age of a piece, how to date it, for example, by knowing about dyes and silver stamps, the difference between a stone and a gem, how to spot a fake. That sort of thing. Everything I learned about this business, I learned from experience. I have made many mistakes, and there is a great deal that I don't know.'

'You mean this is preparation for what I'll have to do when I leave school?'

Simon laughed at the glum look on his son's face. 'I think we'd both better wait to decide that. Eh? When the time comes for you to make that choice you will do as you will do. But meanwhile, this is a great opportunity to learn a lot of skills. Life, my son, does not always go as you wish and it is useful to have a spare string, you see. Just in case.' He was silent for a moment as if something in what he had just said had jogged his own memory. He shook his head and with a sidelong glance at the boy's lowered head continued. 'But you may also find it is something you enjoy. For now, the job I have in mind for you is at least as important as watching the money drawer. Much more, in fact, because it not only requires skill, but also great knowledge.'

Israel hoisted his satchel onto his shoulder. He sent a quick prayer to Abraham's God.

'Is it the gems?' He screwed his eyes shut. Please God, let it be the gems.

'It is indeed the gems first. Then, if you like, gradually the coins and antiquities, the silver.'

Jewels. Israel let his breath out in little spurts. Pearls were pretty, certainly. But to him each contained a centre of sadness. Small moons of light with a Mona Lisa smile. But jewels and stones: here was a different, more exotic story.

That night, Israel dreamed that the stacked drawers of Kozminsky's cabinets spilled open to reveal a cave, the walls of which were studded with jewels of colours so clean and clear and bright he forgot to breathe.

Embedded in the wet and glistening quartz were gems of every colour: pink, orange and golden sapphires, rubies with stars at their centres, jasper and emeralds, bright orange carnelian, blue, yellow and white topaz; and even the olivine mined from the green mountain.

As he looked about in wonder trying to absorb the kaleidoscope before him, the ground began to rumble beneath his feet until there was a roaring, a pounding of drums and clashing of cymbals, and in through the entry of the cave poured a dragon. In the centre of its forehead was the brightest ruby he had ever seen, a stone the colour of pigeon's blood, burning so fiercely it set the space afire. He watched in a trance as the dragon's lumbering body swayed towards him, with the ruby flashing and dimming as the smoke and flame poured from its long tongue. Following its own bulging eyes, the beast pawed at the ground, bowed and swayed, and danced its languid dance.

Israel stood rigid. Even if he had wanted to run, there was nowhere to go, and this was a sight unequalled. His breath was still on hold, his skin prickled and his limbs were quite useless. But it was not fear that held him; rather a thrall beyond anything he'd known before. The dragon's hot breath reached out towards his chin.

But just as it did so, the ground moved a little under his feet, cracking and rocking until a mound formed beneath him raising him up towards the roof of the cave which slid back to reveal a sky of black and silver, so silent and so still that he was caught between the wonder of the two extremes: the music and dance and perpetual excitement of one, and the quiet knowing promise of the other.

He closed his eyes to better savour the moment. When he opened them it was to see Abraham standing in the cave below looking up at him with a half salute before taking the bridle of the dragon, which followed him out as meekly as a pet dog.

On waking, the bedroom came into focus one piece at a time, all the familiar things first like the complicated cornice that joined the ceiling to the wall, the iron railings at the head of his bed, Ptolemy on his bedside cabinet and the realisation that his nightclothes were clammy with sweat.

Israel's gaze turned to the window framing the day that lay ahead. His ears took in the slosh and clang of the morning water cart. All was the same as usual. Why, then, did he feel so different?

15

There was something about turning ten years of age that was particularly special. Numbers, he was beginning to suspect, had a significance way beyond pen strokes on a page or candles on a chocolate cake. Ten, the system suggested, was more powerful than eleven. But for now, this strength he found in his tenth birthday had a practical use. For the first time, he had the courage to put in place the second and final part of a pact he had made with himself years before, on the night he vowed he would one day put an end to the teasing of his name.

He pulled out his watch, one of his most precious possessions. If, as his uncle was fond of saying, life was what you made it, then there was no further time to waste. Time, in fact, was Enemy Time, said Abraham. It had a face, like the face of his watch, but it was finite.

'When people, both individually and severally, badger their memory boxes about the greatest gift to mankind,' said Abraham, 'their minds are so bent on tangible goods that they quite forget that time is the supreme commodity. Because they place such little value on it, they don't realise that time has a habit of running out. Time is limited. When you think of time, Israel, think egg timers, not clocks. Remember the story I told you the other day about Lot's wife? There's a punishment for looking back in time, wouldn't you say? Eh? Row the boat, my boy. Row the boat.'

Israel wished he would drop that maxim. It always reminded him of the strange dream that still occasionally nibbled at the edges of his mind. And although what Abraham said about time was true, he thought now on his way up Collins Street, there was also a balance to be maintained and sometimes pausing to take in other aspects of life was as important as rushing through regardless. The thought had no sooner occurred to him than he drew to one side of the crowd. Skipping up the steps of a nearby building, he stopped to watch the city folk pass, the new rich that were the talk of the town. They certainly looked prosperous: the men with their tall black top hats and frock coats sucking at fat cigars; the women in grand silk gowns, the bustles and flounces colour-matched to their stylish hats and twirling parasols.

When his mother spoke disparagingly about the fine furs and feathers of the *nouveaux riches*, his father was silent and Abraham changed the subject. Israel wondered whether this was because the family she came from was wealthy, while the Kozminsky brothers had each made their own way. Everyone had to start somewhere, Israel thought.

If indeed Abraham had been guilty of overstatement at dinner several months before, when he had clinked the best crystal in honour of 'This marvellous Melbourne, Simon, where the streets are literally paved with gold', his statement made up in essence for what it lacked in accuracy. Melbourne was booming, and it was no ordinary land boom. It was a boom of banks and building societies that lined either side of the 'Golden Street', great temples of commerce built to the drumbeat of their benefactors' egos. Born to be part of their own horizon, they soared sharp against the sky, giant edifices of carved stone, lavish with great pillars and pointed Gothic arches, colourful leadlight cupolas, railings of glossy black iron, statues of gilt and bronze. Throughout the city, the wreckers were moving in on the more humble shops and buildings. The weatherboard dwellings were dashed to the ground, sometimes three or four at a time, and each new building that rose out of the freshly prepared earth seemed higher and more ornate than the one before. It was indeed an era of embellishment.

'The fastest-growing city of the century,' boasted the land-sale placards. The proof was there for all to see.

But as Israel stood there he realised he had erred by basing his judgement on the observable, on the scene before his eyes: the dress of the citizens, the quality and quantity of building. Despite himself, he heard his uncle's voice.

'Yes, but what about the intangible, the subtle, the things you can't see? How do they manifest themselves? What does the less obvious say to you? How does it bear witness to your vision?'

Israel glanced again at his watch. He was early for his appointment, still with a few minutes to spare. He leaned back against a pillar, closed his eyes. Where he had been a part of the crowd, he was now cut off, separate, and so instead of being part of the melee, he found the sounds separating out. He heard discrete words instead of clamour, sometimes whole sentences moved towards him with increasing sound, hovering for a few seconds, and then fading fast away on a little whiff of breeze as if he were on a station platform in the wake of a passing express:

'…such a red-hot tip for a long time. I tell you, you could do a lot worse than buy into the Freehold…'

'…Fink? Oh, there's no doubt he's a genius. I gather one of his next projects is Queens…'

'…afford it, old chap, price of land rules me out…'

'…then he's building a villa out in Kew. Two stories. Slightly extravagant. You must…'

'Bankruptcy! Don't make me laugh. He's got so much money that…'

'…saying at dinner the other night, that it's becoming virtually impossible to get reliable help. Do you know…'

'Direct from Italy. Where else…'

'…hear they caught the Benalla bugger… You think he'll swing?'

'…mark my words, cable trams will revolutionise this…'

Boom. Investment. Power. Land lust. Gold dust. Bull dust. Speculation. Inflation. Elation. Money, money, money…

And filtering through the voices, the clink of harnesses and the shouts of the conductors from the horse buses, the intermittent screech of winches hoisting a load of bluestone one floor higher, the shouts of foremen or the thud of pickaxes digging the drains at the edges of the streets, the explosion of a wrecker's hammer and the collapsing brick of a house that was once someone's dream, music, a band maybe, from a doorway or a window…

A BREAK IN THE CHAIN

A long way under his feet, starting as rumble, the rhythm of the city swelled gradually to a roar. Each strike of a hammer rang through his body, hoof beats pulsed, speech and music in translation vibrated through his mind, and under his two hands the granite pillar became complicated.

'Are you all right, sonny?'

He started as someone placed a hand on his shoulder, opened his eyes to see an old face with the softness of concern about the mouth.

'Oh yes, thank you. I was just...listening.' He nodded and smiled and he went on his way. He was due to meet Abraham at the new coffee palace, five storeys of grand building just completed. He had a coin in his pocket to spend on the celebration.

Abraham was there before him, though Israel was not late.

Typical, thought the boy; he doesn't miss a trick.

'Uncle.'

He held out his hand. Abraham's initialled cufflinks caught and held the myriad lights multiplied by the long mirrors in the huge room.

'Ah, Israel. It's been too long, my boy, too long.'

Israel swallowed. He was not looking forward to this. He had something to say and his uncle might not like it. Settling himself on a chair opposite Abraham, he felt like a black spider with too many legs confronting a bigger and very much blacker spider and wondering which way to move.

For the first few minutes, Abraham said nothing. He seemed preoccupied, not his usual talkative self, and Israel could think of nothing to break the uneasy mood.

He cast around the room for inspiration. Noted the domed ceilings, the arched doors, the way the light flooded through the windows, felt again the city rumbling beneath.

At last, Abraham spoke. 'This city, boy. What do you think of the chess game being played out?'

Israel lightened. 'You know, sir, just now I was thinking the same thing. Well, more-or-less the same thing.'

'You were?' Abraham's eyes glistened behind his wire-rimmed spectacles. He reached for his pipe. 'Go on.'

As the match flared and the tobacco took light, Israel breathed in a soft wave of vanilla-tinted smoke. Ever since his small victory over the school bullies he had found a way to deal with his own nerves. He'd learned to get out of his skin, make himself into someone else.

'On my way here, I stopped to listen.' He spoke softly.

'The city, sir – it spoke to me. '

'Ah! And then? What did the city say?'

'It spoke from all around – of all sorts of things. No one's poor here, Uncle. Buildings are ripped down and built bigger. The talk is rich and all about money. People aren't hurting. There's a vibration of energy.'

'People aren't hurting.' Abraham blew out a cloud of smoke. 'I agree with you. Not at the moment. But people are greedy. People don't look ahead.'

He was silent for a moment and Israel had the horrible feeling that he was going to say, row the boat. But he sat chomping on his pipe like a cow chewing cud. 'On this walk, let me ask you: did you hear cannons or did you hear bells?' he asked at last.

Cannons or bells? Why did his uncle always do this?

'Well, no,' he said. 'I didn't hear either.'

'You didn't listen hard enough, my boy. It's either one thing or the other thing. Bells ring with good news. They create a thrill throughout a city. You can hear it in your ears, in your feet, too. Cannons spell doom. They talk of invading armies and create a tingling of another kind. A chill that travels through your being from the top of your head to the tip of your right toe. That's the difference between bells and cannons. So! Which, do you think, you heard on your journey through the town?'

'Oh, definitely bells, then. Everyone, everything was tingling and happy.'

'So, Israel – what would you do if you had a fortune today? Would you buy shares or perhaps put your life savings into land? Would you plough ahead? Or would you sell your shares and your slice of real estate?'

'I would invest. Just as the people in the street were saying. I would invest everything I had.'

'No qualms?'

'No. Absolutely not.'

'And do bells ring forever? Does the tide run only in one direction? Does day never turn to night?'

Israel moved on his seat. He was surprised Abraham hadn't added, 'And does the sand in the hourglass never run out?' The ceiling looked like an inverted Christmas cake with its scrolls and curlicues. The laughter from the adjoining table was becoming intrusive.

'No, but...'

'But?'

The cake trolley rumbled across the marble tiles and Abraham became distracted by one of his greatest pleasures: viewing a colourful selection of cakes and pastries that stopped the conversation in its tracks.

'You first,' he said to Israel, tapping the tobacco from his pipe, his eyes raiding the tray.

Israel didn't have to think. Chocolate cake won every time, particularly a piece like this, sandwiched together with thick cream and topped with flakes of white and dark chocolate and bright red cherries with leaves of angelica. Abraham, however, took his time, bending over the trolley, examining first one candidate and then the other, his eyes questing his tastebuds, deciding, finally, on a thick slice of apple pie, wobbling tall with a rich golden crust. It was some time before he spoke again. His uncle, thought Israel, alternated between action and inaction with no in-betweens. But whatever he did commanded his full attention. When he had finished eating, he sat back and reached for his pipe and tobacco pouch once again. 'So. Today is your birthday?' Israel nodded.

'Are you celebrating?'

'Yes. Now.'

'Ah. This is your celebration?'

The boy nodded. From his pocket, he drew the coin and placed it reverently in the centre of the table. His uncle sat back in the padded chair, his hands folded under his chin.

'Well, Israel. Thank you. I am honoured.' Abraham observed him for a moment. His flushed face, clenched hands. 'But something is on your mind? Can you tell me about it?'

Israel took a deep breath and squeezed his eyes. It had to be now.

'Uncle,' he said uncomfortably. 'I do have something to tell you.'

His uncle placed his hands on the table, smiled. 'A new school, I hear? Or another city experience?'

'Er, no. That is, a new school, yes. But you see, something even more important, I have decided to change my name.'

The smile didn't slip on Abraham's face. On his raised sleeves, a shaft of sun struck sparks off the gold of his jewellery. 'Yes?'

'I'm not called Israel any more. I would prefer to be known as Isidore.'

As he said this, he imagined that the lights dimmed just a little for a fragment of a second. He imagined his pocket watch ceased its ticking. He imagined all the people at the tables round and about stopped to stare, frozen in their poses. His uncle spoke.

'So now you are Isidore?' He rolled the name slowly across his tongue as if he were tasting it. 'Israel no longer. Isidore Kozminsky?'

'Yes,' he went to say, but the word caught in his throat and so he could only nod.

'Isidore, I see. But you are a Kozminsky, you know. That you cannot change. Cast in stone, as it were.'

'Yes. Yes, of course, Uncle. Kozminsky is fine. It is just my first name. It's only Israel I wish to change. You see, Isidore has a more favourable numerical value.'

Abraham's eyebrows rose. 'Numerical value?'

'The Kabbalah, sir. It attributes a value of five to each name – Isidore and Kozminsky. That's ten, a good number on the wheel of fortune. Better than Israel Kozminsky, which is eleven... This is the Hebrew system, the best I think...' He hesitated, but his uncle was sitting upright. 'The Pythagorean system contains flaws. For some reason, it isn't always right and I think it has something to do with the pronunciation, the silent letters. I'm not quite sure...' He shifted in his seat.

Abraham bent towards him. 'And this...this new name. You think it will change the course of your life, do you?'

The boy nodded. 'I know it will,' he said quietly. 'And yes, I have started finally at Scotch College. With my new name.' He breathed deeply. 'Everything's different. It's a new life.'

His uncle continued to draw quietly at his pipe. From time to time he nodded slightly as if he were having a conversation with himself. Israel itched to move, but there seemed to be some sort of spell at work here, and he didn't want to break it. He knew his uncle could project a face that was a river of calm, but underneath the unruffled surface a mass of connections and interconnections were being established. Gradually the light drew in and the air grew cool as the sun passed beyond the window. The rowdy table beside them got noisier, and still his uncle sat. When at last he spoke, his voice was quiet, controlled.

'I agree with you that a name is important and you are not the sort of boy who does things without self-examination. I would say only: take care with the Kabbalah. On the one hand, it is fascinating; on the other, those who think they are in the know contradict themselves by calling it both nonsense and dangerous, as if it could be both things at the same time. And remember, to work properly, a change of name must be accompanied by attention to the important aspects of prayer and charity.

A BREAK IN THE CHAIN

Effective change has to take place inside as well as outwardly.

'Apart from that, my boy, and the time all this must be taking from your true studies, it is your name and your choice. It has an honest sound and it keeps the initial of your birth name. Clothes may, or may not, maketh the man, but a name... Ah, that's important. Because you will be as you are called.'

He rose and stretched out his hand. 'Congratulations, Isidore Kozminsky.'

The rest of the room with its mirrors and tables and cake trolleys blotted out and there was just his uncle and himself and this final step in the vow he had made to himself after that first day at school.

He walked with Abraham to the horse tram, proud that his legs were now long enough to keep pace with his uncle's gait. When they shook hands, he was filled with an exuberance that threatened to burst. As he watched the tram move away, he fought the urge to run and jump and cry.

A moment later and he would have done all three if he hadn't spied a disturbance about a block away. A milling crowd, flanked on the street side by mounted police, was moving like a funeral procession through the city. So with a scant half-hour to spare before his violin lesson, he sprinted in the direction of the throng that was growing by the second.

He was out of breath by the time he arrived at the corner of Russell Street and almost too late to see the bloodstained figure of a man, heavily chained and closely guarded, shuffle into Melbourne Gaol. As the gates clanged behind him, the strangely hushed crowd fell back, their mouths slack with disbelief, rubbing their faces, whispering uneasily.

'It's Ned Kelly,' said one fellow in a conspiratorial whisper, bending down to him. 'They got the poor bastard. He'll hang, that's for sure.' He sounded surprised. As if he didn't want to believe the conviction in his own voice.

Isidore hung at the edges of the crowd for as long as he could, and when he finally dragged himself away to his lesson his thoughts were full of the man with the tangled beard and the chains dragging behind him.

That night in bed he pondered. Was his new name already changing him? Isidore at school, Isidore at home. That much was already established, but late at night there was only this boy in a bed that felt much too big, in a room too spacious, beyond the walls of which was a universe that hung over the whole like an umbrella that might snap closed quite suddenly without any warning at all. He felt unreal, as if he were playing a stage role suspended between two characters.

He squinted into the darkness. There was, he thought, a period of nakedness between putting aside one name and taking on another. Like a chick before it grew its feathers. A new name was not just an overcoat, a robe over a person's normal day clothes. It was, in a way, a change of personality.

And, overall, it was much more: not only was it a complete change that came with an interlude of inevitable vulnerability, but it also required the recognition that there was a two-way consequence. Although it had been his intention to change the way the outside world related to him, what he hadn't considered was that it also affected the way in which he related back to that world.

Why had he been so nervous of today's meeting? His father had accepted his name change with a degree of irritation and a shrug. His mother had just looked at him, her head on one side, her brow creased, but there was nothing disapproving in her stance. Had he thought Abraham wouldn't have approved? Was acceptance as simple as gaining Abraham's support?

And they'd caught Ned. Finally. But from the mood of the people the only ones happy were the newspapers that made profit from others' misfortune. For ages now the paperboys had been singing the headlines: 'Stringybark Shooting', 'Hart and Dan Kelly Dead', 'Ned Kelly Captured', and tonight's finale in the late-night edition of *The Age*: 'Extermination of the Kelly Gang'. Was Ned Kelly really a rat? The people didn't think that.

Why was every happiness diluted with unease? Perhaps that was what being older held in store? It was a strange ending to a birthday which had begun with the number ten.

Part Four

Isidore

1906

16

The disagreement erupted quite violently and without warning. The catalyst was not, for once, Isidore's inability to settle down, but quite the opposite: his desire to marry. After all the women he had met or half-heartedly courted, he had at last – if it were not too absurd to put the complexity of his feelings so simply – fallen in love. The conversation with his father had not gone well. It had ignited violently, in fact, somewhat like a spark set to a stagnant puddle of energy.

He had mentioned it quite casually the week before as he worked his way through a collection of Chinese razor coins and garment pieces, some of which he estimated dated back to 1250 BC when the barter system was replaced with coinage as a method of acquisition.

Calling across the store from his den in the corner to where his father stood crouched and absent over an item he was examining, he asked: 'Will you be at home on Saturday afternoon? I'd like to bring a friend to meet you both this weekend. A young lady.'

'A young lady?' Simon looked up, vague for just a second before he gathered himself to catch his eyeglass deftly in the palm of his hand. 'Ah, Isidore, this is excellent news. And serious?'

Isidore turned over another coin, held it close to the light, a Tsen Dynasty bronze from the reign of the emperor Wang. 'Of course I'm serious. How many girls have I brought home so far? None.' He looked up briefly and then back to his work. This coin, he estimated, could be fairly accurately dated around 520 BC. It needed cleaning; an old toothbrush, a bit of whiting and a little yellow soap would take off the worst of the muck. Then a light coating of Vaseline would bring up the shine perfectly. He put the coin down, looked his father in the eye. 'I'm very fond of her.'

'Excellent. And the lovely lady herself? Who is she? Tell me more.'

He had his father's attention now. 'Yes, she is lovely. Lovely in nature and lovely to look at. Fred McCubbin wants to paint her portrait. But clever, too. A journalist.'

'Excellent,' said Simon again. 'She sounds most suitable. I look forward to meeting her. And her name?'

'Her name,' said Isidore, 'is Eileen Watkins. And thank you – I'll bring her over for tea on Saturday.' He looked down again at the pile of metal. 'Come and look at these shapes, Father. I think we have a shirt, trousers... No, two pairs of trousers... And this, it must be an overdress of some sort. Some of the oldest coins in the world. Nearly fifteen hundred years ago these would have been minted. Quite wonderful.'

But Simon stood with the eyeglass still in his hand, a slight scowl forming across his forehead.

'Eileen Watkins? That doesn't sound very Jewish, Isidore.'

'No, it's not Jewish and neither is she.'

'She's not Jewish?'

'No, that's what I just said. She is most emphatically not Jewish.' Isidore looked up, the sudden frown on his face mirroring his father's. 'That's a problem?'

Simon shrugged. 'Well, that depends,' he began, carefully.

'That depends,' Isidore retorted. 'On what?'

'I mean only that it would cause difficulties, family difficulties, if you like, should you marry, for example. But if she is only a friend…'

'You mean because she's not Jewish she's not good enough to marry? Is that what you're saying? Because if you are, it sounds as though there's a double standard operating here.'

Simon raised a hand. 'Enough. You forget yourself.'

Isidore took a deep breath, dropped his voice. 'But, Father, I told you at the outset that I was serious. Very serious. Eileen is a pragmatic, down-to-earth person, quite different from myself. And yet we share so many interests. I have never met anyone with whom I'm more in step. And I fully intend to marry her.' He looked straight at his father. 'I hope we will have your blessing…'

Simon's voice was brittle. 'Have you told Abraham?'

'I can't quite see what it has to do with Uncle Abraham.'

'No? After all he's done for you. Supporting you during your years of study. What's it to do with Abraham? Quite a bit, I would say.'

Isidore rose from his desk, marched across the store and stood facing his father, the counter between them.

'I find it hard to believe that we're having this conversation. This is, after all, the twentieth century.

Believe me, if there was a Jewish girl in Melbourne to whom I was sufficiently attracted, I would marry her like a shot. But there's not. There's a scarcity of eligible women here, let alone Jewish women, and a dearth of beautiful ones of any colour or creed…'

'In Melbourne, yes, perhaps. But in your time away you must have met…'

'Beautiful Jewish girls with lots of money,' Isidore cut in. 'Yes, the occasional one. But no one to whom I was attracted…'

'Michael…'

'Michael is not yet married, but I grant you he is lucky with the lady he is seeing. Father, in the name of God, be reasonable. You can't seem to appreciate the fact that I've fallen in love…'

It was Simon's turn to interrupt. 'Love?' His voice was bitter. 'You sound like a naive youth, not a man of thirty-five.' He leant over the counter so his face was close to his son's quivering beard. 'And shall I tell you what happens to love when the wolf walks through the door? Because I warn you, that will happen when you try to support a family on the secretary-ship of this and that organisation, when you spend your time writing this, that and the other – all those unimportant things instead of making money.'

'You're so sure of that, aren't you,' said Isidore coldly. 'Of my inability to support myself? Despite the fact that I have been doing very well for years now. And all this sudden lack of faith is over a woman you have never even met. Why don't you just meet her before making up your mind?' His father's eyes glared back at him.

'Oh, what's the use!' Isidore cried. He strode towards the door, grasped the handle, and then swung back on his heels. 'I find it difficult – impossible – to believe what you are asking me to do. If I hear you right, you are suggesting I break faith with someone who trusts me. That I give up the only true chance of happiness that has so far come my way. And why are you mixing your prejudices with a discussion of money? That elevates money to a godlike status. Is that what's important here? Money! And after all you've said to the contrary.'

He stepped quickly back into the shop, took two huge strides across the room to his desk, slashed at the pile of coins which fell like metallic leaves to the floor. 'Pah, that's what I think of money,' he shouted. 'I hate money. And I hate religion. Evil. Yes, that and more. I can't believe that you, my own father – after all you have taught me about values and honesty and truthfulness – have suggested a course of action so at odds with the way we live our lives.'

He took a deep breath, released it slowly.

'And, yes, I am, after all, thirty-five. Old enough to know the difference between lust and love. Old enough to feel lonely. Old enough to know my own mind. For heaven's sake.' He sat down heavily, put his head in his hands. The silence was broken only by the sound of their breathing until Isidore scraped back his chair. He began to pick up the coins, placing them one by one in the drawer with such gentleness that he could almost be apologising to the coins themselves. Simon moved out from behind the counter, walked across to the door, swung the open sign to closed, turned the key in the lock and moved back to his post behind the counter.

In the coldness of the silence that followed, the two grappled with their separate angers. Simon was no less angry than Isidore. But he knew his feelings were the rough-edged disappointment of an old man, while from Isidore spilled the white-hot rage of frustration. As Simon had leaned over the counter with his son's flashing eyes and dark beard inches from his own face, a memory had dislodged from the archive of Simon's brain and he saw himself younger, very much younger than Isidore was now, closed in battle with his own father. Relentless as a tide at the whim of the moon, the memory brought with it a fragment of the foaming adrenaline that had accompanied the wrangle, a smattering of the original emotion. But now mixed with it was something of what his own father would have felt, this keen displeasure with his son – and the sad knowledge that Isidore had set in train a series of events he may live to regret and, not least, the unpleasant recognition of Simon's own responsibility. He had never forced religion on his children. But then wasn't that an important tenet of his faith, that it not be forced on another, that they should come to it of their own free will? It had worked with Minnie and Michael, who had come to the Jewish religion quite naturally and remained keen observers. Less so Isidore. But had it always been like that? Simon's eyes flickered. He had to admit that while his elder son's interests were broad and constantly changing, most were connected with the faith in one form or the other: his enthusiastic support of the Jewish literary society, the Anglo-Jewish Association and the many times he was called upon to play his violin to raise funds for the synagogue or the Hebrew school or to act in a fundraising play for the Montefiore Club. And there was no question of his passion for the Hebrew language, its history and its literature. But for all that, he didn't observe in the way his siblings did. And his focus wasn't solely Jewish. There were his secretary-ships for various institutions all over the city, his sponsorship of the aboriginal mission child, his interest in other religions and his stargazing.

Simon shifted his feet, pressed his shaking fingers against the counter. The fact remained that Isidore had never conformed and some of this was undoubtedly Simon's fault.

In his senior years at Scotch College, Isidore had insisted on taking elocution, not just for one year, but for the next and the next. At the time, Simon had believed that his son's persistence stemmed from his embarrassment of his own still-thick European accent and that Isidore was persevering to ensure that not a trace of it appeared in his own voice. The lessons had done that, yes, but it was at times like this he realised the full value of Isidore's diligence. Not only was his voice clear of any accent, but Simon suspected that his mental agility and his ability to play with words and their meanings as if he had a dictionary in his head was due in no small measure to this rigorous training. Isidore would never have to scratch and scramble for words as he did. And though these skills were as useful on the lecture circuit as in the theatre, it meant that his son was constantly performing. One moment Simon felt as if he were on the receiving end of a prepared speech, the next as if he had been drawn into some other-worldly dimension, a heightened reality where he, too, was playing a part. His other concern was Isidore's passion for the occult. It was something he didn't understand, something that frightened him and no amount of persuasion on Isidore's part could convince him otherwise.

But, on the other hand, there was the matter of Isidore's undoubted contribution to Kozminsky & Co. Although there had been long gaps when he was travelling or lecturing, his son had shared a working space with him for over twenty years. What's more, he had to admit that even Isidore's absences had benefited the business: his not infrequent summons to an Egyptian archaeological dig as a specialist authority on dating and identification, for example, or his invitations to lecture in New York on jewels or stones or curiosities, or the buying trips to Europe – Italy, Germany, Austria – and the subsequent arrival of crates of carefully sourced antiquities or rare coins and the years in London where he completed his extensive studies, returning jubilantly with the precious certificate that proclaimed him Doctor of Science. There was no doubt that the firm – and, as an extension of the business, Simon himself – had been the primary beneficiary from each of these ventures.

What to do now? Simon's hands wouldn't stay still. It was at times like this he missed Marks most, wished he was still alive. Although he had seen little of his brother once Simon moved to the city and Marks further north to Swan Hill and then across to Nhill in the west of the colony, a warmth remained that was more than memory. Sudden things happened to Marks, both good and bad. On one trip to Europe he had met and married his Rebecca. They had a son, he had written, who was the centre of their world. Once they had moved to Nhill, stories of his brother's many works on behalf of the townspeople – of the numerous projects he floated or was involved in, his unfailing generosity – filtered through to Simon. And then within hours of falling ill, he was dead. Mushroom poisoning, they said.

It must have been over ten years now, so why didn't the pain diminish? If he were honest, was there guilt still that he didn't go with Abraham up to Nhill that day to bring back his brother's body? He'd heard that once the townspeople received news that Marks was to be buried in Melbourne, they defied the numbing cold of the May night to wait outside the Kozminsky-owned Commercial Hotel where Marks had lived and died. It was after midnight when the coffin was loaded into the hearse and the procession of townsfolk – accompanied by a band playing 'The Dead March in Saul' and the Nhill fire brigade – headed for the train station. A whole town in mourning for his brother. In the press they'd called his passing a 'public calamity'. And why hadn't he gone – was he too busy? Simon shook his head. No use wishing back the past. No use trying to magic up his brother every time he faced a crisis. What could he do in the present situation? He forced himself to think.

So integral was his son to the firm that Simon couldn't recall when last he had given a thought to Isidore's future, always assuming it lay in the business. Although both his sons were involved – his daughter, too, in her earlier years and then her husband – it was on his elder son's shoulders that an increasing responsibility fell. It was Isidore the collectors demanded to classify their collections; it was Isidore who travelled out to the country areas to value curios for probate or assess the wealth of antiques in the big squatters' mansions; it was Isidore who verified the authenticity of an article; Isidore who was asked to answer the queries flooding the editorial offices of *The Australasian* or *The Age* or the *Melbourne Herald* or any one of a number of national papers; Isidore whose knowledge of Hebrew and Aramaic enabled him to translate strange hieroglyphics into English; Isidore who kept in touch with antiquity experts and Egyptologists all over the globe.

Just the other day, he had overheard an interview between his son and a journalist. The words floated back to him from the dim corner of the store where they had sat huddled and he imagined his son's fingers deftly sorting through his collections, holding up first one piece and then another.

'Here you have, in coins,' Isidore had explained in his clear voice, 'metallic leaves, illustrating the entire history of the world from about 1000 BC to the present day. You can see how we get our portraits of the ancients: there's the head, just here, on the obverse. Then there's the art side on the reverse which shows the type or design. But besides giving us the only true likeness of some of the old rulers, many of the traditions of the past are preserved in these round pieces of metal. These, for example.' Opening another drawer, Isidore had withdrawn the collection of which he was the most proud.

'These Greek coins are the most artistic. This is a tetradrachm – or three shilling piece – of Alexander the Great, worth, to a collector, about five pounds. It shows on the obverse the Emperor's son, who wears a curious headdress made from the skin of an elephant. On the reverse, Pallas is seen in the act of throwing a spear.

'Your lady readers can judge, from this type, the mode of a Grecian dress in 300 BC; and, in this Syracuse tetradrachm, they can observe how a Greek woman wore her hair in the same period. The latter coin is worth about thirty-five shillings. Here is another coin…'

Simon had glanced across the room to where his son was tucking the coins into a box with as much delicacy as one would treat a newborn baby. Behind him were arranged a host of certificates, the books he had published, the papers he had given. He applied himself to everything with total focus and dedication. How he made time to do it all was a mystery. There was, Simon thought, no question of the value his son had brought to the business. But a measure of what he had achieved had been done with Abraham's help, at least in his formative years. And Abraham wouldn't like this proposed match. Of that Simon was convinced.

As he put himself through the familiar process of setting the collection to rights, Isidore's emotions soared and swooped like a swallow on the wing. Arguments between himself and his father were not infrequent, but usually they retreated to their separate corners before they became vehement. On the one hand, he felt a mounting anger at the injustice of his father's ill-considered reaction, on the other, the uncomfortable realisation that his own sudden anger had shown up as bombast. Abhorring pomposity as he did, his anger turned in on itself and he regretted the haste and nature of his replies. Suddenly Simon was not an antagonist, not a father even, but merely an old man who had become quite shockingly small and stooped in a short space of time.

He wanted to apologise, but he couldn't work out whether he was sorry for the haste of his reaction or for the fact that his father had so abruptly become old. He had a suspicion that it wasn't, after all, his father he was fighting and that it wasn't really about Abraham's fictitious reaction, whatever his father thought or said, and it wasn't even about being or not being a Jew. His father had never forced religion and had made his own observances in his own way – the beautiful Yod in the synagogue that Simon had bought as a tribute to his mother, Hendel, was proof of this. Beyond that, he had shown pride in Isidore's Bible studies at Scotch College, his leadership of the Jewish debating society and the setting up of the short-lived Hebrew Students' Society. But Simon had never insisted that Isidore take these things further. Isidore realised now with some surprise that there had not even been a suggestion of a bar mitzvah and that it was Abraham, not Simon, who noted his thirteenth birthday.

What he was battling, then, was a type of block that was not prejudice and neither was it so much a question of bias as it was being suddenly shut off to reason. One of his uncle's clever parables slid into his mind. The one about the bitter landlady whose fear of being alone had led to her alienating her student tenants and brought about the very loneliness that so terrified her. If he took this approach, if he put his father's rigid insistence in gazing through the wrong end of the telescope down to fear, what then was he frightened of? Losing his son? Not doing the right thing by his religion?

He glanced towards the front of the store where his father was hunkered low over his counter. In the end, perhaps, there were no answers – things just happened the way they happened. And that, in the end, was that. The coins were back in the case Isidore had had made for them and he reached for his overcoat. But before he moved, his father spoke again.

'I do have one suggestion.'

Isidore strove to keep his voice even. 'Yes?'

'If you were not to meet this woman for a period of one year, say...'

Isidore wondered afterwards whether his jaw actually dropped open or whether he just thought it did. Never, on any stage, would he be able to repeat the authenticity of that action.

'A...a year?' he had stammered. 'A whole year? Of not seeing each other? And what would that achieve?'

'A year is not so long when you have the rest of your lives together. It would prove, I suppose, that your feelings for each other are sound. Give others time to accept the situation.' His father's voice had gained an edge of certainty.

'Like a test, you mean?' Isidore shrugged on his coat. 'To show the family what we know ourselves to be true?' Suddenly weary, he shook his head. 'I'll put it to Eileen and see what she has to say.'

17

Isidore found he was spending a disproportionate amount of time staring out of the window. As if the answers to all his questions could be found there. In the way the clouds spread or banked or in the way the leaves of the trees shivered in the breeze. Or in the configuration of migrating birds. Flocks of swallows flew in shapes like spearheads. Ducks in groups of three. Rainbow bee-eaters arrived in pairs, sat on the fence knocking their prey against the wood to render them unconscious. Sacred ibis flew alone. The ubiquitous dove saved its energy for procreation.

He blew out his breath slowly, brushed aside the artwork for the first issue of *The Antiquarian Gazette*, a journal for the antique industry he was in process of founding. It was hard to concentrate on the things of the past when the present, his present, was about as steady as a canoe in white water.

His office at 339 Collins Street, not really much more than a room, was filling fast with boxes of books in one corner and packages in another, and under his desk a mounting assortment of collectibles waited for valuation or identification. Filed in another cranny, part-hidden by the door, were the ones already dealt with: last week's mail-order items, valued and ready for advertising. These were more of interest rather than great value, including an eclectic collection of weapons, a sword found – they claimed – at Waterloo, a rather large antique pistol quite attractively chased, a boomerang.

Worth a little more, given his recent death, was an interesting document written by Pope Leo XIII in sound condemnation of egalitarianism – that might go for fifteen shillings.

The list for the *Gazette* was now complete. On top of the clutter of books, almanacs, letters and envelopes on his desk was the introduction to this issue of 26 June 1906, just returned from the typesetters. He picked it up for a final proof, cleared a space and settled to read.

It made sense to see how it went as a monthly paper. To get it out there as widely as possible he had fixed subscriptions at twelve pence for the first year with postage free of charge. There would be little money in the journal itself, but as an advertising medium for his valuation business he was satisfied it would work.

He liked the idea of combining the history of the past with the reality of the present in this way and of the mix of the arts and science. Both disciplines fed into each other in such a manner that, despite new-fangled views to the contrary, they shouldn't be separated at all. Pushing back his chair, he rubbed his hands together briskly.

And then his mind returned to the immediate future. He checked his watch. He was meeting Eileen at The Fed for coffee at five o'clock. The day was already gone and the stack of mail would swell after he had been to the post office. After that it was back down Collins Street to the Austral Club.

Perhaps it was part of her charm that he could never predict how Eileen would react. He had expected a bout of Irish temper to greet his announcement of Simon's condition. But when he told her, she gazed at him steadily, her head tilted as she considered.

'A year?' she repeated slowly. 'Well, that's not really so terrible. After all, if it makes them happy…then there'll be less pressure all round.' She nudged his hand. 'It's a nuisance, yes, but really what's a year, Izzy, when we'll have the rest of our lives together?'

Having been prepared to soothe her, he felt a sharp stab of irritation that her words were so close to his father's. Was he the only impatient one?

'It's so arbitrary, that's what bothers me.' He ran his hands over his beard, tried to put his thoughts into words. 'A sudden whim of an old man. There's no real sense to it, and it's more than just the Jewish thing. If we'd been brought up as a strictly observant family, I could understand it. But we weren't, so it's more than that. His own guilt, perhaps? Or panic? That he married out of the faith and now it's happening in the next generation? Fear that I might leave him in the lurch now I'm starting my own family? Or maybe something similar happened to him and now he's taking it out on me? I don't think so – he's not like that. But it does make me realise how little I know of his life despite all the years we've worked so closely together.' Isidore shook his head.

'There has to be something behind it. It has to be more than just the fact he's just getting old. I keep turning it over and over in my mind, but I really have no idea. Ironic, isn't it, that this is the only time in my life I've happened to copy his own actions and it's upset him so badly.' He took a gulp of coffee. 'But it's nothing to do with you, Eileen. He doesn't even know how long we've known each other anyway. He doesn't care. He's just hoping we'll change our minds. But what about all the things we do together? And our friends? Do we see them separately? Do we tell them about this childish ban?'

Leaning back in his chair, he set his cup down sharply so it chimed against the saucer. His fingers automatically caressed the edge of the china, feeling for a chip.

'It's all a bit ludicrous, don't you think? I don't know whether to talk to him again, or to talk to Mother. Or whether we should just go ahead anyway.'

When Eileen set her mouth in just such a way he knew she was about to disagree. She stared into her empty cup as if she hoped the answer lay there, and it gave him a moment to study her. Her long dark hair was gathered into a loose knot under a small straw hat angled to one side, and she wore a dress of pale yellow silk with a rose of a deeper shade pinned to her shoulder. When she was in this sort of mood – half-pensive, half-determined – he was hard put to tell whether her eyes were brown or black. When she lifted her gaze to his once more, he knew only that he could see why they wanted to paint her and why she had been photographed for the cover of more than one of the social magazines.

'It never works – defying the family,' she said as she lifted her head. 'At the moment, it's just an argument that can be fixed. But if we go about it the wrong way, quicker than you can blink it'll cause a real rift. And what'd happen then? I know enough of you to know you would regret it for your whole life. And that would affect me, too. It's only because it's important to him – to them –

and not to us that we think it unreasonable. If it were the other way round…' She paused. 'But why on earth didn't you tell him we've known each other for years?'

Had there been an opportunity? Isidore tried to cast his mind back, shifted on his seat. 'The conversation didn't go quite like that. It was…difficult. Unexpected. It took me by surprise. To tell the truth, I don't think I handled it very well.'

She nodded, sat quietly, considering. 'No, I think we should do the year. No cheating. And hope like hell it all turns out all right.'

He looked at her helplessly. 'No cheating?'

'No cheating, Isidore Kozminsky,' she said firmly.

He said nothing until they were out of the coffee palace and around the corner. Grasping her hand firmly, he slipped into a side street. Pulling her with him, he asked, 'Starting from when?' and took her in his arms.

When they walked the Block later that night, her long fingers resting lightly on his arm, Isidore found it difficult to focus on anything other than that he wouldn't see her for twelve months. The wretchedness of time again, a period so short and yet so long. They stood to watch the giants strike the hour and then he steered her to Kozminsky's window and stopped.

'What are you doing tomorrow after work?'

She looked at him, a query in the tilt of her brow. 'Going home. What else?'

He took her hand. 'Will you marry me, Eileen Watkins?'

If she was surprised by the suddenness of his proposal, she didn't show it, simply fixed him with her direct gaze.

'You know I will – this problem notwithstanding. But what's it got to do with what I'm doing after work?'

He drew her hand through his arm. 'Tomorrow morning I'm going to sound out some of my favourite dealers. And I'm going to get together a collection of the prettiest diamond rings in town. There are some good stones coming out of South Africa these days and De Groot has some connections. And then I'm going to put them in this window. See, just there, to the right of the watches.' He pointed through the night bars.

'My father and I have some antiques to value from one of the old squatters' mansions up in the Mortlake area – the big place Chatsworth is coming up for grabs – over the next couple of days, so neither of us will be here. But Alfred Levin, my sister's husband, will be holding the fort. So what I'd like you to do is to come by and pick your favourite without me standing at your elbow. And then get Mr Levin to put it on hold. When I get back I'll size it and we can celebrate our engagement – and start this embargo from then. Does that sound a good plan to you? There's nothing to say we can't get engaged, is there? Make something of the year nonetheless. What do you say?'

'But you don't know my size.'

He looked at her, smiling, and touched the gloved hand tucked in the crook of his elbow.

'I know your size, my dear. I know your size.' He was about to move off, when he stopped and turned to face her again. 'And one other thing. I am at my desk at the Anthropological Society at precisely nine o'clock each morning, which means that I walk slowly – very, very slowly – along this street in the fifteen minutes prior. I don't think it would be a breach of the embargo, do you, if you happened to be going to your office along Elizabeth Street – on the opposite side of the street, of course – at around about that time? It might be possible, for instance, to at least acknowledge each other?'

She regarded him seriously. 'On the odd occasion when we might see and smile at each other from such a distance? I think that would be perfectly proper.'

They walked to his office where he showed her his first issue of the *Gazette*, pulling up a chair for her and clearing a space on the crowded desk. She read it carefully, nodding from time to time while he sorted through the mail.

When she'd finished, she said, 'It's good. An interesting read and a clever idea to combine the paper with a valuation service. Why not? That's where a vast area of your experience lies. But why not have a query column as well? Readers love that. Makes them a part of the publication and it's something they can get for free.'

The morning after, he rose early. The rain during the night had softened the air and Isidore had decided long ago that just before first light was his favourite time of the day – after the dawn and before the sun rose over the horizon – while the stars and sometimes the moon still lingered. Although it was the opposite time of day to that of the poem, it had something about it of *Gray's Elegy*, a sense of aloneness so precarious that the senses could not help but be heightened – extended, too, so there was something more in the mix, big things like awe and wonder perhaps, and a feeling of humility as the sun finally tilted up to light the day.

A BREAK IN THE CHAIN

He paced back and forth until the stars had disappeared and in their place Fitzroy Gardens was a mass of diamonds: little droplets twinkling from the tips of the mown lawn, resting in the centres of the flowers and along the strands of a spider's web, hanging from the elbows and fingers of the statues, and swinging from the she-oaks in necklets more perfect and more beautiful than anything that had ever crossed a dealer's desk. Today was going to be his day for diamonds.

Bending to the ground he pulled at a shoot of grass only to find that an entire yard of runner came loose with it. He flung it away. Damned rhizomes. They had a lot in common with extended families. Not much to be seen on the surface, but underneath you could be sure there was a vast network of tentacles working away in their subterranean hide-out, linked for the term of their natural lives in dark and closeted conspiracy.

'Row the boat.' He had dreamed that dream so often the words often flipped unbidden into his mind. Why had his uncle deserted him just when he needed him? Perhaps his handing across of the oars functioned as a sort of baton. Perhaps it was a show of confidence in that however turbulent the waters, his nephew would reach the shore?

He had once thought that Abraham's abrupt departure in the dream had a sink-or-swim element to it. That while the sun was shining their relationship would progress happily enough, but if troubled waters arose, his uncle would withdraw altogether. But that was too easy. There was too much hidden in the world to accept that a dream would be so obvious. It was precisely that which couldn't be seen that was so critical.

He would visit Abraham, he resolved. There was, after all, no point in hiding the fact that he was planning to get married and every possibility that if his uncle found out about it from another source it would make for an even worse upset.

Irony upon irony, Isidore smiled grimly. Having played Romeo so many times, now he was cast in a real-life role.

Consigned to waiting in the wings. As above, so below. What was the message in the stars?

Back in his office, he drew towards him two strong envelopes marked with the embossed crests of the Rosy Cross, slit them open with the silver paper knife he'd spotted amid junk in London's Portobello Road. This early part of the day was the only time he had spare to study.

But the Rosicrucian crest brought with it another thought. Some of the fine pieces of silver that were finding their way into his own collection begged for a coat of arms, his own crest. Sometime soon he would act on that. But he needed a strong motto, something with personal meaning.

He checked his watch. An hour's study would leave him just about enough time to get across to Lincoln's Inn Chambers where he acted as corresponding and organising secretary for the Royal Anthropological Society. Although he doubted that Eileen would act on his suggestion so soon, he could certainly practice his slow stroll along Elizabeth Street. From there he would call around the diamond dealerships before meeting up with Simon for the Mortlake trip.

A BREAK IN THE CHAIN

Later that day, Isidore was back at his desk, a letter he was writing to the English astrologer Agar Zariel before him. A line in Zariel's 'Vibratory Forces' printed in *The Theosophy* some years back concerned him, and he was sifting words in his mind when the telephone rang, a shrill discordance that made him start. He grabbed it from its cradle, continued his letter with the other hand.

'Hello?' He'd been expecting this. However well they'd done the previous week, the bookies were always nervy by Thursday.

'Dr Kozminsky, it's Dave Blake here. How's it going?'

'Very well. What's up?'

'Can you check my sun/moon thing again, mate? I need some help with the first race at Flemington this Saturday.'

'What time?'

'One o'clock.'

'What's in the running?'

'Only six horses, so it's perfect...'

As Blake listed the field, he immediately picked one potential error. 'Not Hidalgo,' he interrupted. 'It's pronounced *'idalgo*. It's Spanish. The name of a Spanish nobleman. Remember what I said: pronunciation is vital. The name is vibrated as it's spoken...in this case as IDALGO. 1.4.1.3.3.6 = 18 = 9. How did you go last week?' He continued writing as he listened. 'Excellent. You'll do well on Saturday. Just remember the need to study the phonetics closely and faithfully. Don't spare yourself and don't be disheartened if an event confuses you. We are too often terrified by appearances in this world.'

A BREAK IN THE CHAIN

'Something else, Dr Kozminsky,' Blake said, as he was about to hang up.

'Yes?'

'If all you say is true, why doesn't the wealth of the world fall into your own lap? Why would you waste your time on the likes of me, for instance?' His voice became apologetic. 'I'm only asking because that's what the blokes ask me.'

'Mr Blake. I, myself, am not a betting man. Nor am I particularly interested in the speculative branch of the sport. My interest lies in the unravelling of hidden things. My associates do what their inclinations lead them to do, and I am well enough repaid through them. Good day.'

18

Somewhere inside the big house someone was thumping out a tune. Waves of uncertain sound falling somewhere between a frightful racket and what might be called music. He was greeted by his uncle's butler, a man somewhat on the thin side and a little frayed around the eyebrows, caused, Isidore guessed, by trying to please too many people all of the time.

He followed the butler into the large drawing room, a space he had always liked with its large planes of light that drew the eye upwards to the elaborate ceiling roses, the deep cornices. But today more warmth came from the flickering of the crystals in the chandeliers than from the fire itself, so while he was waiting he wandered around the room, unable to stop himself from appraising such an unusually good collection of artwork. The height of the walls was broken by a picture rail from which hung a number of significant works, some painted by the Heidelberg crowd. No Streeton, but a Withers if he was not mistaken: good tone, colour and atmosphere, the bush brought inside.

There had been some interesting stuff happening in the art world over the last ten years and it was something that Kozminsky's might think of branching into. A gallery.

But then there wasn't much room in the present place. In a separate building, perhaps…

Abraham broke into his thoughts with a welcome and an apology for his wife's absence before turning to his man and ordering tea, cake and a stop to the piano practice in the other room. As quiet, competent and thoroughly focused as ever, thought Isidore. His uncle rested his full concentration on one thing at a time and it had been so ever since Isidore could remember. No wonder he had been so successful in business.

'Don't get them to stop on my account; I don't mind the scales,' Isidore said with a grin as he took his seat on the edge of one of the deceptively plush sofas. The day was not far off, he thought, when his own son would be playing, but it would be the violin rather than the piano.

'It's human nature, isn't it? What amounts to a mind-numbing tedium for one person is soothing to another. What do they say? One man's meat is…'

Isidore nodded. The din in the next room ended in an angry sweep of the keys: a climax cut short. Into the silence he said: 'Excellent news on the cable trams. I hear…'

'…another man's poison.' Finishing his quote, Abraham held his gaze, still smiling. 'That's how it goes, isn't it?'

Isidore shifted. These seats were clearly not designed for comfort. Just as plainly, he had stepped into a game of mental chess and he had a horrible feeling that this was one he wasn't going to win. He stepped out of it.

'So you know?' He kept his voice light, his smile pleasant.

'Know?'

'About Eileen?'

'Eileen...?' His uncle raised his eyebrows.

Isidore sighed. This wasn't going to be easy. Maybe Eileen had been right and it would have been better to leave it alone. But he was here now and the front door was far away.

'I think you must know my intentions, Uncle. Did Father not tell you that I am very keen to marry a young woman I have known for some time?'

'Isn't there some problem with her not being Jewish?'

Isidore forced himself to breathe evenly. 'I don't see it as a problem. But unfortunately, yes, Father does. But I'm hoping...'

'But you have, I understand, given yourself a space of a year? During which time, of course, it's quite conceivable that you may change your mind?' Clattering lightly over the polished floorboards, the tea trolley arrived. 'And so this storm in a teacup, as it were, will be for nothing. Milk?'

The clichés irritated him. He preferred Abraham's parables. 'Uncle,' he said. 'I don't think I made it clear enough to Father that I've known this lady for some years. She is a dear friend on whom I look with growing affection. I have no doubt that she will make a good and constant wife.' And a fun companion, he wanted to add. Instead he said a little more firmly than he had intended. 'And the year's interregnum was not my idea. It was his.'

Abraham passed him the tea and the sugar bowl, offered him cake.

A BREAK IN THE CHAIN

'Your father is no longer young,' he said at last, sitting back against one of the over-stuffed feather cushions, his own cup resting gently on his knee. 'It's only natural he's somewhat disappointed. I must confess that I, too, would rather you were marrying into the faith.' He leant forward. 'You know, Isidore, it is all too easy to forget about God, to go one's merry way and flout the traditions that have held up so well over the centuries. You started so well with the accolades from school on Bible studies and Hebrew and so forth. Then there were the stories for the *Jewish Herald*. Eh? Clever Jewish stories with a good moral. From there what happened? You have become an acknowledged expert in all sorts of areas from antiquities and Aborigines to the zodiac studies. But nothing Jewish. Anymore.'

Isidore cleared his throat. 'It hasn't been a conscious thing,' he said. 'Just that I'm so busy. There are all sorts of interests that I no longer spend the time on I would like.'

His uncle cut in. 'I'm not suggesting that you necessarily attend synagogue. But just that you take into account the future. The life of your Uncle Marks, bless his memory, was a good example. In the early days of Swan Hill and Nhill, there was no synagogue, but it didn't stop him from being a good Jew. He did a lot for the community and eventually married a lovely Jewish woman. And I hasten to add that this is not about the lady herself. I am sure she is a fine person, a good friend. We all need those. But marriage is a serious thing and what is appropriate in one sense is not necessarily so in another. With assimilation, a lot is lost. '

A BREAK IN THE CHAIN

Outside the wind was getting up. Flailing against the glass of one of the long sash windows were the purple blooms of a bush.

His uncle continued. 'But I'm happy enough about the one-year break. I have to agree with Simon that if you are both of the same mind after such a period…'

The crystals of the chandelier merged, and the myriad lights turned into a fuzzy mess. Isidore knew without looking that the small teacup in his hand was Dresden, a delicate thing hand-painted with bright pink roses with darker centres – the yellow background banded with gold leaf and more suited to the hand of a woman than a man. He gritted his teeth. The blur of his uncle's voice, the steady beat of a clock somewhere. Spelling out the seconds. Somewhere towards the back of the house a baby cried. Then a small snapping sound, almost imperceptible, an eggshell giving way, and the saucer fell apart.

Isidore sprung to his feet. Hurriedly, he placed his half-empty cup on the small filigree table at his side, collected the pieces from the carpet, his hands shaking as he fitted the two halves together. 'I'm sorry. So sorry. I think it's a clean break – no chips. I'll take it with me. I might even be able to find a replacement.'

Abraham didn't blink. 'I'm sorry, too,' he said. 'But not about the china. Saucers can be mended…'

All the nerves in Isidore's body alerted; now was the time to leave. While it could still be done with grace, before one of them said something that might never be forgotten. But he had loved this man. It was worth another try. Feeling like the student still, he placed the pieces of china on the table in front of him and sat again on the edge of the sofa.

A BREAK IN THE CHAIN

'Uncle, you talk of God, but this is not about God. Let's leave him out of it because I believe there's no question of our mutual commitment in that regard. It's just that we go about it differently. I do what I can, but I no longer have the time, or resources, to do more.

'Do you remember, when I was a kid, how you told me some of the Besht's stories? Well, that was the beginning for me. I became fascinated with the Chassidic with its deep-thinking core of intelligence, its joy and happiness, music and dancing. For me, life is never going to be about making money, but more about learning on the one hand and keeping that centre of joy and hope on the other.' He drew a deep breath. 'My father may be upset, but I too am disappointed. Disappointed in his reaction – and in yours, too, for that matter.

'It isn't that I don't understand your own need for observation. It's just that, in myself, I don't have any feeling of...of *Yiddishkeit*. But, reluctantly in this case – in terms of the conditional year apart – we will do as you both wish.'

When Abraham said nothing, he went on, his voice unsteady. 'You have helped me a great deal – you have guided and inspired me.' Isidore smiled a little sadly. 'Listen,' he said, shoulders hunched in concentration, staring unseeing at his hands on his knees. 'When I was a child, before I knew you even, I had a dream, which became a recurring dream.' He looked up. Abraham nodded. The man's focus was formidable. His gaze hadn't wavered from Isidore since he'd walked into the room. 'In this dream there's a boat on a fairly rough sea and we're both in it. Me as a child, you as a man. You are different, with wild hair and beard. But you're you, nonetheless.

A BREAK IN THE CHAIN

The essence of you, as it were. You have the tiller tucked under your arm and are rowing strongly.

'There's a wind,' he nodded towards the window, 'like that out there today, but the boat sails up and down the waves and somehow I'm not scared. No sight of land but the boat shoots along powered by your confidence. Then suddenly you're not there anymore.' He was frowning, his gaze now as steady as his uncle's. 'The first time I had this dream Mother said it was a nightmare. And it was, but not in the way she meant.'

He leaned forward. 'I could interpret your sudden disappearance as your regret for some of your generosity of the past. But that's too simplistic. The frightening bit was that you were no longer there to move the boat along so efficiently, to guide me the way you did when I was a kid. Over many years now I've had to learn to row my own boat.' He grinned suddenly. 'I seem to remember you saying that more than once.' Abraham started to speak and Isidore raised his hand. 'I know that's what you think you're doing now, providing guidance. But forgive me if I say that there's a world of difference between guidance and interference.'

Isidore rose from his seat. He felt strangely tired. When he started across the room, Abraham set his own cup down and followed him to the hall. His uncle made no move to open the door, but instead placed his hand on the architrave as if he were blocking the exit.

'You know, Isidore, there is something rather wonderful about our culture,' he said quietly. 'That could sound trite, but it's not so. The Jewish way of life – it's good for us, good for our children. Guidelines. How often do you witness disrespect of Jewish children for their parents? Don't you think that your dream could be telling you that? You have interpreted guidance differently, but think on it. There's something solid in a sense of community, in not travelling life's path alone.'

Isidore straightened his shoulders, looked directly into the older man's eyes. 'Uncle, please understand. The only thing I have against religion is times like this when practicalities are overridden in the name of faith, when friends are split up, rifts are caused in families, whole nations destroyed through internal strife.

'What both you and father cannot seem to grasp is that I am not Jewish. My mother isn't Jewish and I was not brought up as a Jew. All this ruckus, all the judgements that are being made now over a woman neither of you have met – that's one thing. But why was there not more fuss made over my not having a *bar mitzvah*? Was everyone too busy making money to note, beyond the book you so kindly gave me, that my thirteenth birthday came and went? Surely that would have been the time to stage a protest? For heaven's sake, even Father didn't marry a Jew, so why all this fuss now?' He reached for his coat on the hallstand.

'No one understands better than me, believe me, the loneliness of never quite fitting in. Of always being neither one thing nor the other. But by being observant, by attending the synagogue, by marrying a Jewish woman, what would that achieve in terms of identity? Would that make me Jewish? Or would I still be on the outside? Not quite a Jew, but the man who married a Jew and had Jewish children?'

He heard his own voice rising, went on more quietly. 'Is that how you'd define a Jew, Uncle? Someone who follows the rules just so they fit in? Do they sell identity down at the corner store along with the candles and the unleavened bread? And what about this Jewish woman marrying the man who is not quite a Jew? What would that do for her sense of self, if self is so tied to observance?' Just one word, he thought, just one word to show he understands what I'm trying to say. That's all it will take for us to be friends again.

'What is it with you, Isidore? Always the questions! You get so caught up in words that you don't listen to the answers – to what people are saying underneath.' Abraham's eyebrows were raised, his voice charged with a voltage that reverberated in the hallway. Isidore dropped his gaze.

'Why can't you realise that our generation finds it difficult to express ourselves in the way you do? You talk disparagingly of money, but then you've never wanted for bread – leavened or unleavened. One day you might ask your father about hunger, about how he and your Uncle Marks arrived in a new country with the clothes they stood up in and no language to make themselves understood. About making a home with strips of bark and rags stuffed in the gaps to keep out the cold. About sitting in the sand watching the rats scour the rubbish and feeling lucky to have anything at all to eat, let alone bread. As to your father's marriage. I am not quite sure of the circumstances or of what he was thinking... But there were few Jewish women in the country at that time.'

'I'm not sure that my father thinks beyond his standing in the synagogue.'

'If you think that, then you do him – and me – a very real injustice.'

A BREAK IN THE CHAIN

Isidore shrugged himself into his overcoat as his uncle swung the front door wide.

Isidore welcomed the bite of the wind. Bending into it, his feet crunching in the gravel of the driveway, he did up the buttons of his coat, and it was not until he was outside the gates that he remembered the saucer. He stopped and turned, looked back down the long drive, wondered whether he should go back for it. That this may be interpreted in a different sense made him pause.

The gates were painted black and finely wrought and as his eyes travelled up the iron bars to where they looped and bent into curves and scrolls, he resisted a childish urge to trace the metal with his finger. He lifted his head to the house. The windows glinted back at him. Behind one in the upper storey there was a movement and he thought he saw a curtain drop into place.

Abraham was right in that saucers could be mended. But broken families or friendships – not so easily.

19

'Would you mind waiting on the line?' The voice of the operator impersonal. This was where his life was at the moment, Isidore thought. Waiting. Always this waiting. He switched the receiver to his other hand, pulled the latest set of *Gazette* proofs towards him. Added a few lines.

'My Query Column will, I think, prove an interesting addition, and I am assured that readers will make good use of it. If private replies are needed, a special fee of five shillings will be required, and a fee of five shillings will also be required for a signed opinion on any special object.'

He completed his call, put the handset down, lit his pipe. Fifty weeks to go. This was impossible. He would have liked to write to Eileen, but he didn't know whether that contravened the bargain. Most days he'd glimpse her walking in the opposite direction on the other side of Collins or Elizabeth Streets. He would doff his hat and he'd see the answering wave of her hand and imagine the intensity of her smile, and it would stay with him through the day. But Haines had done him proud. She had liked the ring.

So much to do, the will to do it missing.

A BREAK IN THE CHAIN

The telephone again. His mother.

'Isidore?'

'Yes?'

'What's this business with your father?'

Useless to feign ignorance, but he was not in the mood for another argument.

'It's not quite convenient, Mother. May I telephone you later?'

'Don't telephone. Come around. I'll be at home from four o'clock.'

Emma rose to greet him as he was shown into the drawing room of the large house in Robe Street later that day. She settled herself back into her chair and waved him to the seat opposite, lost no time in repeating her question of earlier.

'Tea's on its way,' she said. 'But what's going on between you and your father?'

'Tea, ugh.' Seeing broken saucers, Isidore winced. He flung himself into one of the armchairs opposite her own, the wing chair that had recently been re-covered in a pastel chintz that didn't really fit with the dominant colours of the Robe Street house. But then his mother always had been somewhat of a law unto herself. She had recently taken over the running of Kozminsky's and he wondered now what effect this had had on his father.

Time had treated her more kindly, he thought. Her hair was silver, but her rather long face had held its structure and her dark eyes were as intense and as passionate as ever. She was a favourite with the bank manager, he knew, whether for her sharp mind or for her account he could never be sure. Probably a bit of both.

Her bid for the London Hotel in Market Street had been successful. She'd had it redecorated, installed a new licensee and it was starting to make money.

For years she had done the accounts for S. Kozminsky and Co., and a few years back she had registered the business in her own name, quite why he had never been told. But with the two houses she owned outright in St Kilda, she came a worthy second to his uncle in terms of her investments. Isidore's own deficiencies in this respect were drummed into him on each of his uncomfortable visits to the ES&A Bank to ask for yet another loan. 'A shrewd businesswoman, that mother of yours,' said the manager. Compounded by a glance that said more than the words.

He coloured at his sudden urge to wrap his arms around her and get her to make it right for him. But he couldn't do that any more now than when he had been a child. There was a paper wall between them which, nonetheless, hadn't stopped them protecting each other and there had been times when he'd soothed his mother as much as the other way round.

Laying her tapestry on her lap, Emma continued. 'He's like a bear with a sore head. Keeps muttering. Something about you and a woman?'

'Not just a woman, Mother. Not just any woman, but the person I'm in love with and intend to marry. She is, in fact, my fiancée.' He jumped to his feet. 'This wasn't the way I wanted you to hear about it. What's happening here, Mother?' Clasping his hands tightly behind his back, he strode about the room. 'First, I wanted to do the proper thing and bring her to meet you both. Then as soon as I mentioned she wasn't Jewish…' He sighed. 'It upset my father tremendously, so much so that he laid this ban, an embargo actually, on our seeing each other for the next year. Two weeks and a day of which have passed...painfully. I agreed reluctantly. I mean, do I have any choice?' He paused. 'Well, I do – though it's not much of one.

'But that's not the end of it. Next, Uncle Abraham had a go at me, and now you. For heaven's sakes, we've agreed to wait. Isn't that enough for everyone?'

Emma sat very still and silent. Isidore dropped into a chair and put his head in his hands.

'May I smoke?' he asked a few moments later and when she nodded he reached for his pipe and a small tin of tobacco.

'Izzy,' Emma began quietly. 'I don't know what to say. Obviously you are old enough to make up your own mind and it is quite unjust of us to judge this lady without knowing anything about her, let alone meeting her. Yet that, it would seem, is what has happened.' She breathed deeply, picked up her work, holding it up to the light as if the answer lay in the intricacy of the pattern. 'People lose their rational selves where religion, politics or money is involved...'

'But how, in the name of God, did religion suddenly become so important? Minnie, yes, granted, she's done the right thing by Father, twice as it turns out. And it looks as though Michael has found a suitable partner. But I've gone my own way all these years and now, suddenly, it's become a problem.'

'Eileen? Is that her name?'

'Yes.'

A BREAK IN THE CHAIN

'It's pretty. Is she English?' His mother had a knack of rerouting a difficult situation.

'Irish. Her father, William Watkins, is a medical doctor. Until recently he was the administrator for the mental hospital up at Beechworth. He's a lovely man, warm and caring. Beau, they call him, and it must be for his nature, not his looks.' Isidore laughed, his face suddenly alight. 'Loves children, dogs... He's always getting into trouble with the authorities for the number of dogs on the property. But I don't think that worries Beau. Once you meet him, and to a lesser extent Eileen, you'll know what it means when they say "typically Irish"!'

'A bit impractical?' She didn't lift her eyes from her work, but it was as close as he'd ever seen his mother come to a grin.

'Totally! But such enthusiasm. No, much more than enthusiasm – a vigorous passion for life. Their house is alive with projects and ideas, people coming and going all the time, lots of noise and laughter. Quarrels and arguments, too, sometimes violent clashes of opinion, but somehow there's nothing bitter about them.' He stopped, suddenly conscious of the difference between the Watkins' home and his mother's house. But his mother didn't appear to have made the comparison. She was nodding, absorbed in his happiness, her needle lightly threading the canvas as he continued to talk.

'Eileen makes time to visit the prison each week to spend the better part of a morning talking to the prisoners. She believes there's good in everybody and that if you can just touch their energy that person might recover. And so when I talk about energy, about vibrations, all the stuff I believe in, she understands.' He shook his head. 'You can't begin to know how important that is to me, Mother. The fact that we speak the same language… And we have so many friends in common, the Heidelberg group, musicians. And while she doesn't play music, she has a great ear for a tune. She's altogether and in every way just right for me.' A shadow fell over his face. 'But not, unfortunately, for Father.' Lightly he reached across and touched her knee. 'Mama, tell me, please. What am I going to do?'

'She sounds as though she'll make you happy, and you her. There's nothing quite as bleak…' Emma's lips tightened. She went on quickly. 'But your father is no longer young, Isidore, and he is now set in his ways. Spare a thought for your young lady, too. Difficult for you it may be. But it must be rather unsettling, to say the least, for her to be treated this way by her future husband's family.' She paused for a moment and when she went on her voice had softened. 'She must love you very much to be prepared to wait under circumstances such as these. And I think that's what you have decided to do, isn't it? Do as they wish. To see out the year, difficult though it will be? But it'll be worth it, we both know that. A small sacrifice now to get the best of both worlds for the rest of your life. And make no mistake: being part of a family is precious. People take it for granted and yet that blood connection is something that should rightly be prized above all other…'

His mother stopped, biting off her words as a tone he hadn't heard before crept into her voice. She bent to light the lamp, moved it closer to her work.

His skin tingled. Here was an opportunity to join up some of the dots. He remembered that night, long ago, when he had eavesdropped on a conversation between Simon and Abraham from the top of the stairs. They had been discussing Emma's conversation to the Jewish faith, and Isidore wondered, suddenly, whether she ever had. He thought not: she hadn't attended the synagogue with the rest of the family. But she had supported Simon in all his endeavours and hadn't discouraged the children from observing the faith. Along with the other secrets that surrounded his mother, it was something he doubted he would ever find out with certainty.

'You know, you've never told me, Mother. About your early life,' he said more gently now. 'You always promised you would – but you know you never have.' He could tell he had upset her by the sudden way she compressed her lips.

'What was so terrible?' he asked softly.

She was silent for so long, only her eyes moving in rhythm with her quick fingers, that he thought she had forgotten he was there. It was only when he moved as if to rise, that she gave a sudden sigh and put her work to one side.

'Yes, I did promise you that, didn't I, and you've been very patient,' she said with some difficultly. 'The truth is that time has gone on, Isidore, and perhaps now none of it matters.' He was about to protest, but she knew what he would say and she raised her hand. 'Yes, yes, to you it does. For me, it's still painful. Sometimes the past is best left buried. Consider that.' Her voice had dropped, so he had to lean towards her to catch her words.

'But, you're right, there are some things I suppose you should know. You need to know that my mother's name was Frances Coaten. And that the man who came out here years and years ago when you were quite small – remember him, the man you knew as Uncle? He was your uncle, a real uncle, my brother. Without going into the difficulties, hey sent him out to check...'

He was so intent on what she was saying that he didn't hear the horses' hoofs or the wheels of the carriage in the side driveway. And so it wasn't until the maid opened the front door in greeting that they both started, guilty as children caught stealing humbugs.

Quickly gathering up her wool, Emma straightened her back and she was a different person altogether as she stood to greet Simon. It was clear no more would be said that day.

As the door closed behind him and Isidore adjusted his hat and coat, he wondered how she could be so contained. His own emotions threatened to spill over like a fast-running stream suddenly dammed. To be given such a small fragment of insight into a mystery that had both worried and intrigued him was almost worse than his ignorance. He couldn't help thinking that anyone but his mother would contact him to provide some sort of finale, to complete the explanation in some way. But with his mother, the opposite could just as easily apply. He rubbed his hands and stamped his feet; he had never before thought of the house as cold. And surely it hadn't always been so? Were there raised voices behind him? He hoped not. More likely his imagination. He shivered.

Moving rapidly down the steps and out into the front road, he looked back. The light was gone from the main room and, despite its size, it was just a house, he told himself, as one might draw it in pen and ink with chimneys, windows, a front door and a driveway leading away.

20

The year crept along. He immersed himself in the *Gazette*. From the first issue, its popularity had escalated until he had been forced to rent a second mailbox. His office had run out of space, unopened parcels in one corner, curios piled up against the wall in another. But he was not yet ready to take another room, to set up the gallery. Meanwhile, complementing the banknotes tucked inside blank pieces of paper that accompanied the many queries he received, there was enough in terms of mail-order items and valuations together to supplement his other incomes very satisfactorily.

Yesterday's post had yielded an old Jewish Bible, the biblical text centred on the page in both Hebrew and Aramaic. The only surrounding commentary he recognised was that of Nachmanides, not only an expert on the Torah, but also a mystic, one of the first to include the tradition of the Kabbalah. This was Judaism at its best: the proud and rigorous scholarship that underpinned the teachings.

And then this morning a small book by the English Merlin, William Lilly had turned up. His astrological judgements and observations for the year 1680, printed by Macock in London. A 'Student in Astrology', he had styled himself at eighty-one years of age, this first and perhaps last real horary astrologer and one of the greatest of them all. Quite aside from his books, probably his greatest claim to fame was the annual almanac, the *Merlini Anglici Ephemeris*, which he put out until his death sometime in the late seventeenth century.

There was a loud rap at the door and when Isidore opened it an exceedingly scruffy young lad stood there.

'For you, sir.' The boy held out an envelope, trimmed in black.

Isidore ripped it open, pulled out a folded sheet.

Dearest,
Forgive the lateness of this, but I have been battling with my conscience for the past couple of days. I am sad to have to tell you that Mother died suddenly last Sunday and everything here is very awful. It's as though someone has put a lid on the sun. Father, as you can imagine, is taking it very hard.
There's to be a gathering here (at home) at 3 o'clock this afternoon. Mother thought a great deal of you: I know she would have been pleased if you were able to attend.
I hate breaking The Promise, but do you think that God could look the other way? Just for one afternoon?

With my love, as ever,
Your Eileen

Postscript: Of course, if you decide to be upright and not come I shall respect you even more.

The small clutch of sadness he felt on opening the note was overwhelmed by an explosion of relief and happiness.

He laughed outright. Typical Eileen to set him a fork in the road: come but don't come. But the battle with scruples was fought and won without a scratch on either side, and there was no doubt in his mind what he would do. He glanced at his watch. Getting on for two o'clock. Barely time to get home, wash and dress, catch a hansom cab and get across town to Hawthorn.

Meanwhile, rather as a dog might wait for the opening of a biscuit tin, the lad stood, his head cocked, his eyes following the expressions that danced across Isidore's face.

Reaching into his pocket for a coin, Isidore noticed the toes poking through scuffed leather cut away at the top of the boy's shoes and took a note from his wallet instead. The lad snapped his shoulders back.

'Hurry back. Tell the lady that, yes, I will be there. All right?' He gave the lad the note. 'And take this to buy some decent shoes. Mind you spend it on nothing else. And,' he added, placing a hand on the boy's shoulder, 'make sure you deliver my message. Or else.'

It was not unusual that the Watkins' house was spilling over with people, but today the crush was such that he had to search for Eileen. He stood awkwardly, hat in hand, just inside the front door, his gaze sifting through the crowd.

And then suddenly she was at his side, her eyes dark and bruised in a face all planes and shadows, her heavy curling hair pulled back from her forehead and held loosely in an elaborate knot at the base of her neck. Her face was devoid of prettiness; instead there was a haunting dark beauty that made you want to get below the surface of her, to find her heart or soul or whatever it was at the core of her. Her hand resting lightly on his arm burned through the sleeve of his coat.

'Do you want to see her?'

Given his rather shameful motive for attending, Isidore was not sure he did. But he was here now and he could see it was unavoidable. She drew him deftly through the crowd to the side of the drawing room where the coffin, a shiny black shellacked affair, lay with the lid off.

Eileen looked from the sight of her dead mother to his face and back again, her hand even heavier now on his arm. He bent his head to hear her mutter.

'I can't believe it. The influenza. No one else caught it. Not Father, none of us. Only her.' Her grip tightened. 'Tragic, isn't it, Izzy?'

Isidore could only nod. He would miss Clara, but it was the grief of the Watkins family that moved him, while Eileen's distress tore at his heart.

She must have glimpsed his mind for, with a quick look about her, she drew him outside. Around the corner of the house, the lawn spread out to a suburban fence and there was a bench under a tree of a spreading but otherwise indeterminate nature.

He wondered whether it would be appropriate to put his arms around her, but throwing her head against his chest she took the decision from him. As she cried out her miseries, he leaned against the house and breathed in the glossy tangles of her hair, holding her to him and wondering how he was going to make it through the next three months and fourteen days without going mad.

The first auspicious day after they'd waited out the year was a Monday. And so it was late in the afternoon of Monday, 18 February 1907 that Eileen and Isidore were married in a private ceremony at St John's Church of England in Heidelberg.

As Eileen moved slowly towards him on her father's arm down the centre aisle, Isidore wondered whether it was possible to be happier. His bride was dressed in a gown of ivory silk, and woven into her dark upswept hair was the strand of pearls he had given her as a wedding present. The late sun shafted through the tall stained-glass windows and blinked colour off the crystal hanging from a chain around her neck. Beau's mouth was trembling as he withdrew his arm from his daughter's and stepped back.

Afterwards, under the shade of the gums in the paddock alongside the church grounds, the guests gathered around tables laden with platters of food and carafes of wine, an exuberant scene that reminded Isidore of a Renoir.

It was a small gathering, but most of the Watkins' family and their friends were there: Eileen's father, of course, and her brothers, sisters and their children as well as their artist, actor, musician and writer friends, Melbourne's antiquity dealers, friends from the séance group. Only the Kozminskys were missing. Isidore had added his personal request to the invitations that had been sent, but it seemed that both the day of the week and the distance from Melbourne prevented them all, his mother included, from accepting.

As the last of the sun slanted through the gums, Isidore toasted his new wife. 'To you, my dear, with thanks from my heart for your love and patience.' He turned to his friends. 'And similarly, deep gratitude from my new wife and I for standing by us.'

The beaming faces before him were expectant. What could he give them?

'It's appropriate, I know, on such occasions, to give a speech… But forgive me…' He shook his head. 'My heart today is too full for me to make much sense.' Yet something had to be said. He firmed his voice.

'Those who know me well are aware that I believe there's no such thing as chance. But I believe the planets have finally swung our way and that the heavens, at least for now, are in harmony. In this respect, I can do no better than this short quote from Ecclesiastes:

'To everything there is a season and a time for every purpose: a time to be born, a time to die; a time to plant, and a time to pluck up that which is planted; a time to get, and a time to lose; a time of war, and a time of peace…

'This, I firmly believe, is the right season and the right time for our wedding. And I can only pray that this interlude of peace and supreme happiness lingers with us all.'

21

Sydney and Lane Cove. 1912. Living alongside the river with its changing moods: as smooth as a bowl of molten silver when the air was still, at other times disturbed, flickering bright-white and black and shimmering-blue, as if Van Gogh had dabbed and daubed at it from its underside. On its banks, the gracious old homestead with the four-poster bed where he lay awake at night listening to the rustling in the lathe-and-plaster walls.

'We need a dog,' Eileen had said after Ken had gone off to kindergarten one morning.

'A dog?'

'Yes. For the snakes. Now the heat's come, they're all over this place. Don't tell me you can't hear them at night. In the walls…'

'How could they get into the walls?'

'I'm frightened for Kenneth. There was one in his playroom yesterday.'

'But why on earth didn't you tell me? What did you do with it? Was it venomous? Big?'

Eileen's eyes were an unflecked brown-black, and steady. 'It was…long. Long enough to scare the living daylights out of me. It looked poisonous. And I didn't tell you because first you were working and, after that, sleep-working at your desk. But a dog would protect the lad, silly.'

'And get itself bitten?'

'If that's the case,' she had said, placing her hands on her hips, 'then it's clear we'll have to move. A dog's a dog and that getting bitten is bad enough. But the child is our child and at present he's the only one we have.'

No one in their right mind would argue with Eileen once she took that stance. But with the boxes still not unpacked from the last move, the thought of yet another address was unbearable. Inwardly he'd groaned. He had threaded his fingers together, looked down at his hands and moved the discussion into safer territory. 'What did you do with it, then?' he'd asked again.

'The snake? Well, I grabbed Ken, closed the door and when next I peeked, it was gone. Perhaps it climbed up out the window.'

Isidore nodded slowly, taking in the generous gap between the bottom of the door and the floor. He was having trouble remembering the numbers of addresses over the last few years. But if there were snakes in the house, there was no option. 'You're right. If that's the case, maybe we have to move. There are snakes in paradise, too, it would seem.' He shook his head. 'I suppose it was ever thus. But we can get a dog. After we've moved. Why not add another layer of difficulty to leasing?' he added in a softer tone. But she had kissed him and gone.

He turned back to the water, reflecting that its very changeability was a reassuring constant. It could, for example, be flat grey one moment, the next a reflective mercury; at others so dark it was either black or blue. Or sucked out to sea so the rotting bones of the wreck stood proud within the inlet where the waters lapped among the river weeds.

Letting out his breath, he picked up his pen. He was too prone these days to waste time on internal philosophical debate when there were horoscope appointments to confirm for the following day, readings to chart and the next issue of the *Gazette* to put to bed, but he had no sooner started to set out the planets when his son's high laughter brought his thoughts back to Eileen. In a few months' time, it would be their sixth anniversary. He rubbed his brow. How best could he mark it? Buying a dog was one option.

But another possibility – he tapped the top of his pen on his blotter – was a portrait of Kenneth. Eileen had been delighted with McCubbin's portrait of herself, the Watkins/Kozminsky oil begun in the months leading up to their marriage and completed just a few days before.

'Fred would like you to watch while he puts the last touches to it,' Eileen had told him. 'He's off on his European trip in a few months and he's trying to get as much done as he can before he goes. He wants you to see him working on it. As his wedding present to us. Because this is one he's going to keep, he says.'

Although Isidore had no doubt that from an artist's point of view of light and space and mood, *Daneida*, the city house that Fred had recently rented, was not a patch on his property up at Mt Macedon, there was something about the McCubbin energy that filled the space so the surroundings were immaterial. People coming and going, sitting and talking – it was an atmosphere that reminded him so much of the Watkins' own home he could see why Eileen was so comfortable in their company.

When he knocked Fred waved him into the studio, his hands full with his palette and brush, his mouth hidden under his huge moustache, his eyes smiling sideways. Eileen was wearing a gown he had seen only once before and standing in front of a piece of canvas nailed to the wall. She unclasped her hands to wriggle her fingers at him.

'Fred says another ten minutes. And then you can have a look.'

Isidore leant against the wall and took out his pipe, knowing that time itself would have no meaning for the artist. In the end it was the fading light that caused McCubbin to fling his brush onto his palette.

'Done for the day,' he said. 'Come and take a look at what I've done with your future bride. I'll organise some refreshment. I might even be able to tease some scones out of Annie.' He winked.

Eileen came up behind him and rested her hand on his shoulders while he gazed at the portrait. Which was not, he thought at first, a work that particularly appealed to him.

Study in Blue and Gold McCubbin had titled it, and it was well-named in that it was indeed a study. But Isidore's initial reaction was that the work fulfilled its name too exactly: that it was all about Eileen's gown with its full skirts and deep shades of eau de nil, the long wide sleeves and bodice trimmed with a fall of deep-ivory Flemish lace. McCubbin's subject was less important than the clothes she wore, he thought. She was too pale, her face too solemn, the backdrop too sombre. Fred had painted into her features a sadness that wasn't to him quite part of Eileen. And then he remembered with a small shock that she had looked rather like this at her mother's wake, which after all had only been a few months before. McCubbin would have been well into the work by then, and caught some of that emotion. But it was the setting, too, that bothered Isidore. It was intimidating, dark, a murky darkness, a cave with beasts lurking in the reaches. What had McCubbin done here? Had he painted her as an Eurydice of the underworld waiting for the magic of Orpheus's music and song to bring her home? He'd asked her that as he stepped back from the painting, put his arm around her shoulders.

'Is that it? The mythic Eurydice?'

'You can't be sure. That's what I love about it.' She shrugged. 'Look again.'

Was it the rapidly changing light or his desire to be as pleased as she? Or was it something more, something he'd missed? Now as he looked he saw the portrait differently. The pallor, yes, and the sadness palpable, but along with it a light of anticipation in her eyes, a suggestion of roses painted onto her cheekbones, an overall sense of waiting, of barely checked impatience. It had, he thought, all the ambiguity of the *Mona Lisa*. The background, too, had shifted and out of the darkness emerged an aura that frothed around her head, a cloud of something that could be peacock feathers or eyes or even spirit beings. Eileen spilling into the other worlds she believed in so intensely.

'Yes,' he'd murmured. 'Now I see. He's captured all parts of you.'

But now as the idea grew on him, for his son's portrait, he had another artist in mind.

A BREAK IN THE CHAIN

If Isidore's rooms were cramped, the door to the portrait artist's city studio barely opened. At least two easels looked as though they held works in progress; others displayed paintings that were clearly of a different style to her own. The walls were hung with artworks, and still more canvases were piled on tables or stashed on chairs, against the walls, or anywhere the gaze happened to light. Florence Rodway laughed as he inched his way in and he couldn't help thinking it was just as well she was so thin, any more flesh and she would not be able to move at all. Even the shaking of hands turned into an art form in the cramped space.

She cleared a seat for him and then without a space to resettle them, hugged the canvases while she perched on a stool. Tall anyway, now she had to bend to talk to him.

'Sorry about the seating arrangements, Dr Kozminsky. I'll have to get a bigger room some time. One day. At the moment I'm just too busy to move. So, you said you wanted a portrait of your son?' Unselfconsciously she pushed back her fair hair and, although she couldn't physically have been more different, there was something in the strength of her features that reminded him of Eileen.

'Yes, my son Kenneth, now four going on five. My wife Eileen won't let him cut his hair until this portrait is done, so I'm afraid he looks somewhat too angelic at the moment. My one worry is he won't sit still long enough…'

She crinkled her eyes. 'Ah, but I have tricks, you see. Hold these for a moment.' Passing her armful to Isidore, she hopped off the stool and threaded her way to the other side of the room. She returned with a tin which she rattled and then opened. 'See? Shameless hussy offers irresistible bribe! Chocolate biccies. No kid can resist. Nor adults, for that matter. Here.'

She jiggled the tin. Isidore took one, laughing.

'But there's more to it,' she went on. 'Ideally, I need an hour each sitting. So, see that clock up there with the big hands? If he sits as still as a mouse – and if the fidgeting gets out of hand all I need to do is to look in the direction of the tin – then every fifteen minutes, he'll get a chocolate biscuit. It works. But don't bring him just before suppertime!' She paused. 'If you have a few minutes, Dr Kozminsky, I can show you how I work.' She continued to chat as they moved with some difficulty around the room. 'Things rather took off for me when I sold two portraits to the Sydney Art Gallery a couple of years ago. I've a commission for Mr Henry Lawson and his children coming up – and I hear that the singer Dame Nellie Melba is considering asking me to do hers. So your son will be in good company.' She showed him examples of her work in all its different phases, from the first tentative outlines – the light pencil strokes of disembodied parts that captured shape and suggested emotion that led to the artist's rough draft – and then to the final confident rendering of the chalky pastels.

'What should he wear?' Isidore asked when they were once again seated.

She gazed at him, considering. 'Whatever you like. It doesn't matter until we get to the final sitting and then maybe I'll use this.' She reached for a length of hessian. 'Just wrap it lightly around him to look like a smock with perhaps just a suggestion of a ruff at his throat. What do you think? If he is as you've described, I'd like to try a sort of Fauntleroy effect. I think that might work.'

He had agreed to her fee and taken his leave of her when he turned back suddenly. 'Oh, one more thing. I'd like to keep this a secret.'

'A secret?' She arched her brows.

'Well, more of a surprise, really. It's an anniversary present for my wife, you see, and the way I know it's going to turn out, I can't think of anything she'd like more.'

Miss Rodway looked even more doubtful. 'And your son? Kenneth? Can he keep a secret?'

Isidore smiled. 'But it might take an extra biscuit or two!'

It was hot and muggy, a day that was both grey and overbright, the clouds low, the heat compressed. The moisture was invasive, an envelope of dampness like living in a wet bathing suit, a place on the planet where shoes grew mould and his elbows picked up papers in the most irritating fashion. In the end, Isidore threw down his pen, grabbed his hat and went for a walk.

He walked fast along the river beach, his mood challenging his sweating body; if he was going to be wet, he might as well be thoroughly wet. The river was so still that the houses on the opposite shore streamed their reflections into the water.

What would it have been like when Captain Arthur Phillip landed in these parts, he wondered. No shelter, unexpected dangers and a deal of hard physical labour to get this country moving and you could be sure it wasn't only the convicts who worked hard. That was one of

A BREAK IN THE CHAIN

Fred's masterpieces: his early *Down on his Luck* said it all about the trials of colonising this country – any country for that matter. A lot of *hard yakka* and it didn't always go to plan. Or, maybe, *most* times it didn't go right.

He frowned, a taste of bitterness on his tongue, remembering someone – his father – shouting in anger.

But there would always be differences between his father and himself. Their attitude to work varied for a start, something not major in itself, but which he suspected lay at the core of the problem. For Simon, the store was a means to an end and that end was money. Work and the underpinning skills counted as exertion for which one was compensated with earnings. Education, too, was directed to the same end: increased earning capacity.

Isidore, on the other hand, was unable to regard the occupations he was involved in as toil. Rather they were absorbing ways of passing time from which he counted himself lucky to earn a decent living. But he knew that since most of his earnings came from unconventional activities, his father regarded him as wasting time.

He would never understand his father's parsimonious focus, and Simon would never understand his lack of interest in money for its own sake.

But it did beg the question as to how his father had coped when he first arrived. All the many hours they had spent working together and yet how little he knew of the man who was his father. Beyond plans and techniques for making more money did they ever have real conversations? Perhaps when he was very young. After that, his father was one with his business. Was that how the gaps appeared in generations? Unquestionably, there was one hell of a progressively widening gap now.

The rift was certainly complete. Since the wedding he had had no contact with his family. From then on his life had filled so rapidly with Eileen and the baby, a thriving astrological practice, the *Gazette* and the antiquities arriving daily and the gathering of material on the talismanic properties of gemstones for a new book, that there had been little time to dwell on what was happening back home.

Gradually he became aware of another change in the river. From the way in which the reflections were breaking up, he guessed the tide was on the turn. In more ways than one.

Snakes aside, sooner or later, he was going to have to face another move. If that were so, was this then the time to return to Melbourne? Set up the Isidore Kozminsky Gallery? Never go back, or so went the saying, but the move to Sydney was never intended to be permanent. In effect, it had been a temporary *force majeure*, an essential part of allowing his marriage to work without interference, something that under the circumstances would not have been possible without changing cities.

He drew a line in the sand with the toe of his shoe, stared unseeing at the water surging around the hull of the old wreck. He tried to persuade himself that it was Melbourne he missed, the city that sported a type of grace that grew clumsy sometimes with greed, but which more often than not rose above the morass in style.

'Streets and buildings don't make a home,' he said aloud to the river. 'People do. Be honest.' There was scorn in his voice, a damning, which provided shock enough for him to walk on, and when he next spoke to himself it was in a whisper. 'Just what are you saying – are you homesick? Is it actually the connection with your mother and father you miss? It would be good, wouldn't it, for you to know that your mother was all right? Abraham, too, and the rest of them? Is it your own conscience that's surfacing after this long while? Or is it purely that your brain has become addled with the heat?' He scuffed the loose sand viciously as he walked. 'And it'll be different, you think, do you, once you get back? You think being away for a few years will change anyone's mind towards anything? If you do, you're a clot. No, worse than that: a silly fool.'

There was something of Eileen in the tone of this last, but he knew it wouldn't occur to her that the family would continue to withhold their blessings, until all at once he realised that he was making assumptions, that he had never actually asked her what she thought. Knowing she missed her father and siblings, and aware of his own reluctance to return, maybe he was too afraid of her reaction. There was never going to be an easy answer. How had it all happened? A fight caused by differing interpretations of the will of God? Or were they right and he wrong, and his disobedience was this punishment, a physical displacement of someone who had never really belonged.

The damp in the heat got to him and he shivered. He turned back towards the house. Perhaps the time had come to face up to the fact that it was time to return to Melbourne. This was one case where emotions had subsided to the point where it might be possible to make amends, to smooth things over. He would discuss it with

A BREAK IN THE CHAIN

Eileen tonight. He started heavily up the stairs, only to hear her calling when he was halfway up. Her voice echoed out from the house, excited but a little strained, and he finished the flight two steps at a time.

She was in the kitchen taking a well-risen fruit cake out of the oven. Grinning at him, her face flushed and beaded with sweat, proudly she placed the cake in the centre of the kitchen table.

'For our anniversary. Red Indian cake. You can't begin to imagine how much love and courage it takes to bake on a stinker of a day like this.' Her eyes narrowed. 'Are you all right? What's the matter with you? You're all out of breath...'

'I ran up the last few steps. I...heard you calling.'

She wrinkled her forehead. 'Calling? No, not me. Tea's nearly ready, but there's no rush. And Kenneth's just having a short nap. He's been expending his energy on the wreck most of the afternoon and the sun's taken it out of him. No, I've just been working away. Tonight we'll have a feast.'

He winced, placed his hand on the edge of the kitchen table. 'Eileen, I've been thinking...' He stopped. Maybe now was not the time.

She put down the dishcloth and came around to his side of the table. Putting her arms around him, she said, 'Thinking? What, you? Izzy, tell me something I don't know, would you? There's not a moment in your waking or sleeping life that you're not either thinking or dreaming or planning or doing something different...' Slowly her face lost its mischievous dimple. 'But there's something up, isn't there? What is the matter with you? More than running up a couple of stairs.'

'Nothing's up. Not exactly, but I definitely heard you. I did hear you – your voice…'

She gazed at him steadily. 'I don't doubt that you heard me, Izzy. All I'm saying is that it wasn't me. I haven't been calling you. Thinking of you, yes, some of the time, but not calling…'

He scratched the back of his head. 'Well, I don't know…'

Several nights earlier, they had been to a séance, as they often did on a Friday. A closed room, quite large and completely bare save for a young woman sitting on a wooden chair in the centre and the small audience seated at the far end, some ten yards away. A little earlier, after the doors had been locked and the windows closed, the spectators had been invited to inspect the room, to turn over the chairs, to knock and tap the wood, to stamp on the floorboards, to examine what they could of the ceiling. The girl had been dressed in a thin shift, not much more than a slip, under which it was quite evident she was naked. Beneath the bright light of the bare bulb, she stood and turned slowly in a circle. Once reseated, she sat still, her eyes empty as a Roman statue. When an audience holds its breath, as had happened that evening, the silence is so intense it's almost loud and intrusive.

Amid this noise of his awareness, Isidore had glanced at his watch: four and a half minutes to eight o'clock. Seconds later a huge bunch of coloured chrysanthemums appeared on the lap of the sitter. Nearly four minutes to eight. No one moved, or spoke, for a long time.

A BREAK IN THE CHAIN

Eileen turned back to her task. 'That's why we need a dog here. Get a bit of sixth sense into the place. And so, no, I didn't call you just now, but yes, you did hear me calling you. After all, today is a good day for it, isn't it? A day for vibrations. Lots of stuff happening on other levels when the air is close like this.' She nodded at the clouds. 'Loads of electricity. It's only another instance, my dear.' She reached for a knife. 'Meanwhile we're not going to give this cake a chance to get cold, so put the kettle on, will you, and wake Kenny.'

Isidore and Kenneth waited for Eileen on the wide verandah, the brown-paper-wrapped parcel standing on the floor between them almost as tall as Ken who was squirming enough to give anything away.

Eileen had set up the small rusty table with one of her colourful cross-stitched squares of tablecloth and the pink and turquoise Shelley tea set they used for special occasions. There were at least three varieties of filling he could spy in the small squares of fresh sandwiches under their shelter of wilting lettuce leaves and a plate of Ken's favourite ginger nuts absorbing the damp air and growing softer by the minute.

'And there,' she said, whisking away a fly and setting down the Spode bone china platter topped with chunky slices of fruit cake. 'Bit too warm to cut properly. But this should do us until supper, don't you think? Let's eat it before it attracts all the flies in Christendom. It's all this warm weather.' She picked up the teapot and was about to pour when she noticed that her son was having trouble sitting, while Isidore was leaning forward in his chair with his head down and his hands lightly clasped between his knees. She set the pot down again.

'What's up with you two this afternoon? Why are you fidgeting like that, Kenneth? You're both so quiet…' Her eyes rested on the package. 'Oh!'

Released at last from the bondage of keeping the secret, Ken glanced at his father.

'Open it, Mother. Quickly. It's a surprise. From us both. You'll like it. Here, let me help. I'll help you take off the paper.'

When it was unwrapped and propped against the wall of the verandah, Eileen had no words. The boy danced from foot to foot, clapping his hands, his face alight with laughter.

'Do you like it? Don't you like it? Father said you would like it. He said he knew you would.'

'Like it?' she said eventually. 'I love it. Love it to bits. There's not a present in the world you could have given me that I would treasure more.' She took her gaze from the pastel and let it rest for a moment on her husband and son. 'Nothing.'

Once they had retired for the night, he tentatively told Eileen of his decision to return to Melbourne. But once again he had underestimated her pragmatism.

'It had to happen, didn't it? We can't avoid them forever. It was only a question of when. Let's get it over and done with. They are only people after all, and they probably regret the whole difficulty as much as we do. To be honest, it's hard to tell who was in the right or wrong…'

A frown knit his forehead and he was about to protest, but she raised her hand.

'No, wait a bit. Let me finish. We believed that we were right because we'd waited out the year as they'd asked. But then we came rushing up here to put some distance between them and us when maybe, just maybe, we could have been a bit more patient...'

'Patient!' He exploded. 'Patient? Do you realise what that year was like? How long it was? How easily one of us might have met someone else? Missed out on everything we have together, everything we do together? The son we both adore? They had absolutely no right to do that. And then...' his voice broke, 'after all that, to go back on their word.' He turned away only to spin back. 'And, what's more, they didn't *ask*. They demanded, threatened...'

'Stop storming around like that, Isidore. At the end of the day, none of those things happened,' she said reasonably. 'We married and we do have Kenneth. And most of the time we're rather keen on each other. Except when you're unreasonable. All I was going to say was...' There was a clap of thunder and she dropped backwards onto her pillow. 'Ah! Blessed rain, let's hope. At last the weather has broken. We might get some relief now. All I've been trying to say is that if we hadn't gone away we could all have made a bit more effort to get to know each other. You know, a middle way through all this.'

Despite himself he laughed. 'You're thinking "the middle way is the best way"?'

'You find that funny, do you?'

'It's funny the way you've used it in this instance.'

'Oh?'

A BREAK IN THE CHAIN

'From Ovid. *In Medio Tutissimus Ibis*. Literally translated as "in the middle of things you will be safest". It stems from the controversial theory that travelling in the centre of the army is safer than leading, bringing up the rear or patrolling the flanks. But by "the middle way", you meant, I think, all things in moderation?'

She nodded.

'Whereas, it could be construed as an injunction to watch one's back. Quite appropriate given the context, I think. And you've given me an idea for our family crest. Watch your back. *In Medio Tutissimus Ibis*. How very appropriate. What will the generations that come after us think of that, I wonder?'

She pulled out her combs so that her hair swung the way he loved it, thick and glossy about her shoulders. 'Sometimes I don't understand you. You are not an arrogant person; yet sometimes you come across that way. And you're so angry, Izzy.'

'Understandably angry,' he protested. 'One day I'll set the record straight.'

'Whatever that means. And stay angry until then?'

'I'll go away somewhere else. Back to London. We'll go to London. What do you think. Change my name again. Completely this time. Take my grandmother's name – Frances Coaten. Perhaps simplified slightly. Francis Coton? He spelt it out slowly. 'Coton. That will show them.'

She shook her head sadly. 'I sometimes find it hard to remember you're an adult,' she said. 'What is this hate you won't let go of? It's not part of the man I used to know. The only person you are going to hurt is yourself. And me, too, by the way.'

A BREAK IN THE CHAIN

He was silent for a few moments. Then he reached for her hand. 'I don't *hate*, Eileen. I am not the hating sort, you of all people know that. I said just now that they – my father, uncle and, to a lesser extent, my brother and sister – are disappointed in me. Well, I too am disappointed in them. And it's not us who are refusing a peace offering.'

'We haven't contacted them either,' Eileen said. 'Sounds like a bit of an impasse to me. Why not just sacrifice a pawn – let go a bit of pride – and move ahead? Why let a silly quarrel continue to fester?' She thumped the bed. 'We've got so much, Izzy. So much. Who cares about the bloody past? When we get back to Melbourne, let's sit down and plan how we might at least make our peace with them. We may never be close friends, but at least we'll have tried.' Her eyes softened. 'I love you. I love you completely, you complicated man.' She moved across to kiss him, and then leaning back into the pillows, closed her eyes. Moments later her breathing settled into a peaceful rhythm. It never ceased to amaze him how smoothly she moved from one mood to another and how easily she fell asleep. The Irish conscience was a wonderful thing.

22

By the time they were settled back in Melbourne, with Ken at prep school and booked in for his senior schooling at Melbourne Grammar, the newspapers were full of the rising tensions in Europe. Ferdinand of Austria had been assassinated and all signs pointed to a world at war.

Isidore's own conflict was never far from his mind. He suspected it would remain an internal aggravation, clinging to his back like a monkey, until he did something about it. He had been both pleased and surprised at Ken's increasingly warm friendship with his brother Michael's son Geoffrey. It boded well, perhaps, for an end to this stalemate of family relations. And so, over breakfast one morning, he looked up from the front page of *The Age*.

'I've made an appointment to talk to Father,' he told Eileen. 'Which in itself is quite strange, really. I mean how many people make an appointment to speak to their parents? I'm meeting them later this afternoon. I thought Kenneth might like to come along. After all, they are his grandparents and they haven't met…'

His wife put down her fruit spoon. A small crease appeared between her eyebrows. 'It won't be a whole barrel of fun for him, will it? Two old people and the little boy.'

'And me.'

She looked at him. 'Oh yes, Izzy. And you, feeling awkward in the centre of it all. I almost forgot...' She shrugged.

'I beg your pardon, but I seem to remember,' he said slowly, 'that all this getting back together was your idea. Let me see if I can return my memory to a few months ago...' He tapped his head. 'Ah, yes, a bit of a storm going on outside the house – and inside too. You'd gone to bed, I think. Remember that evening? And that bit about the importance of families and about letting bygones be bygones, et cetera, et cetera. That was you, wasn't it?'

He was pleased to see her flush. She gave in too easily. 'You might as well take the lad, then,' she sighed. 'Certainly there'll be no harm in it.'

Pressing his advantage against her sudden collapse of defence, he said. 'You can come, too, if you like.'

'No,' she said hastily. 'Leave me be, will you. I'll do things in my own way.'

They were ushered into the drawing room, heavily draped and altogether stuffy with something indeterminate hanging about the margins. Isidore fought the urge to raise his head and sniff like a beagle. His father rose unsteadily, leaning heavily on a cane. Isidore shook the hand with its long cool fingers and crossed the room to greet his mother. They all looked at Ken.

'This is my son, Kenneth,' Isidore said, proud of the way his son, apparently unconscious of the mood of the room, walked tall across the carpet to shake the hand of his grandfather who had already collapsed back into his chair. But Emma proved more difficult. So forbidding was she, sitting back against her old high-backed wing chair, that Ken's mouth trembled. He held out his hand.

'Hello Grandmama.'

History suggests otherwise, but it is possible she smiled slightly. That would have been all. Certainly she made no move to take his hand. Isidore had forgotten how intimidating his mother could be if she chose. Or was this a new thing, her daunting demeanor lifted to this degree? Ken was confused for a moment. He looked around at his father and his hand dropped slowly to his side. Simon motioned to the sofa at the far end of the carpet where they obediently sat, Ken on the very edge.

Was there a sense of comedy in all this that made him want to laugh? Isidore wondered. Or was it the edge of hysteria, this incipient gurgle rising in his throat at the incongruity of it all – at the way they were seated in the big room at the apex of an isosceles that further divided the participants, none of whom wanted to be there anyway?

How would it be if he rose and danced a bit of a caper on the carpet? Or if he got down on his hands and knees, wagged his tail, licked his father's boots? The non-conformist son. He forced himself to breathe evenly.

They were seated so far from each other that Isidore would have difficulty hearing his father, who had begun muttering to himself. His mother had still said nothing. Ken looked like an animal in an iron trap. The gap in time and space that had elapsed had not made anything easier for any of them, Isidore realised for the first time.

A BREAK IN THE CHAIN

The meeting continued as it had started by assuming the shape of a monologue: Simon talking, Isidore nodding, Ken looking from one to the other and Emma staring out of the window. Simon made an effort to be affable. He had all but retired from the business itself, he said. For many years now the firm had operated under Emma's name and was heavily subsidised by her property dealings. For all the effect his words had on his wife, she could have been the pet dog. But this wasn't a house, Isidore reflected, where a dog would have been comfortable.

And then his father spoke about renting the shop next door to the present business and installing Isidore as manager at a salary of five pounds a week. As a stipend it was not a lot, Simon admitted, but it would give his son an income which would allow him to pay back the loan he understood he owed to the bank as well as freeing him to work on his other projects during the quieter spells. In that respect, it was generous. That was one Simon speaking. But it soon became clear that there were two people in one.

The other broke loose not in words but in actions, glaring at him with something close to hatred after a perfectly genial sentence, picking disgustedly at the fabric of his trouser leg as if trying to remove something, to dislodge a piece of fluff, to rid himself of something that only he could see. He kept his eyes firmly averted from Ken, his only acknowledgement of his existence coming in the remark that should Isidore take up his offer, then the boy might like to clean silver for an hour or two after school each day.

A BREAK IN THE CHAIN

Isidore was aware that his father had relinquished the running of the firm to his mother some years ago. He appeared now and again behind the counter, but grew tired easily and some months before he'd had an altercation with a customer which had resulted in a charge being laid. Simon had apologised and the charge was withdrawn, but these days he was absent from the business more often than he was there.

Emma sat silently throughout. Sometimes her lips moved, but it only served to make her look more disapproving, and Isidore was unable to work out whether it was involuntary twitch or whether she was holding back from something she wanted to add.

Emma's thick hair was quite white now, drawn back from her face into a knot at the back of her neck, so that there was no relief from the strained lines that netted about her eyes and mouth. She was more remote than he remembered, her gaze fixed on something distant, on something that must be happening out through the window, in the garden or further away perhaps, while all the time he was quite sure that her mind registered every word and every action in the room with absolute precision. She had an inaccessibility about her that rendered her both untouched and untouchable. That she loved him, he once thought he knew. But did she still?

There were sounds from the kitchen, but as time passed the likelihood of refreshment diminished. His father's voice, disintegrating into a mutter from time to time, droned on. Fortunately Ken was intimidated enough not to fidget. The anger, never far away, started to stir in Isidore, but he pressed it back. 'They probably regret this whole thing as much as we do,' he heard Eileen say. 'They are only people, Izzy, with their own sets of hopes and expectations.' That was true. They were only people doing, he supposed, their best as people tended to do. What he found hard, almost impossible, to understand was his own inability to find some way to connect.

He had lectured and acted in front of audiences all over the world and, even if there were a disagreement or a divergence of views – or even, as on one memorable occasion, the straight-out condemnation of a thesis he was putting forward – there was something coming back from the audience in the form of a vibe, an energy. Any opening, however small – including dissent or lack of understanding – presented an opportunity for adjustment on his part or gave him a chance to mount a reasoned defence. But here there was nothing; that was the problem. No energy at all. So that the air itself was lifeless and when his father stopped speaking, the silence took the form of a clammy chill that wrapped around him as if the room were full of ghosts. Isidore did not dare look at Ken, but he had to have one last try.

He sat forward, tried to make eye contact with Simon. 'Look, Father,' he started. 'I know we haven't always seen eye to eye and perhaps this isn't the right time or place, but we don't get much of a chance to talk and this needs to be said.

'First, you know already, I think, how much I appreciate the job offer and I accept with thanks. It's very generous of you and the income will certainly be handy after the move and so forth.

'But, secondly, and perhaps more importantly. Eileen and I – and Kenneth here – came back from Sydney to try...' He had been about to say 'to make amends', but that was the wrong way round. The onus was not on him to make amends. This wasn't a question of atonement on anyone's part, more a matter of adjustment on everyone's part. He looked down at his hands. 'We've come back from Sydney to try to... God damn it, this ridiculous seating!'

He jumped up, dragged the central ottoman over to his father's chair and perched on the edge just a yard away from him.

'That's better. I can see you now. Father, you know, you have to know – and with all the things I do, I know it's hard to keep track of – but the direct inspiration for two of my great loves, astrology and gems, comes from you. Do you remember, as I do, our night rides? The sky and the stars, and how you'd point out the planets and get me to recite them. Remember Mortlake? I never forgot that introduction and astrology became my first love, my living. I have you to thank for that. You planted the seed in that respect. You, Mother – and Abraham too – in different ways you all inspired and encouraged me.' He thought he could see some sort of flicker, something stirring, in his father's eyes though Simon continued to sit passively, one hand on his stick, the fingers of his other hand working away at the fabric of his trouser leg.

'However, my other loves are my wife and my son. And there will be a new baby soon. They are equally important to me.' He could feel his son's eyes hot on the back of his head and he thought he heard a sound from his mother. He had gone too far to stop. 'If I had one wish, it would be that we can find a way between us...' He had been about to say 'to be friends', but he was speaking now from his heart. He started again. 'If I had just one wish, it would be that we could love each other. That we could regain the warmth and understanding that was once there. Surely something of that must still exist?'

For answer, Simon simply looked at his watch and started to get to his feet. When he spoke, the words were indistinct. It was something like, 'The time for that has gone.' But Isidore could have been mistaken. The meeting was clearly over.

As he went to take his leave of his mother, Isidore realised how wrong he'd been to imagine his absence had affected her. It was clear that emotion of any sort had long gone and with it any chance to find out why. Her mind might be active but Emma's eyes were dead. For the first time he understood the full extent of the chronic unhappiness that had filled her for many years.

Outside, once the door was closed firmly behind them, Ken looked up at his father. Even Florence Rodway's broad palette of colours could not have captured the scarlet of his cheeks.

'Heck.'

'I agree with you, son. Heck is the only word for it.'

In bed that night, Isidore moved restlessly. He had mucked it up. They weren't ready for that sort of thing. May never be. Damn religion for driving a wedge between families! But then he had another thought that made him sit up so suddenly that Eileen groaned in her sleep. At the end of the day, was this really about religion? Was this really about being a Jew or not being a Jew? Or was it more of a question of control? And, if that were the case, there was nothing further he could do.

Not long afterwards – on the wintry day of 3 July 1916 – Simon died. The cause of death was senile decay. Or so it said on his death certificate, when what they meant was his quick mind had sunk by slow and difficult degrees until he could reach it no longer.

Emma insisted that in his grave be placed a small carefully wrapped parcel, its shape something like a book, and a fiddle, so scratched and battered that it, too, was only what it was because of its shape.

'I didn't know Father played,' Isidore said to his mother.

'There was a lot you didn't know about him,' she said shortly. 'But yes, there was a time when he played well.' And then, as if aware of the hardness of her tone, she added, 'No one knew him very well, I suppose. Your father wasn't a man anyone understood easily.'

In his last will Simon left his estate to Emma, appointing his three children equal trustees and beneficiaries should she predecease him. But as a codicil to that will, on 3 October 1907, some six months after the marriage of his eldest son and while his estate remained divided between the three, Simon had revoked the appointment of Isidore as one of the trustees.

23

'You're telling me that you've asked the Archbishop for dinner? The Catholic Archbishop? Tonight?' Eileen stood up from what she was doing, put one hand on her hip.

'Yes.'

'Why? You're not Catholic.'

'I'm not? Unless I've got the definition wrong, I'm very catholic. And so are you.'

'Oh Francis,' Eileen groaned. She'd taken to calling him Francis on occasion, ever since the night of the storm. It suited him in some of his iterations, she said, but now she passed her hand over her eyes. 'Not words again. Give me a break. Just for once. We can't have him here with these awful orange boxes to hold up the door and no proper tablecloth.'

Isidore swept his hand at the room. 'Granted, it's not the Vatican. But then neither is he the Pope.' Suddenly he stopped and stooped forward a little. Placing his hand above his eyes as shelter from an imaginary sun, he swung around on his heel, first left then right and back again.

'Where is she?' he asked.

'Where is who?'

'Eileen?' he called. 'Eileen?' Eventually he turned back to her, his face a furrow of concern. 'I'm looking for my wife,' he said. 'Have you seen her? She seems to have gone missing. Lovely looking woman she is, with a heap of dark hair and dark brown eyes. One of the city's best lady feature writers: she gets to the point without mucking about. Great character, too. Game for absolutely anything. I can't do without her, if the truth be known.' He looked under the door recreated as a tabletop. 'Eileen? Eileen? Where's she gone?'

'You really are a clot,' she said.

'So are you,' he said, putting his arms around her. 'What's all this suddenly about a damned tablecloth? Not everyone has a sheet as snowy white as ours with fancy stuff at one end. Why would you want to swap it for a cloth? Besides, I bet he eats from a wood trestle table at his institution...'

'And that's another thing,' she interrupted.

'What?'

'No dining table.'

'No, but at least we have a dining room.' He tilted her chin so she had to look him in the eye. 'What's up with you, Eileen?' he asked, suddenly serious. 'All this,' he swept his hand around the room, 'has done us proud for years. And look at the people we've had here. Some of the best wits and conversationalists in town, and genuine people all of them, artists, academics, the Heidelberg folk, the orchestral practice sessions, even a politician here and there, bless their hearts. They all congregate here because it's a neutral uncomplicated space. They want to relax, unbend, talk, opinionate. We don't preach politics or religion or follow precise and fanatical rules for living. We just make a welcoming space – and it's appreciated.

A BREAK IN THE CHAIN

Jelly or junket. Cover or cloth. In the scheme of things, they're so unimportant. Who the hell cares?'

He tapped the door-turned-table-top. 'This may not have started its life as a table but I'm willing to bet that what we have here can tell more stories and has witnessed more fun and genuine laughter than any dining table in the colony. When we front up to the pearly gates at the end of the day, isn't that the stuff that's important?'

'It wobbles.'

He let her go, laughing. 'It only wobbles because Kenneth borrowed the orange crates for his woodwork and when he put them back he didn't bother to centre them. Look, we need to coordinate our efforts here.' He pushed her gently into a chair. 'You sit there and I'll sit at the other end. Now, listen. When the big bloke thumps the table – and he will because being a man of God he'll have some salient points to make and a thump is equivalent to several exclamation marks – we'll hold up the table underneath. Grip it, just so, and then we'll catch each other's glances and do our best not to become hysterical.'

'And the menu?'

'What's that you had in the kitchen just now.'

'Fish. Vegetables for you.'

'Well, that sounds perfect. All clerics like fish.'

'I'm having trouble getting the head off.'

'A knife. Have you tried that?'

'It's a big fish. I should have got them to do it in the market. The knife's not sharp enough.'

'I'll borrow one of Kenneth's chisels. A sort of exchange for the loan of the crates. Then I can fix that screw on the saucepan lid at the same time.'

A BREAK IN THE CHAIN

'Kenneth isn't too keen on your using his chisels as screwdrivers. Remember the last time?'

Isidore nodded, but his mind was already on something else that would, he thought, make amends for springing the Archbishop on her without notice. Reaching into his pocket, he withdrew a clipping.

'Listen. I told you Florence Rodway stopped in at the store the other day, didn't I? You'll like this. From the *Bulletin* of 19 March: "Florence Rodway the tall smiling girl artist who specialises in pastels was in Melbourne last week, but talked of returning to Sydney where she does all of her work. She had been holidaying in Hobart – her birthplace. She intends to show some of her art in Melbourne during August and a few charming specimens are already in town. A portrait of Isadore Kozminsky's son is a clever piece of work and Henry Lawson's children seem ready to step out of their frames." Spelt my name wrong, as usual.' He shrugged. 'But "clever piece of work"? Don't you like that?' He glanced at his pocket watch. 'Which reminds me. I told Florence that we'd let her hang it as part of her exhibition. Strictly not for sale, of course. I'd better be off. Billy Hughes is in town for a short time, too, and I promised I'd show him how to wish on the Dog of Foo. If anyone needs a bit of luck, he does.'

'I'm glad about the *Bulletin*. Thank you for sharing it, but it doesn't tell us anything we don't already know, does it? And it was a clever way to change the subject.'

'Ah, I've found her! That's my Eileen back.'

She sighed. 'The trouble with you is that you're always play-acting or playing with words. You take a lot of keeping up with, Izzy.'

A BREAK IN THE CHAIN

Once he'd left, she moved into the kitchen to face the fish, took up the knife again. Placing a dishcloth over its eyes, she grasped it firmly by the tail and began the distasteful business of separating head from body. Despite the lack of enthusiasm she had for the task, a smile passed over her face.

'That bloody Francis,' she said aloud.

As the silver scales spun off the knife, she set her mind to working out a further conciliatory move towards the family. She hadn't had to ask how the meeting with his parents had turned out. Isidore's set mouth and Ken's flushed face had told her most of what she needed to know; Isidore had said only that he would be managing a new store, an extension of the business next door to the one in the Block.

With Ken already booked into the Grammar school, the offer was timely. Her husband had an unshakeable faith that if one worked hard and did the right thing by other people, the money side of things would take care of itself, and somehow, by the Grace of God, so far it had. He refused to worry about it openly and there was no indication it stopped him sleeping at night. His only concern was one that swamped all others: that it was his inability to be other than true to himself that had disappointed his family, a disappointment that was non-negotiable. Neither party was prepared, nor able perhaps, to find a middle way and so the deadlock remained. The original cause of dissention had either been forgotten or remembered as just another example of filial disobedience she suspected, and what was left was a civility picked as bare as one of their Red Setter Piper's lovingly gnawed bones.

A BREAK IN THE CHAIN

'I'll have one last try,' she said out loud. She flicked the final pieces of silver from the fish. 'Invite them all for tea and cake. That's what I'll do. And I won't tell him. Just get on and do it.'

For some time now, Isidore had been aware of the intertwining of the two supposedly opposite forces of magic and science that were to form the core of his thesis on gemstones. A piece of red coral, for example, that started life as a leafless polyp-infested bush on the sea bed, once subjected to the laws of transmutation became the substance calcium carbonate, a carbonate of lime, c. rubrum, a piece of orange-red talisman. Easy to see and thus explain.

He had finally reached Z in his own personal encyclopedia, which was of particular interest since it pertained to the zircon, the jewel that related to his zodiacal sun sign. Shielding the light from the lamp, he scooped the small glassy crystal onto a fragment of black velvet where it shone, emitting its own phosphorescence, another proof that these gems were alive and electric. Turning up the lamp and holding the stone under the circle of light, he teased it with the end of his pen, observing how small shreds of velvet fluff appeared to be attracted to it.

The door opened and he glanced up, still attached to his thought waves. Seconds passed before he registered that it was Eileen and that she did not look happy. He braced himself against the back of his chair while she flung herself into the armchair usually reserved for Piper.

'Well,' she said. 'That's that, then.'

There was something about his wife that always made her start her stories at the finish. What was it about the Irish that made them so constantly perverse? He sighed. 'I beg your pardon?'

She glared at him, her face burning. 'They all came when I didn't think they would…'

'Who came?' Irritably he passed his hands through his hair.

'The family. But they looked so disapproving, so stiff and – oh! I don't know. And they whispered to each other that my cake would fall apart when I cut it. A loud whisper.' She put her head in her hands, ran her hands through her hair. 'So, so awful, Isidore. I can't believe it. I can't believe they said that. And of course that upset Kenneth who protested rather loudly that his mother's cakes didn't fall apart. And so now, to make everything worse, they are going to say that we've brought up a son who is rude and undisciplined.' She bit her lip. 'I made matters worse, Izzy. I didn't mean to, but in the end I think that's what I did.'

'In the name of God, who cares what they think or what they say?' When he took her in his arms it was to soothe her, but he was unprepared for the violent surge of his own anger meeting hers. He bit down on it hard, forced a measured tone. 'They're jealous, that's all.'

'Jealous? What of? What of, for Christ's sake?' Her voice rose. She pulled away and flung out her hand. 'Of this? Of this…stupid stuff?' She was incredulous. His gaze followed hers around the room, which was not large but big enough, with its comfortably used sofas and the oak desk in the corner so covered with books and manuscripts that it was a wonder he could work at it at all.

Piper was sprawled over the rose carpet while that other dog, the Dog of Foo, stood guard at the open French windows.

The breeze that stirred the curtains touched the roses, too, so that the heavy heads swayed, lush colour against the green of the lawn. Aside from their breathing and the occasional murmured snore from the dog, the only sound in the lazy day was the buzz and drone of bees.

His voice was quiet but bitter. 'Exactly. What could they be jealous of?' He leaned towards her. 'Eileen. Do you realise just what we have? I'm not sure you do. They don't like any of this. Jealous is an uneasy word and I hesitate to use it. But don't you see? We have so much. They are resentful of all this. Of the freedom, if you like, from convention.

'And this "stuff" as you call it.' His hands waved. 'These antiques and what-not. They're nothing by themselves. Each part is only a part of something else. But as a part of the whole, it's powerful.' He rubbed his hands together. 'Now, good wife, by any chance, is there any of that excellent cake left for tea?'

Later that night, when everything was quiet and the house was a dark shape against the sky, Isidore lit his pipe and walked out into the garden. He stood awhile drawing at the tobacco, gazing at the stars, the bit of a moon which gave the garden colour. That he was deep in thought was not unusual, but that his eyes were hard and unyielding was.

After some time, he knocked the ash from his pipe and dragged a large piece of tin into the centre of the lawn. Back in the house he went methodically through his desk drawers, through files and folders, certificates and degrees, framed and unframed, and it was only when he had a thick sheaf of papers and a pile of frames in both hands that he went back out to the garden, placed them in the centre of the tin, and striking a match, set them on fire.

There was a blaze as the paper caught light and settled to the steady burn he recognised within himself.

'Much good they've done me,' he muttered, kicking at the embers.

But he knew they had, and something inside him snapped. He felt a traitor standing there in the dark, burning up the evidence of his life, his many accolades and his studies. He put a hand to his eyes.

24

Ken wasn't quite sure just when the idea came to him. But he had overheard his parents talking often enough to know that it was this 'family thing' that from time to time cropped up and disturbed both his mother and father. Life would go on very pleasantly and then, wham, the upset would surface again.

He hadn't been able to work out whether it was a sadness or a bitterness, perhaps because one became the other as time went on, but now he had a plan. He would call on his great-uncle Abraham. See if he could patch things up a bit. He didn't live too far away, no more than a bus ride, and as he had heard his mother say often enough, people were, after all, just people.

And so, after school one day, he decided he would pay him a visit. It was late enough that he might be home from the city by now. Although a soft breeze came off the water along Marine Avenue, the hot late-summer afternoon provided sufficient excuse for an ice cream at the stall by the Luna, so that by the time he knocked at the door of his great-uncle's house, his mind was not so much on the meeting as it was on the sugary aftertaste.

The door was opened by the butler and Ken was about to speak when he heard Abraham's voice from the hall.

A BREAK IN THE CHAIN

'Who is it?' The man started to answer when suddenly his great-uncle was there in front of him, his frown deepening when he saw Ken. He had met him only once and he remembered a man taller and altogether larger than the man who stood in front of him, or perhaps it was only that he himself had grown. His great-uncle wore spectacles which magnified the cool blue of his eyes and the dome of his head shone through the darkness of the hall as if it had been polished. His moustache was carefully curled and he was dressed to go out, his cravat a snowy white, his three-piece suit carefully pressed.

'Yes,' he said, his voice short. 'What do you want?'

Ken licked his lips, suddenly dry, no trace of sugar remaining. He felt the colour rising in his cheeks. At the back of his mind he heard his father quote: *Summon up the blood*. He shook his head not so much to clear it as to ground himself, to get on with what he had come to do.

'Good afternoon, sir,' he said, and when Abraham merely nodded he forged on in a hurry, words tumbling over each other and then a blank. But this was the man about whom he had heard his father talk so often in the Sydney days, pain in the lines of his mouth. 'He was generous to me, Kenneth. Very. He didn't have to be. He had his own family, his own commitments. But he believed in me.'

Ken squared his shoulders, started again. 'I've come to say this,' he said flatly. 'That is, well, what I would like to say is that my father wants to be friends. He wants things to be the same as before. He regrets – that is, he wants...' He looked up at his uncle. 'Sir, I do wish you could both...'

Placing one hand on the doorframe, Abraham cut in. 'You are involving yourself in something you do not understand. Our quarrel is not your quarrel. Please don't interfere in this matter.' He turned to his butler. 'Get the boy a sandwich.' He nodded curtly at Ken, glanced at his pocket watch and was gone.

Shaking, Ken followed the butler into the big hall. He waited for a minute or two, and then his mind started working again. There was little point in staying, he realised, and no sooner had the thought registered than he took to his heels and clattered off through the suburbs. Never again, he said to himself. Never again.

Ken had been at Melbourne Grammar for some years before Isidore got word Emma was dying. She had been ill for so long it was hard to believe she would ever die. But the call had come, so Ken accompanied his father through the streets to the Charnwood Road house wondering whether the whole family would be at the bedside and if they would close ranks to leave his father and himself a self-conscious island.

But it wasn't like that at all, so much for his anticipation. Instead they were the only visitors, and once they were up the stairs with the bedroom door closed behind them a change came over his father. He dropped to his knees and clasped his mother's hands in his. This wasn't a replica of the dutiful son he had played out in front of Simon. This was someone who unreservedly loved, who looked as if at any moment, he might start to cry or wail or worse although, after all that had happened, Ken wondered how it could be so.

A BREAK IN THE CHAIN

They had said she was paralysed, and Ken wondered whether, despite the physical lock on her body, she could still feel and think and reason or whether the disease had stolen everything away. The answer, perhaps, lay in her eyes.

Because, surprisingly, the eyes he remembered as expressionless were now bright, clear and full of energy, darting searchingly over his father's face as if they had borrowed every last scrap of strength from the body that had let her down.

After some time her head sank further into the pillows and she was still staring into her son's eyes as the light dimmed in her own.

Gently his father took his hands away. Rising, he went to the window to stand gazing down at the raindrops bouncing off the verandah roof below.

Part Five

Francis

1936

Epilogue

The sounds he had been waiting for all morning came at last. A metallic squeak, the clatter and bang of the brass mail flap, letters whispering their way onto the hall carpet, the soft thud of something heavier, more substantial, a final click, the soft whirr of bicycle wheels retreating.

But it was not just this morning he had been waiting. It was most of his life. And now it was done, with no going back, because he knew with the same certainty he felt each time the envelope with the crest lighted on the hall carpet that today would be the day. Today was the day it would all be made legal. Final. So he promised himself. Just this last moment of the in-between, the compromise, the neither one thing nor the other thing, the really nowhere at all. This time, like all the other times, he knew he was right.

More than once he had wondered how he would feel. Relieved, perhaps, just a little light-headed as someone might after a divorce? Or would his heart thump hard, just as it did when he held one of his books in his hands, straight from the press with the pages still smelling of ink? Or, after all the difficulties of the past, would he have a feeling of reverence, like when he held in the palm of his hand a pearl that he knew, even without his eyeglass, was as perfect as any ever formed?

It was August, a London August, just a few days before his sixty-sixth birthday. It was, in fact, the eighteenth day of the eighth month in the year one thousand, nineteen hundred and thirty-six, and he knew he would spend time later in the day determining the exact significance of this sequence of numbers.

Meanwhile, the sun colluded with his mood, streaming hot and thick across the garden, falling into the room as patterns on what little of his desk could be seen among the stacks of papers and pages of manuscript, and turning the smoke from his pipe into ghostly circles about his ears.

He was working on a new book. *My Key Treatise*, he would call this one; he was confident that his system of predicting race winners was as good now as it would ever be. The demand for his writings was more prevalent than ever and on the whole he was well-satisfied with events in that direction. Humouring the sun, teasing himself with this small delay, he took up his pipe again, sucked hard at the elusive hint of vanilla, speculated on the message in the wreathing, rising spiral, saw things he knew weren't there, and those that were.

It was a year, more now, since he'd sold the Melbourne business and left for London in the months following Abraham's death. Over a decade since his mother had died, nearly two since his father had passed away. Longer still since Uncle Marks. And the other uncle, the elusive English uncle? He had thought that by moving here he would be able to find out more. But even at Somerset House, the bound volumes with the relevant pages were missing just as the people themselves had gone. But their personalities remained, almost palpable and certainly less ephemeral than the spiralling smoke before him. Was this the spirit that was so tangible in the séances? Was this what he thought, what he hoped or what he dreaded?

Back in Melbourne, the business, too, had gone up in smoke. Little Collins Street, his 'commercial museum'. The papers had liked that. He'd tried to patch it up, keep it in the family, and there had been a great deal of generosity and goodwill from a lot of people. If it hadn't been for the Depression, when antiques and jewellery were the last things people were buying... The bank loans, too. If it hadn't been for the weight of the loans, the credit finally, after all that time, running dry. Although perhaps things hadn't been the same since the days of the Hopetoun family at Government House. They'd one of the most stunning collections of silver he'd ever valued and had certainly sparked the lust for collecting that followed. And that was what he was. He had thought of himself as a dealer in antiques, but in truth he was a collector. It was in his bones. He realised that now. Too late. A collector without a collection. Well, a diminished collection at best. His gaze rested on the Dog of Foo, swung left to the watercolour of Lord Nelson and around the room to the green cut-glass bowl he'd bought with Abraham in Venice. His uncle had been as excited about it as he was himself. Bits and pieces he'd kept and every piece had a story to tell.

Eileen usually brought him the post along with the tray of tea and biscuits they shared, but today she was out and eventually there was no excuse not to walk down the corridor. He knew that one of the letters would be the long envelope that arrived every fortnight and which, for the past six months he had ripped open, eagerly scanning the contents only to be disappointed. Today, as always, it would be different.

He bent to pick it up: the August issue of *The London Gazette* with its crest of the lion and the unicorn. He flipped to the contents at the back which directed him to page 5449. Still standing on the mat inside the front door, his eyes raced down the familiar phrases, the varying passions that pushed people to declare their past lives 'renounced and abandoned' or 'formally and absolutely renounced, relinquished and abandoned' and stopped, finally, at long, long last, at his own name.

He smiled now. Read each word slowly with the pedantic care of a proofreader. He was still smiling at the end of the short paragraph. But it was not, somehow, a smile of happiness. The creases between his eyebrows and at the outer corners of his eyes said something else. There was a degree of pain – no, not pain exactly, but something more complex in the set of his mouth that said that perhaps this was the end of a journey rather than the beginning of a new one. That this was a more a thing of sadness than an occasion for jubilation. It was an occasion that was both momentous and of no note whatsoever, as if the two opposites were reconciled – or cancelled out – in the one.

He went back along the corridor to his study. The room that had been warm and sunny felt suddenly hot and stuffy. He knocked out his pipe, opened the window. Taking a deep breath, he picked up the phone. Along the wire he imagined a row of welcome swallows thrilling as the vibration passed through their claws, wondered whether they could pick up on the essence of his own thrill along the wires across London. The ring tone, his son's voice.

'Hello?'

'Ken. Are you there? It's official. Official at last. I'll read it out. Word for word. Listen. It's brief. For the record, here we go. "Notice is hereby given that by deed dated 31 December 1935, and enrolled in the Supreme Court of Judicature on the 14th August, 1936."' He broke off, took a breath. 'A full eight months it's taken. Never mind. Listen.

'"Francis Coton of 7a Abbey Road London NW8 and Kenneth William Coton of 75 Warrington Crescent London W9 have abandoned the names of Isidore or Israel Kozminsky and Kenneth William Kozminsky respectively, and adopted the names of Francis Coton and Kenneth William Coton respectively."'

His voice was quiet. 'It's through, Ken. After all the anger, the grief, the waiting. Just these few lines. But finally, after all, it's done.'

And at the other end, a silence, because after all, after all the acrimony and bitterness, the anger, hostility and self-questioning, it was hard to believe that this bare paragraph from the Supreme Court of Judicature could make good the past.

After Francis had hung up the telephone, he sat for a while. The sun had moved so the open window was in shadow and his face hung there, reflected in the glass, vague and disembodied.

A BREAK IN THE CHAIN

Was that really all it was, his past – a series of names he had discarded like the sloughed-off skin of a snake? How was it, he asked himself, that even moments of extreme sweetness could be so sad, so uncertain? And why was it that of all his predictions, the most unreliable would always be his own feelings?

The rattle of teacups in the corridor interrupted his thoughts. Eileen was home; he hadn't heard the door. The sudden smile in his eyes flashing in the window pane as he turned to greet her. He rose unsteadily.

In the doorway, Eileen stopped. She took in the look on his face, the journal trembling in his hands.

'Yes,' she said, 'I had a feeling…'

Postscript

In her 1993 introduction to *The Golden Notebook*, Nobel-prize winner Doris Lessing concludes with the observation that 'fiction is better at "the truth" than a factual record. Why this is so is a very large subject and one I don't begin to understand.'

In the nearly thirty years that have passed since Lessing wrote those words, it's becoming increasingly recognised that like the somewhat arbitrary lines on the old maps that are fading here and there, so it is with that once inviolate border between fiction and non-fiction. A rigorously referenced work of dates and 'facts' provides the essential framework of setting and staging. But the stage is bare without the players, lifeless without their personalities and idiosyncrasies, without the stories handed down from generations past.

My grandfather died just two or three years before I was born and very little in terms of primary material existed of his life.by the time I came to set it down. And, yes, Isidore did indeed burn all his journals, diaries, letters and his many certificates until all that was left were his printed works – a couple of which are still available in one form or another nearly a century after they were first published.

A BREAK IN THE CHAIN

And so it is to Dad that I owe the rich resource of stories that runs through this book. Towards the end of my father's life (at one month short of 100), the story of the rift in the family was one he wanted told, but his memory of his own father's emotional turmoil was such that, despite his own talent as a journalist and published short story writer, it was one he was unable to bring himself to write. As a result, this is a story based largely on my father's recollections. I say 'largely' because there were few factual details to Dad's tales. No names were ever attached, no dates or ages, places were undefined. Although the anecdotes themselves were vivid and impassioned, the relationship between these characters of the past and our family of the present was smudged and vague.

My father's name was Kenneth Coton, my grandfather Francis Coton and I grew up as Tangea Coton. It was not until well into my adult life that I discovered with a mix of puzzlement and disorientation that Francis Coton and Isidore Kozminsky were the same man. Through the dizzying pace of a life spent in many different countries juggling marriage, career and children, a picture began to emerge. Yet it wasn't until my children were themselves young adults that I had any knowledge of my Jewish past.

As the story took shape, I felt strange, as if I'd entered a new world that was over-bright and a trifle uncomfortable until, little by little, I began to sense a feeling of more space, room to move. Gradually, encouraged by my reading and by the people I have met in the course of writing this book, I am gaining an appreciation of the charm and ritual of Jewish tradition.

A BREAK IN THE CHAIN

My own life journey, as a result, has been greatly enriched on a number of levels.

Had I been more curious at a younger age, the cream- and maroon-covered book titled simply *The Jewish Cookery Book* that accompanied our family travels and which was packed and unpacked all through my childhood (though never opened) might have given me a clue, or at least launched a discussion. Or there was another book, well-thumbed – *The Magic and Science of Jewels and Stones* written by an Isidore Kozminsky – that contained photographs of rare jewels and Egyptian icons, which was filled with the stories and myths and for some reason sat alongside our *Blackie's* dictionary on one bookshelf or another in the many houses we inhabited in those years. Since this was one of the books that eventually gravitated from my parents' bookshelf to my own equally nomadic one, you would have thought it would have provoked some inquisitiveness on my part. But not so.

I would like to think that nothing was deliberately concealed. It was just that, after their name change, neither my father nor my grandfather recognised any connection with the Kozminsky side of the family. They simply didn't exist. The rift would have been complete save for the link to the past through Isidore's published works. Even my mother, if indeed she knew, didn't let on in all our many discussions of family and background.

So we were brought up knowing that our grandfather was both an astrologer and a Doctor of Science, and that he had written a number of books, one of which *was The Magic and Science of Jewels and Stones*, but somehow we never connected one with the other. Other clues were there, but never picked up. From time to time, alongside Dad's stories of old Melbourne, its tramways and arcades, of the giants Gog and Magog that had so fascinated him as a child, was a mention of Kozminsky Jewellers. And it was not until the beginning of my research I learned that Isidore was born Israel.

Although Dad's half-Irishness meant his stories were as vibrant and alive as only the Irish can make them, as I have said, few people were named or connected. Included in this 'disconnection' was my father's grandmother. 'I would say, "Hello Grandmama,"' Dad once told me, '…and she would sit in her special chair and say nothing. She had been badly treated by her family and she rarely spoke. One day someone came out from England to make sure she was all right. My father asked what he should call him and he said, "Call me Uncle". That's all he would say in his stern voice. He came with a personal valet, a very hard and arrogant man. They – the children – had bought a pair of slippers for the uncle as a present and the valet said, "He would never wear these" and handed them back with a look of disgust.'

And then another story. A long, long time ago, Dad said, there was this rather grand and somewhat haughty young lady who landed at the Melbourne docks accompanied by a maid and a pile of expensive luggage. She was met by the manager of the English, Scottish and Australian Bank and taken to accommodation in the city. Each month she received a payment through a London bank from her exceedingly wealthy and well-connected family back in England, who wanted her 'out of the way'. Dad told my sister and I this story hundreds of times, but somehow always omitted the critical link: that this remittance woman was our great grandmother.

My father's other strong memory was of the love between his grandmother and his father. 'My father and I were there when she was dying. He loved her very much and she him. But not his father. There was no love there.'

This inevitably led to another recollection about a man who wasn't named until our discussions at the end of Dad's life: his grandfather Simon Kozminsky, who was 'not much of a person and always after money', and who picked up a sovereign on the wharf on his arrival. There was never a suggestion that Simon subsequently married the remittance woman.

There was an oft-repeated account, too, of another uncle, this time Isidore's uncle who was 'very kind to him and took him all over the world – America, Egypt, Europe – to study and lecture.' Since Isidore only had two uncles – and Marks spent most of his life in country Victoria – this, by deduction, was Abraham, his half-uncle. Clearly, my father wavered between an uneasy respect for Abraham (he was not spoken of with the same aversion as Simon) and his own great resentment at the trauma his father suffered with the rift caused by Isidore's decision to marry out of the Jewish faith.

That Isidore and Eileen were required not to meet for a year – and that they cheated just a little by passing each other on opposite sides of the street each morning when he would 'doff his hat and she would smile and incline her head' – was one of the few anecdotes that did have names attached. At the end of that year's 'ban', there came what Dad described as 'the double-cross.'

It was a double-cross because this agreement was reneged on by both Simon and Abraham and perhaps Emma, too, (Marks does not seem to have become involved). When the couple became more determined than ever to marry, the disapproval and censure of the family continued and Isidore was in a bind. He was by now well into his thirties, working part-time for his father, immersed in Melbourne's bohemian world of acting, art and music, and facing a situation where he had to choose between his family and his Irish sweetheart.

The loss of his family for this kindly man was savage. It came, firstly, in the difficulties that his relationship with a non-Jew caused a mother he loved dearly. Secondly, he had to come to terms with the fact that the bonds of religion mattered more to his family than his friendship and affection. In particular, he was unable to forgive them for going back on their word. In the end, according to Dad, he 'got clear of the whole lot of them' by going off to Sydney for four or five years. While on his return to Melbourne Isidore continued to work for his father on and off until Simon's death, things would never be the same. In a fit of rage and grief, he burnt his many certificates as a symbolic obliteration of the past and with it everything Jewish, aside from his beloved Kabbalah.

When he moved to London in 1935, Isidore and my father changed their names by deed poll to Coton, the surname of Emma's mysterious mother. Indicative of the depth of meaning this change of name had for Dad was that among the scant few papers handed to me on my father's death was the original copy of the government gazette that recorded the change of name, still in its original envelope and further protected by what looks like a purpose-made folder.

I'm happy to be able to relate that Isidore's marriage to Eileen, gained at such cost, was extraordinarily happy, lasting nearly forty years until his death during wartime Britain in 1944/45. Sadly, I was never to meet this man with the fabulous enquiring mind, the man who according to Dad was 'always doing something different' but always with immense focus and scholarship.

His widow, my Irish grandmother Eileen, travelled to Africa in a converted warship in 1946 with the woman who was later to become my mother. Eileen died in Uganda when I was four years of age and I remember her as a warm, uncomplicated and easy-to-love woman who continued to tell me stories as she lay on her deathbed in Entebbe hospital – and who, incidentally, didn't change her name as had her husband and son, but who remained Eileen Kozminsky until her death in 1952.

The divergence between how my father might have written this story and my own version of events comes in two major areas: in any mention of Simon and in my more sympathetic portrayal of both Simon and Abraham. Since I am a further generation away from the hurt that was caused, it is easier for me to believe that there was another side to the story. And I don't think there would have been so much pain had there not also been love and feeling.

Moreover, I do not believe that Simon was as bleak as my father would have him. There are a couple of reasons for this. Firstly, Isidore didn't return to Melbourne with his family until around 1912/13, when Simon had only a few years to live and my father, Kenneth, was no more than four or five years of age. As Simon died of dementia in 1916, it is quite likely that by the time Dad met him, he was already affected by this disease. That and his already strained relations with his son would have altered his behaviour. Under these circumstances, my father's distasteful memory of the old man, whom he'd only met a couple of times, was probably accurate enough, but not necessarily indicative of Simon's character overall.

Additionally, as late as 1914 – according to the ES&A Bank manager's notes – Simon had plans to lease the premises next door to the existing Kozminsky store which he wanted Isidore to manage, so it is quite possible that in his own Victorian way he was trying to make amends to a son he didn't understand any more than that son understood him. Each generation separates itself further from the very real difficulties our ancestors faced when they first arrived in this country. Simon came here with nothing and, Emma's wealth notwithstanding, he created a dynasty and a business which remain to this day.

The late 1850s and early 1860s is the most likely period for the establishment of S. Kozminsky & Co. There's an apparent contradiction between an advertising pamphlet that gives the date the business was established as 'the fourteenth year of the reign of Queen Victoria' (1851) and documented evidence of Simon's arrival in Melbourne in 1856 and his presence in the Ovens goldfields in 1857. Over the next ten years, he appears both in Melbourne and various country areas, including Mortlake from 1869–71. But this doesn't rule out the possibility that there was a coin and curio business on this site established in 1851 which Simon later bought. It's plausible that the arrival of Marks in 1862 and their subsequent business partnerships – in Buangor as well as

A BREAK IN THE CHAIN

Mortlake – gave Simon the freedom to buy a store in the city and operate between the two stores. We know that for a time Simon and Marks were in business as watchmakers, that the focus of his Mortlake business was as a drapery and general store, but that once in Melbourne he specialized in coins, gemstones, pearls and rare items, Kozminsky's growing progressively into the elite jewellery store we know and love today.

As mentioned earlier, I remain unconvinced that Abraham was unaffected by the quarrel. There is both anecdotal and written evidence that the argument affected the older man, too, more deeply perhaps than Isidore would ever know. It is clear he was a great influence in Isidore's life from childhood onwards and that there was a genuine affection between the two. This, I think, makes the rift doubly sad.

One day when my father was a young boy of eight or nine, he walked to Abraham's house which was not far from where his parents lived in St Kilda. This is how he recollected the incident:

'Seeing my father still so upset and wanting things to be right between them, I had some thought of trying to talk to the uncle. But the door was opened by his man and when the uncle finally came he was very annoyed to see me. He barked at his man: "Get him a sandwich." And then he turned to me. "Stay out of this," he said. "Go home, Kenneth. Our quarrel is not your quarrel." And then off he went.' At this point, Dad's courage failed him and he 'hopped it and ran off before the man came back with the lunch'.

In addition, a simple sentence in Abraham's will, executed the year before his death in 1934, reads, 'I express my sincere desire that all members of my family shall live together in amity'. In deconstructing this sentence, I read a sincere regret about the past. It is interesting, too, that Isidore and Eileen, with their unmarried daughter Nan, left Melbourne to join my father in England soon after Abraham's death.

That *A Break in the Chain* is only about Abraham in the way his life touched that of Isidore is clear, but there is no doubt that he was quite a character in his own right. He was a prominent Melbourne figure during the boom years, generous and with a high degree of altruism. The same could be said about Marks, who certainly left his stamp on country Victoria – although Marks's business dealings were of a different ilk. The three brothers were quite dissimilar and yet all made their mark on early Victoria.

When I first started my research, this was going to be Emma's story. I was quite certain – despite my father's adamancy that Isidore had done everything possible to trace his mother's family of origin – that the sophistication of today's research tools and the passing of whatever family embarrassment had caused her to be banished to the colonies meant further information would be relatively easy to trace. However, my father was right: the trail from the London end was well hidden, the manager of the ES&A Bank in Melbourne sworn to secrecy, and the relevant files burnt in a fire many years ago. (Over the course of my life's research I have come across an alarming number of 'fires' of files and documents.)

Kozminsky family stories present a number of alternate backgrounds for Emma. For instance, Mena

A BREAK IN THE CHAIN

Kozminsky-Meyerovitz wrote to me of 'rumours...that she was the illegitimate daughter of Lady Francis Coton who was either the wife or daughter Lord Coton, a onetime Lord Chief Justice of England'. When I finally persuaded him to talk of the past, my father insisted she was the product of a morganatic marriage of one of Queen Victoria's siblings whose mother was exiled to France where she took the name 'Coaten'. There are other opinions, none of which I have been able to substantiate – and in this work she remains the enigma she was in her lifetime.

Although I was determined my interpretation be as close as possible to the real personalities and emotions of these people of my past, and I have done my best to keep faith with the stories and documentation as far as possible, in several instances I have manipulated dates for the sake of the story. In particular, Simon and Emma left Mortlake when Israel was around a year old – not the three or four years he is in the story – and both Minnie and Michael were born in Melbourne. Abraham came to Australia considerably earlier than the date I have him arrive. Ned Kelly was escorted to Melbourne jail a couple of months earlier than Israel's tenth birthday and the headline quoted from *The Age* is from the edition of 29th June 1880.

But in the end this is Dad's book. In the best of oral traditions, he handed down these tales. Way back then, when we were kids, he spoke about 'the family money that was lost when the bank closed its doors'. Other times, his voice thick with admiration, he'd tell us about the time 'she saved his life, you know, my father's mother... She grabbed him and jumped from the runaway cart...a brave woman.'

A BREAK IN THE CHAIN

As children, we who had heard these stories time and time again, received them with rolling eyes and badly concealed boredom. What a change to my attitude of recent years when every nuance that accompanied those tales became of significance and I have cause now to regret how casually I once treated this precious store of history, memories and stories.

Tangea Tansley, 2022

Acknowledgements

The first thank you is to the late Mena Kozminsky-Meyerowitz – a prominent figure in the Jewish community and author of *Keeping the Promise* – and to her late husband Bob and children Michael and Rosetta for their friendship and encouragement. Mena and I formed our friendship through a flurry of information-exchanging emails while we were working on our respective books and it is one I continue to value and remember with respect.

It was through Mena I learned of the existence of Frederick McCubbin's portrait of Eileen and the existence of the prayer book that Michael Solomon sent to Simon with the inscription I've quoted.

I am also heavily indebted to Captain Henry Leighton – who married into Abraham's side of the family – and who generously shared both his meticulous research on the Kozminsky family tree and excerpts from the Jewish chronicles and newspapers which helped round out Isidore's earlier interest and involvement in Jewish societies and fundraising.

I am grateful also to Lionel Sharpe of the Jewish Genealogical Centre, Melbourne historian Jill Barnard, Scotch College archivist Jim Mitchell, my early readers for their insights and comments, especially June and the late Walter Vivian, Toni Weston, my son Viv for making the first connection with the Kozminskys and my daughter Tammy for progressing it into a friendship. My thanks also to archivists and librarians at the National Library of Australia, State Library of Victoria, University of Melbourne, my own local Manning Library, Murdoch University Library and the National Gallery of Victoria for their kind permission to reproduce Frederick McCubbin's portrait of my grandmother on the cover. Special thanks, too, to my agent Averill Chase for her faith in this book, for her friendship and sound advice, and to Martin Hughes and all the folks at Affirm Press, including my editor Rebecca Starford for her patience and thoroughness during the editing process.

Secretary of the Mortlake and District Historical Society Craige Proctor deserves warm thanks for the wealth of information he provided on Simon's years in Mortlake, as do Florence Charles and Ann Dodd for squiring me around their lovely town. Thanks, too, to Tim Allender's family – whom I met by chance when I got lost in the Buangor district trying to track down Marks's old sawmill on Mt Cole – and who gave me a copy of Tim's book on Buangor *Coaches Called Here* with its many references to the Kozminsky brothers. Other historical societies that have been particularly helpful are those of Nhill and the Royal Historical Society of Victoria.

A number of texts have informed the writing of *A Break in the Chain*. I relied heavily on the works of Edward Dyson and Michael Cannon for descriptions of goldfields conditions and the boom years of early Melbourne. Lola Pescott's *Early Settlers' Household*

A BREAK IN THE CHAIN

Lore was particularly helpful in this respect. For a description of atmosphere of the times I found Marshall Browne's Melbourne trilogy absorbing and extremely helpful. Andrew Hassam's *Sailing to Australia*, was invaluable in reconstructing Simon's trip from Liverpool to Melbourne. The scenes on the Polish album were inspired by and drawn from Justyna Beinek's excellent essay "Forget-Me-Not? National Identity in Nineteenth-century Polish Albums" in *The Samaritan Review* (September 2004). I have quoted from Isidore's discussion of rare coins in his interview with *The New Idea* ("An Antiquary", part VII of their series *The Common Round of Uncommon People*, 6 October 1903). I drew on the death notice in the *Nhill Free Press* of 7 May 1895, for a description of the circumstances surrounding Marks's sudden death.

And finally, my husband Richard Wheater has lived this book with me. Without him – and without my wonderful family and friends – it wouldn't have been written. I am deeply grateful.

Chronology

1828/1835	Birth of Simon Kosmanske/Kozminsky in Raoskow, Prussia (exact date unknown)
1838/41	Birth of Marks in Prussia
1854	Birth of Abraham in Prussia
1848	Birth of Emma Solomon in Knightsbridge, London
1856	Simon's arrival in Melbourne from Liverpool on the *Black Swan*
1862	Marks arrival on the *Red Jacket* from Liverpool
1860s	Establishment of Kozminsky's. See postscript
1868/9	Emma's arrival in Melbourne
1869	Marriage of Emma and Simon on 13 October

A BREAK IN THE CHAIN

1870	Israel Kozminsky born in Mortlake
1872	Birth of Minnie Kozminsky in Melbourne
1874	Birth of Michael Kozminsky in Melbourne
1881	Birth of Eileen Watkins born to Dr William Longworth Watkins (Beau) and Clara Clark in Beechworth
1887	S. Kozminsky, watchmaker and jeweller, moves his store to the corner of Elizabeth and Bourke Streets
1880–87	Israel/Isidore attends Scotch College in Hawthorn
1888–1905	Isidore studies, travels, lectures, establishes himself as an acclaimed amateur actor in Melbourne and overseas
1895	Death of Marks in Nhill
1898–1905	Isidore writes some of his early works – *The Occultism of the Australian Aboriginal* Vols I and II and his first book on numerology, *Numbers: Their Magic and Mystery*. All published by J. C. Stephens in Melbourne

A BREAK IN THE CHAIN

1906–1911	Isidore launches and edits the *Antiquarian Gazette*
1906/7	Fred McCubbin's painting of Eileen Watkins-Kozminsky
1907	Death of Eileen's mother Clara Watkins
1907	Isidore and Eileen marry on 18 February at St John's Church of England, Heidelberg
1907	S. Kozminsky & Co. move to their first address in the Block Arcade
1907/8	Isidore and Eileen leave Melbourne for the first of several addresses in Sydney
1908	Birth of Kenneth Francis Kozminsky on 12 April in Sydney
1912	Painting of Kenneth by Tasmanian artist Florence Rodway
1912	Isidore, Eileen and Kenneth return to Melbourne
1913	Emma purchases the London Hotel, corner Market and Little Flinders streets
1915	Birth of Nancy Kozminsky in St Kilda
1916	Death of Simon Kozminsky

A BREAK IN THE CHAIN

1923	Emma, Michael, Minnie and her husband Alfred Levin turn S. Kozminsky & Co. into a private company and the wealthy Lansells of Bendigo subsidise the business
1924	Death of Emma Kozminsky, aged seventy-six. Both Isidore and her grandson Kenneth at her bedside. Buried beside her husband Simon in Brighton Cemetery. My father Kenneth, was adamant that it was *not* a Hebrew ceremony
1928	Isidore establishes his 'commercial gallery' in Collins Gate, Melbourne
1929–32	The Great Depression
1934	Directors of S. Kozminsky & Co. resolve to go into voluntary liquidation
1934	Death of Abraham Kozminsky, aged eighty
1935	Following his decision to emigrate, Isidore sells his 'commercial gallery'
1935	Isidore relocates his family to England
1936	The name change for Isidore and Kenneth from Kozminsky to Coton becomes official

A BREAK IN THE CHAIN

1944/5   Francis Coton aka Isidore aka Israel dies in London

1946   Eileen travels to Southern Rhodesia with June Daynes who will shortly marry her son Kenneth and become her daughter-in-law

1952   Eileen dies in Uganda

www.ingramcontent.com/pod-product-compliance
Lightning Source LLC
Chambersburg PA
CBHW030430010526
44118CB00011B/571